FEARLESS SIMPLICITY

RANGJUNG YESHE BOOKS • *www.rangjung.com*

PADMASAMBHAVA • *Treasures from Juniper Ridge* •
Advice from the Lotus-Born, Dakini Teachings

PADMASAMBHAVA AND JAMGÖN KONGTRÜL • *The Light of Wisdom,
Vol. 1, & Vol. 2, Vol. 3, Secret, Vol. 4 & Vol. 5*

PADMASAMBHAVA, CHOKGYUR LINGPA,
JAMYANG KHYENTSE WANGPO, TULKU URGYEN RINPOCHE,
ORGYEN TOBGYAL RINPOCHE, & OTHERS • *Dispeller of Obstacles* •
The Tara Compendium • *Powerful Transformation* • *Dakini Activity*

YESHE TSOGYAL • *The Lotus-Born*

DAKPO TASHI NAMGYAL • *Clarifying the Natural State*

TSELE NATSOK RANGDRÖL • *Mirror of Mindfulness* • *Heart Lamp*

CHOKGYUR LINGPA • *Ocean of Amrita* • *The Great Gate* •
Skillful Grace • *Great Accomplishment* • *Guru Heart Practices*

TRAKTUNG DUDJOM LINGPA • *A Clear Mirror*

JAMGÖN MIPHAM RINPOCHE • *Gateway to Knowledge,
Vol. 1, Vol. 2, Vol. 3, & Vol. 4*

TULKU URGYEN RINPOCHE • *Blazing Splendor* • *Rainbow Painting* •
As It Is, Vol. 1 & Vol. 2 • *Vajra Speech* • *Repeating the Words
of the Buddha* • *Dzogchen Deity Practice*

ADEU RINPOCHE • *Freedom in Bondage*

KHENCHEN THRANGU RINPOCHE • *King of Samadhi* • *Crystal Clear*

CHÖKYI NYIMA RINPOCHE • *Present Fresh Wakefulness* •
Bardo Guidebook

TULKU THONDUP • *Enlightened Living*

ORGYEN TOBGYAL RINPOCHE • *Life & Teachings of Chokgyur Lingpa*

DZIGAR KONGTRÜL RINPOCHE • *Uncommon Happiness*

TSOKNYI RINPOCHE • *Fearless Simplicity* • *Carefree Dignity*

MARCIA BINDER SCHMIDT • *Dzogchen Primer* • *Dzogchen Essentials* •
Quintessential Dzogchen • *Confessions of a Gypsy Yogini* •
Precious Songs of Awakening Compilation

ERIK PEMA KUNSANG • *Wellsprings of the Great Perfection* •
A Tibetan Buddhist Companion • *The Rangjung Yeshe
Tibetan-English Dictionary of Buddhist Culture & Perfect Clarity*

Fearless Simplicity

The Dzogchen Way of Living Freely in a Complex World

TSOKNYI RINPOCHE

Foreword by
SOGYAL RINPOCHE

Compiled and translated by
ERIK PEMA KUNSANG *and* MARCIA BINDER SCHMIDT
Edited with
KERRY MORAN

RANGJUNG YESHE PUBLICATIONS
BOUDHANATH, HONG KONG & ESBY
2003

Rangjung Yeshe Publications

P.O. Box 395,
Legett, CA 95585

www.rangjung.com
www.lotustreasure.com

3 5 7 9 8 6 4 2

Third paperback edition 2016
Printed in the United States of America

Distributed to the book trade by:
Persues Books/Ingram, Inc.

Publication Data: ISBN-10: 962-7341-48-7 (pbk.)
ISBN-13: 978-962-7341- 48-2 (pbk.)

Authors: Tsoknyi Rinpoche (1966-). Translated, compiled and edited by
Erik Pema Kunsang (Erik Hein Schmidt) and Marcia Binder Schmidt.
Edited with Kerry Moran.

Title: Fearless Simplicity:
The Dzogchen Way of Living Freely in a Complex World.
Eastern Philosophy—Buddhism
Vajrayana—Dzogchen. I. Title.

Cover art: Lhadripa Nawang Zangpo
Cover design: Marcia Binder Schmidt
The verse on page 38 was translated by the
Nalanda Translation Committee.

Contents

FOREWORD

I am very happy to introduce this collection of teachings by Tsoknyi Rinpoche, which bears the beautiful title *Fearless Simplicity*. On many occasions I have had the great pleasure of watching Tsoknyi Rinpoche teach, and I am always struck by his truly remarkable qualities. For me, he is a master who combines both ancient and modern. Recognized by the 16th Gyalwang Karmapa, he was trained in the Nyingma and Drukpa Kagyü traditions of Tibetan Buddhism by the foremost masters of our age: Kyabje Dilgo Khyentse Rinpoche, Tulku Urgyen Rinpoche, Khamtrul Rinpoche, Adeu Rinpoche of Nangchen and Nyoshul Khen Rinpoche. Now, when he teaches, Tsoknyi Rinpoche remains totally faithful to the authentic word and spirit of the teachings, as passed down in the great practice lineages of Mahamudra and Dzogchen. In the depth of his understanding, he reminds me of the outstanding masters of the past, and I find it incredibly encouraging that a master as young as he is can embody so deeply the wisdom of this tradition. And in the generous, direct and careful style of his teaching, he bears an extraordinary resemblance to his father, the great Tulku Urgyen Rinpoche.

At the same time, Tsoknyi Rinpoche speaks to us with an exhilarating freshness, being fully aware of the complexity of modern life, and the needs of men and women today. He is gifted with an ability to unravel the most profound of topics in a way that is clear and easy to understand, and as he maps out the teachings, he draws listeners constantly back to their own experience, allowing them to discover the truth of the Dharma within themselves. From his teachings at my centers at Lerab Ling in Europe and elsewhere, I know at first hand just how much he is appreciated by the many Rigpa students around the world who have heard him teach. One of the qualities everyone remarks on is his kindness—his humanity and his unfailing eagerness to help. I count myself most fortunate that I can number him among my closest friends.

It is our great good fortune that for fifteen years now, Rinpoche has been teaching in Europe, North and South America, Australia and South East Asia. I know that what motivates him is an unshakeable commitment to bring benefit to people and to the teachings, as much as possible. In fact, he has played a vital, perhaps historic, role in opening up the Dzogchen teachings to many individuals from the west who are prominent Buddhist teachers. From many long and fascinating discussions with him, I know of his deep concern for the future of the Dharma, and about how best to present the teachings to make them ever more accessible to modern people. I rejoice at this book; it will be a tremendous blessing for practitioners, and I pray that it will allow his voice and the teaching of Buddha to reach out to people everywhere, and bring them closer and closer to liberation.

—Sogyal Rinpoche

PREFACE

Fearless Simplicity is a collection of various talks, approximately seventy-five of them, given by Tsoknyi Rinpoche in diverse types of locations in different countries, to groups large and small and to individual students, between 1998 and 2002. In some cases, teachings on similar topics were synthesized and combined; other teachings are presented as they were originally spoken. Throughout the process of collecting, transcribing, selecting, and editing, Rinpoche was instrumental in directing and refining the work that culminated in this book.

Quite recently a manuscript of vajra songs of realization from masters of the Nyingma lineage compiled by Kyungtrul Rinpoche was brought out of Tibet. This precious text contained a song by the first Tsoknyi Rinpoche. Upon hearing this, the present Tsoknyi Rinpoche asked that it be translated and included in this book. Finding this song was like finding a treasure in that it condenses the meaning of the entire *Fearless Simplicity*.

In earlier drafts, we called the manuscript *A Feast of Merit and Wisdom*. This is a double play on Tsoknyi Rinpoche's name, being the two accumulations (*tsok-nyi*) as well as the word for feast (*tsok*). Later, Rinpoche decided on the current title, as it seemed more true to the contents. We have tried our best to keep the flavor of Rinpoche's teaching style through the process of codifying the live transmission into the written word.

We have traveled this exceptional journey with many friends. Our thanks go to Sogyal Rinpoche for making time in his busy schedule to write the foreword; to the transcribers, Joanne Larson and Michael Tweed, who also helped edit; to the Rigpa Sangha for sharing some Lerab Ling transcripts from 1999; to the primary editor, Kerry Moran; the copy editor, Tracy Davis; the proofreaders Daniel Kaufer and Christine Daniels; and to our kind patron, Richard Gere.

Please approach this book as you would an exquisite banquet, a feast. Understand that the kitchen staff has prepared it with the best possible intentions, ingredients, and skills. Let it nourish you with a delightful frame of mind. And as a dedication, may all we aspiring Dzogchen yogis attain accomplishment and rebirth in the pure realm of the Copper-Colored Mountain at the table of the master chef, Padmasambhava.

—*Erik and Marcia*
Nangkyi Gompa

VAJRA SONG

A la la ho!

Vajradhara, lord who pervades all families,
Gracious father guru, I supplicate you.

Within the sky of nonarising mind,
The myriad appearances, no matter how they emerge,
When I don't accept or reject, confirm or deny, they dissolve
    into space.
The mind of this yogi of nonarising is completely at ease!

I shall sing you a song about the empty bliss of this ease.
Listen here all of you fortunate men and women!
Since it is hard for people of this dark age to pay attention,
Listen here you worthy men and women!

Even just to see or meet me,
A yogi with whom every link is meaningful,
Is a meeting with one who is very rare to meet.

All your myriad mundane deeds
And all your possible deluded thoughts—
Let them be in the nondual state beyond concepts.

Free of the notion of seer and seen,
While you sustain the essence of your mind,
Meditator and meditated dissolve into space,
And there is not even the words 'meditation beyond concepts.'

This empty bliss that is unceasing
Is the kindness of the glorious father guru.

I am a yogi who gladly accepts
Meat, wine and mudra.
Like the Indian peacock feasting on poison,
All the emotions, no matter which,
Are my great adornments, the five wisdoms.
If you want to share your father's experience, follow me!

No matter which emotion I experience,
I am an untainted yogi who brings the five poisons to the
path.

All of you benefactors, male or female, high or low,
Every link you make with me will be meaningful,
And surely, you will gain rebirth on the glorious island of
Chamara.
To be free of doubt has inconceivable benefit.

I am a yogi who enjoys whatever arises.
This is the domain of the vajra vehicle.
Having crossed the lesser vehicle's conceptual boundaries,
I am a yogi who delights in the greater vehicle.

By singing this song free of mental constructs,
May your minds enjoy the vajra vehicle
And may it bring you to the glorious island of Chamara.

*In the sacred place known as Serkyam, as my worthy disciples Drodön Tsogyal and
Döndrub Drölma provided the auspicious coincidence with precious gifts, this was uttered
by Ngawang Tsoknyi (Drubwang Tsoknyi, the First) while taking as path the vajra
vehicle of Secret Mantra by enjoying the spontaneity of whatever arises. May it be virtuous. May it be virtuous. May it be virtuous.*

PART ONE

APPETIZER

A Daily Dose of
Dharma

All the great teachers of the past have taught this same, identical message: Gather the accumulations, purify the obscurations, and receive the blessings of a qualified master. In the tradition I represent, the preliminary practices and the accomplishment of the yidam deity are considered very, very important. I do not think that the buddhas and all the past masters have created them just to lead us astray.

Vajrayana contains many methods for reaching enlightenment, while presenting relatively few hardships. Some of the easiest and most accessible of these methods are devotion and compassion, along with the recognition of mind nature. Combine these with the preliminary practices and you will progress quickly. While Dzogchen is the pinnacle, the epitome, of the vehicle that is Vajrayana, it does not make sense to grab at the highest teachings and reject the rest. Similarly, it is pointless to invent your own private, personal idea of Dzogchen to train in. To do that makes your "Dzogchen" something fabricated, something you have made up. Calling your own theories Dzogchen is a foolish pretense that has nothing to do with the genuine, authentic teachings.

You see, Dzogchen is not made up of bits of information that you can collect and take home. Dzogchen is about *how to be free*. It is not sufficient merely to receive the Dzogchen teachings: you must apply them, live them. Right now we are still enveloped in deluded experience. We have created a cage for ourselves out of our own emotions and our sense of duality, and here we sit, day in and day out. Once we clearly understand our situation, we have a choice: either we can remain in this cage or we can use the Dzogchen instructions to break it open and become free.

With the openness of devotion, the blessings can enter our stream of being. When we fully let go with a sense of deep trust, it is possible to recognize the state of original wakefulness. This practice is not some new philosophical position, not a new concept that we acquire, but a way of completely and fully letting go of all conceptual attitudes.

To arrive at thought-free wakefulness is not impossible, nor is it necessarily very difficult. However, it does require us to accumulate merit, purify obscurations, and make a connection with a qualified master. These three extremely important conditions are repeatedly emphasized in the teachings.

Sure, we can be told, "Sit down and let go completely; just be natural." But can we really do this? We try to let go, but actually we do not. We are still holding on—keeping hold of the letting go. We grip something else; then again we try to let go. We are always holding on to something, putting up resistance. Actually, we do not really want to let go. It is against our nature, so to speak. We prefer to retain ego control, which is a very strong habit. It does not matter how many times we are told to drop everything and be 100 percent uncontrived and natural; we still hold on to the letting go. We keep hold of what we are recognizing: "Now, now I recognize the nature of mind." We cling to the natural state, holding on to the concept "This is it."

In other words, although we try to let go, a part of us is still holding on. Therefore, it is never the genuine natural state. Something is needed to completely shatter this conceptual attitude, to smash it to pieces. The atmosphere of devotion provides one essential way. When we thoroughly open up in the moment of devotion, it's as if all the coverings of our philosophical ideas, all of the wrapping, all of the concepts that we use to compartmentalize reality are totally stripped away. To be full of genuine devotion is one of the purest conceptual states. Then, if we have received the essential instruction in recognizing mind essence, we can recognize self-aware original wakefulness.

Being full of genuine compassion offers a similar possibility. When you feel sincere empathy toward all sentient beings, the purity of this emotion disperses conceptual mind. Simultaneously, your mind becomes wide open. And again in that moment, there is the opportunity, if you have received the essential instructions, to apply them. You can recognize self-knowing original wakefulness and genuinely and authentically arrive in the natural state.

Otherwise, it appears that we just refuse to be in the natural state. Certainly it is our habit not to be, and that is a very hard habit to break.

This is why there are many practices to facilitate the recognition of mind nature—to break the normal habits of conceptual mind and ego. Heartfelt devotion and compassion are the foremost facilitators for arriving in the original state.

The preliminary practices facilitate recognizing and training in the nonconceptual meditation of Dzogchen. If we feel that it is difficult to simply let be, the preliminary practices are a method to make it easier for us. They are a conduit for purification, accumulation and blessings. Ultimately, we must rely on our basic intelligence. The preliminary practices strengthen and sharpen this intelligence.

Accumulating merit or using conceptual methods is like making a candle, while the Dzogchen pointing-out instruction is like lighting the candle. You must have both—the candle and a match—to illuminate the darkness. With inadequate merit, you can perhaps recognize mind essence, but the recognition quickly disappears. You cannot concentrate; you lack the candle. Like a match in the darkness, the recognition flickers and dies. You need a stable basis to carry and nourish the flame, and accumulating merit forms that basis.

Many positive conditions must come together in order for us to practice a spiritual path. Some people really aspire to practice, but their life circumstances make it very difficult for them to do so. Others wish to spend three years in retreat, but they do not have any money. Still others have plenty of money but cannot get any teachings. Sometimes people have a very good teacher and teachings, but their situation is complicated: they are always fighting with their spouse and don't have a moment of peace at home, or their job takes up all their time. You may need to change your circumstances, but to do so you must have merit. For that, there is no better method than the preliminary practices.

It is the kindness of the buddhas to provide us with a complete path, and the preliminary practices are part of that complete path. Often students refrain from doing them because they do not understand their purpose. Some students even think the preliminary practices are a kind of punishment! Actually, the preliminaries are not a punishment meted out to torture people—not at all. Your own laziness might say, "Oh, no, the preliminary practices are so difficult. They are probably meaningless. I don't want to do them." But you have to smash that lazy tendency. Indeed, the main obstacle to practice is laziness. Crush it from the very beginning, and your laziness gets scared and runs away, whimpering,

"Oooh, I can't go near this person; it's too much for me." Prostrations make mincemeat out of your physical laziness, just as mandala offerings chop up your attachment.

To truly progress in spiritual practice, you also have to develop the proper motivation: "I want to engage in meditation to purify my obscurations, particularly my main enemy, ego-clinging, and benefit all sentient beings." With that type of motivation, you progress toward enlightenment, not toward simply building up a strong, healthy ego. There is a big difference here.

While you are generating this motivation, ego might kick up a fuss and try to create doubts in your mind. Just ignore it. Ego might say, "This can't be true. How can *you* help all sentient beings? How can *you* purify yourself?" Watch out when this voice kicks in, and don't listen! Remember that our progress is completely dependent on the purity of our motivation. Spiritual practice is dependent on mind, and that means our attitude, our motivation. And proper motivation is absolutely crucial, as it ensures that our actions lead us in the right direction.

Often people come to my retreats because they want to be free of suffering. They think, "I'm going to do Buddhist practice in order to free myself of unpleasant emotions." This is one type of motivation, and it is fine as far as it goes. Another type of motivation is broader in scope: "I want to help all sentient beings recognize their self-existing awareness." This is the motivation of altruistic kindness. The best of all attitudes is to be motivated in a true, unfabricated way. Very often, however, it is not possible, and we must instead begin by fabricating it with the *bodhichitta* resolve.

Nowadays it seems that many people feel dissatisfied with themselves and their lives, as if normal worldly aims are not enough. Somehow, ego is tired of the ordinary; it needs different fuel. If you take spiritual fuel and give it to your ego, your ego grows stronger and you can go back into worldly life with renewed vigor. But this is not the purpose of spiritual practice. Quite honestly, many people find that their normal ego is fed up with worldly society. They want to pump up their egos, but normal fuel is not good enough. They hear about a certain spiritual fuel from the mountains of Tibet, and they think, "That will pump me up! Let me get my hands on some of that! Then I'll be better, bigger, and greater. It'll work even when I'm walking through Times Square." So they head off to the mountains to get an injection of Tibetan fuel to pump up their egos. That attitude might be all right insofar as it brings someone into contact with the teachings, but it does not serve the true purpose of Dharma.

Ego-clinging is very subtle. Virtually everything we do seems to be another way to feed the ego. The ego coaxes us into assuming a path that seems to be a genuine spiritual practice, but then the ego goes right ahead and usurps it! Even chanting OM MANI PADME HUNG can be appropriated by the ego. We sit down on our meditation cushion and assume the posture, but it is out of ego. We light incense and prostrate before our statues in our little retreat room, but it is still all for our ego. We need something to break free from the ego's grip. The very effective remedy for this is the accumulation of merit and the purification of obscurations, in conjunction with devotion and compassion.

If you don't know how to initially motivate yourself in the true way, Dharma practice may be nothing more than another way of popping your daily vitamin, a remedy guaranteed to make "me" strong and healthy. When you use spiritual practice as a dietary supplement, you apply it whenever you feel a little low on energy or a little upset. You sit down and practice to feel better. You try to balance yourself through practice, and then you return to your normal activities and forget all about it. Some people have this attitude, believe me! They tell themselves that they need spirituality in their lives—after all, it is not politically correct to be totally materialistic. So they give themselves a little dose in the morning and another in the evening. They apply the gloss of spirituality to put a shine on their normal lives. This is a distinct trend, and some so-called teachers emphasize this approach by telling their students that they will be much happier if they just sit down and meditate for a few minutes every day. In doing so, they are trying to make spiritual practice easier, more appetizing, more palatable—trying to bend the Dharma to fit people's attitudes. But that is not true spirituality. Don't make the mistake of confusing this type of practice for the real thing.

Even if you only practice a little bit, try to do it in a genuine way, with a true view, meditation, and conduct. Even if it is only for a short while, let it be real. Otherwise, it is better to give it up altogether, because you may wind up using the Dharma to further ensnare yourself in confusion. To pretend to be a spiritual person and wear prayer beads around your wrist is useless in itself. If it happens naturally, fine, no problem. But if your intention is to be respected by others, to create a better image because you meditate or are spiritual, you are merely being pretentious.

Nor should you apply "Dharma polish," spiritual practice that is used to make your deluded state appear prettier and more pleasant. One can advertise the value of spiritual practice just like advertising an exercise machine: "Use it twice a day for three weeks, and your confusion is guaranteed to clear up!" It sounds nice, but it doesn't really work.

To really embrace spiritual practice, you need to be honest with yourself and sincerely appreciate what it is you are doing. True honesty and appreciation give you confidence in life. Do not cheat yourself. If your practice is only to boost your ego, the Dharma becomes nothing more than a mask. You are simply fooling yourself, which is useless— you might as well not bother. But if your motivation is pure, you don't fool yourself.

Who is it that knows whether you are fooling yourself? Karma does. Karma stays with you continuously, and it never closes its eyes. Even when you are alone in the bathroom, karma is watching. Be careful! No matter what you do or where you are, karma never sleeps, because it is the natural result of all your actions and intentions. Karma is a constant witness to all you do, now and in the future. Whether other people acknowledge your actions or not really does not matter: karma and the buddhas will do so with 100 percent accuracy. Trust yourself; trust your pure motivation and the good actions of karma.

Pure motivation is really not so difficult to understand. All you have to do is take it to heart and *live* it. Don't be like the person who comes to me with a cup containing water, ten spoonfuls of sugar, ten spoonfuls of chili, ten spoonfuls of oil, and many other things all mixed up into a big mess. He says, "Rinpoche, this doesn't taste good. I want it to taste better. Can you do something?" I say, "Sure, I'll try." And I start to pour some of the water out. The person jumps up and yells, "Oh, please, don't pour any water out! I refuse to take anything out." Wondering what I should do, I ask, "Can I add more sugar?" Again he objects, "No, no, I don't want to add anything—just make it taste good. I don't want to change anything except the taste." What is one to do? For me, it is very easy. I simply say, "Fine, fine, I will pray for you." Because there is nothing else for me to do except pray. People like this refuse to change, let alone let go of ego. Yet they still want something to happen! They are waiting for a miracle that will never come. All I can do is pray.

I am not saying that one should be completely fanatical here by insisting that Buddhism has nothing to do with improving one's present situation in this life and is only for future lives. Genuinely practice the Buddhist path and this present life automatically improves, as if by default. You may also want to assume the responsibility for improving your future lives during your present one, but it is so much easier to accomplish that aim when you have the complete Buddhism.

In this book, I will discuss the reasons and ways to access the perfect spiritual path. The short version of how to do this is that we need to generate bodhichitta. To generate bodhichitta we must first calm our minds. That is done through shamatha practice. Through shamatha practice we attain a state of calm abiding. Having reached a certain peace, we are able to come closer to making all sentient beings feel at ease with loving-kindness and helping them be free of suffering through compassion.

The main point of the Buddha's extraordinary teachings is the view that emptiness and compassion are indivisible. Neither compassion nor emptiness by itself is sufficient. Emptiness is free of the grasping to a self. Compassion is benevolence for all beings, which, by the way, includes oneself. These two are inextricably interconnected.

There are two approaches in Tibetan Buddhism. One starts with the methods of compassion and loving-kindness. Through these, one accumulates merit and is slowly led to realizing the view of emptiness. In the other approach, because one has arrived at the correct view by means of the extraordinary teachings of the Great Perfection, compassion naturally manifests as an expression of emptiness. The essence of mind is recognized as being empty and awake. From the expression of this empty essence, compassion originates. It's as if one way proceeds gradually upward, while the other gazes down from above. The point here is that, regardless of where you happen to start from, the noble qualities of compassion, devotion, loving-kindness, and bodhichitta are always needed. This is true when you are trying to recognize *rigpa* and also after you recognize rigpa, when these qualities should be present in its expression.

I will discuss both of these ways further in this book. Some themes will be employed as an aid to recognizing mind nature in one context and as an enhancement in other contexts. Although we may glimpse the natural state through the blessings of a qualified master, we are unable to sustain this recognition unless we gather the accumulations and purify our obscurations. Based on the skillful means of Dzogchen, we are introduced to the unconfused aspect of our minds—the very essence of mind. *Sem*, or discursive mind, is the deluded aspect. From the very beginning of our training in rigpa, we explore the difference between being confused and being unconfused. As we meditate, meditate, meditate on the unconfused aspect, we gradually become more open. As this openness grows, from the state of emptiness compassion naturally arises. This compassion is the ultimate compassion. It is undivided emptiness and compassion, a topic I will cover in more detail later.

As I do not wish to repeat what I said in *Carefree Dignity*, please familiarize yourself with that book. The terminology is important for understanding the material I will present here.

Motivation

Whether our Dharma practice will progress in the right direction depends on our attitude, our intention. Motivation is extremely important: it is what everything stands or falls with, and this is true not only in spiritual practice but in whatever we set out to do. Therefore, in Buddhist practice it is of utmost importance to continually correct and improve our attitude.

The attitude we need to cultivate is one that is suffused with bodhichitta. This enlightened attitude has two aspects. The first aspect is the urge to purify our negativity: "I want to rid myself of all shortcomings, all ego-oriented emotions such as attachment, aggression, stupidity, and all the rest." The second aspect is the sincere desire to benefit all beings: "Having freed myself of all negative emotions, I will benefit all sentient beings. I will bring every sentient being to the state of complete enlightenment."

This compassionate attitude of bodhichitta should encompass oneself as well as all others. We have every reason to feel compassionate toward ourselves. In the ordinary state of mind we are helplessly overtaken by selfish emotions; we lack the freedom to remain unaffected when these emotions occupy our mind. Swept away by feelings of attachment, anger, closed-mindedness, and so forth, we lose control, and we suffer a great deal in this process. In such a state, we are unable to help ourselves, let alone others. We need to relate to our own suffering here with compassion in a balanced way, applying compassion toward ourselves just as we would do with others. In order to help others, we must first help ourselves, so that we can become capable of expanding our efforts further. But we shouldn't get stuck in just helping ourselves. Our compassion must embrace all other beings as well, so that having freed ourselves of negative emotions we are moved by compassion to help all sentient beings.

At this point in our practice, it's okay if our attempts to experience the attitude of bodhichitta are a little bit artificial. Because we haven't necessarily thought in this way before, we need to deliberately shift or adjust our intention to a new style. This kind of tampering with our own attitude is actually necessary. We may not yet be perfect bodhisattvas, but we should act as if we already are. We should put on the air of being a bodhisattva, just as if we're putting on a mask that makes us look as if we are somebody else. The true, authentic bodhichitta only arises as a natural expression of having realized the view. Before experiencing this spontaneously and fully, however, we need to consciously try to move in that direction. Even though our efforts may feel a little artificial at this point, it is perfectly okay—assuming of course that this is the good and necessary kind of artifice.

The need to improve our attitude, to correct our motivation, is not particularly difficult to understand, nor is it that difficult to actually do. Although it may be simple, this does not mean that we should belittle its importance. At this point, we should repeatedly cultivate the bodhisattva attitude. This is very important. To look down upon it as an inferior or unimportant practice seriously detracts from real progress in spiritual practice. Therefore, again and again, in all situations try your best to motivate yourself with bodhichitta.

In Tibet there is a lot of livestock: many cows, sheep, yaks. The skin from these animals needs to be cured in order to be useful; it needs to be softened by a special process. Once the hide has been cured, it becomes flexible and can be used in all sorts of ways: in religious artifacts, to bind up certain offerings on the shrine, as well as for all kinds of household purposes. But first it needs to be prepared in the right way: it needs to be softened, made flexible. If the hide is simply left as it is, it hardens and becomes totally stiff; then it is nothing but an unyielding piece of animal skin. It is the same way with a human being's attitude. We must soften our hearts, and this takes deliberate effort. We need to make ourselves gentle, peaceful, flexible, and tame, rather than being undisciplined, rigid, stubborn egocentrics.

This softening of our heart is essential for all progress, and not just in terms of spiritual practice. In all we do, we need to have an attitude that is open-minded and flexible. In the beginning this act of improving our attitude is definitely artificial. We are deliberately *trying* to be a bodhisattva, to have the compassionate attitude of wanting to help all sentient beings. This conscious effort is vital, because it can genuinely soften us up from deep within. If we do not cultivate this attitude, our rigidly preoccupied frame of mind makes it impossible for the true view of ultimate bodhichitta to grow. It's like trying to plant seeds in a frozen block of ice atop Mount Everest—they will never grow, they will just freeze. When, on the other hand, you have warmed up your character with bodhichitta, your heart is like fertile soil that is warm and moist. Since the readiness is there, whenever the view of self-knowing wakefulness, the true view of Dzogchen that is ultimate bodhichitta, is planted, it can grow spontaneously. In fact, absolutely nothing can hold it back from growing in such a receptive environment! That is why it is so important to steadily train in bodhichitta right from the very beginning.

The word "Dharma," in the context of this book, means method. The Dharma is a method to overcome the delusion in our own stream of being, in our own mind—a way to be totally free of the negative emotions that we harbor and cause to proliferate, and at the same time it is a way to realize the original wakefulness that is present in ourselves. There are ten different connotations of the word "Dharma," but in this context we are speaking of two types: the Dharma of statements and the Dharma of realization. The Dharma of statements is what you hear during a lecture or a teaching session. Within the Dharma of statements are included the words of the Buddha, the Tripitaka, as well as the commentaries on the Buddha's words made by the many learned and accomplished masters of India and Tibet.

Through hearing the explanations that constitute the Dharma of statements, and through applying these methods, something dawns in our own experience. This insight is called the Dharma of realization, and it includes recognizing our own nature of mind. In order to approach this second kind of Dharma, to apply it, we need the right motivation. Again, this right motivation is the desire to free oneself of negative emotions and bring all beings to liberation. We absolutely must have that attitude, or our spiritual practice will be distorted into personal profit seeking.

Basically there are three negative emotions: attachment, aggression, and closed-mindedness. Of course these three can be further distinguished into finer and finer levels of detail, down to the 84,000 different types of negative emotions. But the main three, as well as all their subsidiary classifications, are all rooted in ignorance, in basic unknowing. These are the negative emotions we need to be free of, and their main root is ignorance.

Someone might think, "I approach Dharma practice because my ego is a little bit upset. My ego is not very intelligent, not quite able to succeed. I come here to practice in order to improve my ego." That attitude is not spiritual.

Here's another attitude: "My ego works so hard. I must take care of my ego. I must relax. I come here to practice and become relaxed, so that my ego gets healthier and I can do my job." That type of attitude is okay, but merely okay; it's just one drop of a very small motivation.

We can, in fact, have a much larger perspective. As long as we harbor and perpetuate the negative emotions of attachment, anger, closed-mindedness, pride, and jealousy, they will continue to give us a hard time, and they will make it difficult for others to be with us as well. We need to be free of them. We need to have this attitude: "I must be free of these emotions."

When you leave this retreat at Gomde, I want you to go home naked. You can think that you left your negative emotions there as a donation! Honestly, that is the purpose of such a place. It is not right to go on retreat or hear teachings with the attitude, "I must go there in order to get something; I must achieve something." Instead, have this attitude: "I am practicing a spiritual path in order to lose something—to get rid of my attachment, my anger, my closed-mindedness, my conceit, my competitive jealousy."

Next, I would like to suggest that you practice in such a way that you are at ease with the whole process. Gradually expand that attitude of ease to encompass more and more. Once you've freed yourself of all these annoying emotions and become naked, it's not like you can just lean back and take it easy. That is not sufficient. You can awaken a sense of responsibility for all the other sentient beings who are exactly the way you used to be, tormented by negative emotions. You can begin helping them—first one, then two, then three, and finally all sentient beings.

Otherwise, what Gampopa said may come true: If you do not practice the Dharma correctly, it could become a cause for rebirth in the lower realms. That may happen for many people. In fact, it happens more frequently among old practitioners than with beginners.

Someone may relate to Dharma merely as a kind of remedy to be used when confused or upset. This of course is not the real purpose of spiritual practice. In this kind of situation, you do some practice till you have settled down, and then you set it aside and forget all about it. The next time you get upset, you do some more practice in order to feel good again. Of course, reestablishing one's equilibrium in this way is one of the minor purposes of practice, but it's not the real goal. Doing this is a way of using the Dharma as if it were a type of therapy. You may of course choose to do this, but I do not think it will get you enlightened. Feel a little bit unhappy, do some Dharma, get happy. Feel a little bit upset, then feel fine, then again feel unhappy. If you just continue like this, holding this very short-term view in mind, then there is no progress. "Last night I didn't sleep—my mind was disturbed, and the dog was barking next door. Now my mind is a little upside down, so I need to do a session to cure it. Okay, this morning I'll meditate."

Do not practice in this way. Dharma practice is not meant merely to make oneself feel better. The whole point of spiritual practice is to liberate oneself through realization and also to liberate others through compassionate capacity. To practice in order to feel better only brings one back up to that same level—one never makes any real progress. At the end of one's life, one just happens to feel good till the end of one's last session and then that's it—nothing happens beyond that. With this attitude of *merely feeling good* becoming the type of Buddhism that spreads in the West, we may see a huge scarcity of enlightened masters in the future. They will become an endangered species.

Please understand that the pursuit of "feeling better" is a samsaric goal. It is a totally mundane pursuit that borrows from the Dharma and uses all its special methods in order to fine-tune ego into a fit and workable entity. The definition of a worldly aim is to try to achieve something for oneself with a goal-oriented frame of mind—"so that I feel good." We may use spiritual practice to achieve this, one good reason being that it works much better than other methods. If we're on this path, we do a little spiritual practice and pretend to be doing it sincerely. This kind of deception, hiding the ego-oriented, materialistic aim under the tablecloth, might include something like "I take refuge in the Buddha, Dharma, and Sangha, so I must be pure." Gradually, as we become more astute at spiritual practice, we may bring our materialistic aim out into the open. This is quite possible: people definitely do it. But if this is how you practice, you won't get anywhere in the end. How could one ever become liberated through selfishness?

There comes a point when we start to lose faith in the illusions of this world: our level of trust in illusions begins to weaken, and we become disappointed. Using spiritual practice to nurture our ego back into good health while still retaining trust in these illusory aims does not set us free. True freedom does not mean having a healthy faith in illusions; rather, it means going completely *beyond* delusion. This may not sound particularly comforting, but it is true. It may be an unpleasant piece of news, especially if we have to admit to ourselves, "I have really been fooling myself all along. Why did I do all this practice? Am I completely wrong?" What can you do to pretend this isn't true? Facing the truth is not pleasant.

The real help here lies in continually correcting and improving our motivation: understanding why we are practicing and where we are ultimately heading. Work on this and bring forth the noble motivation of bodhichitta. Then all methods and practices can be used to help you progress in that direction.

Again I must emphasize this point: if we want to approach ultimate truth, we must form a true motivation. This includes compassion for all other sentient beings who delude themselves continuously with the contents of whatever arises in their minds. Compassionate motivation says, "How sad that they believe so strongly in their thoughts, that they take them to be so real." This deluded belief in one's own thoughts is what I call the "granddad concept." First, we hold our thought as true. Next, we accept that delusion, and it becomes our granddad. You know what it's like to suffer from this delusion yourself, in your own experience. Bring to mind all other sentient beings who let themselves get caught up in their granddad delusion and, with compassion, form the wish to free them all. That's the true motivation: please generate it.

Unless we have completely pure and true motivation, the practice of Vajrayana and Dzogchen doesn't turn out well. Paltrul Rinpoche was a great Dzogchen master. He did not have any major monastery, but he had an encampment of thousands of practitioners that was called Paltrul Gar, Paltrul's Camp. Over and over again, he taught those gathered around him the importance of having pure motivation. He created a situation named the Three Opportunities to improve the motivation of these practitioners. The first opportunity was at the sound of the wake-up gong in the early morning. Upon hearing the sound, people had the opportunity to think, "Yes, I must improve my motivation. I must put myself into the service of others; I must get rid of negative emotions and assist all sentient beings." They would repeatedly bring that to mind in order to adjust their aim.

The second opportunity arose at Paltrul Rinpoche's main tent. To get into it, you had to pass by a stupa, and at the opening to the enclosure, you had to squeeze yourself by to get through. The entranceway was deliberately made narrow so that you paused for a moment and thought, "This is the second opportunity to adjust my motivation."

The third one occurred in Paltrul Rinpoche's teaching itself, at the times when he would say directly, "You must correct and improve your motivation"—just like I am telling you now.

If these Three Opportunities did not work, then for the most part, Paltrul Rinpoche would kick you out of the encampment. He would say, "You are just fooling me and I am just fooling you. There is no point in that, so get out. Go away and become a businessman, get married, have children, get out of here! What's the use of being neither a spiritual practitioner nor a worldly person? Go and be a worldly person! Just have a good heart occasionally." What he meant was, it is not all right to dress up as a Dharma practitioner and merely pretend to be one. To act in this way is not being honest with others, and especially not with oneself.

Motivation is easy to talk about yet sometimes hard to have. We always forget the simplest things, partly because we don't take them seriously. We would rather learn the more advanced, difficult stuff. And yet the simple can also be very profound. When a teaching is presented as a brain teaser and is hard to figure out but you finally get it, then you may feel satisfied. But this feeling of temporary satisfaction is not the real benefit. To really saturate yourself, your entire being, with the Dharma, you need the proper motivation. Please apply this thoroughly, all the time.

In Vajrayana teachings, we find many instructions on how to improve our motivation. In fact, if you really learn about how this motivation should be, the whole bodhichitta teaching is contained within that. Cultivate the correct motivation within your own experience, and it turns into bodhichitta all by itself.

I have been teaching now for fifteen years. To teach on the view, on emptiness and so forth, all of that is of course great, but when I look through the whole range of teachings, the real dividing line between whether one's practice goes in the right direction or the wrong direction always comes down to motivation. That is the pivotal point.

Without pure motivation, no matter how profound the method is that we apply, it still turns into spiritual materialism. To train in being a bodhisattva and cultivate bodhichitta so that "I can be happy" means something is twisted from the very beginning. Instead, embrace your practice with the genuine bodhichitta motivation.

Nyoshul Khen Rinpoche, who is one of my root gurus, would teach on motivation over and over again. He talked about it so much that, frankly, I sometimes felt a little bored, thinking, "He talked about it yesterday, he talked about it today, and he will probably talk about it tomorrow. This is a little too much. I've already heard it." This kind of resistance is actually very good proof that ego doesn't like teachings on pure motivation. Right there, at the moment one feels resistance against the altruistic attitude, that is the precise spot to work with, touchy as it may be. To admit this and be willing to deal with it right at that point is very practical, very pragmatic. I think that the whole point of practice is using Dharma teachings at the exact point of resistance. Otherwise, we just end up practicing when we feel good, and we avoid it when we feel bored or restless. At the very moment of feeling depressed, restless, or unhappy, take these moods as a really good training opportunity, as a blessing, and put the Dharma to use right on the spot. Think, "I am so glad I have this opportunity to practice meditation. I am deeply delighted. Please come here, unhappiness, depression, every type of suffering! Please come closer, I am so happy to see you!" When we train in this type of "welcoming practice" on a daily basis, we can progress and become truly transformed. Otherwise we are just postponing the main problem until some indefinite future time, tomorrow and then again tomorrow. We postpone it again and again, until the doctor says, "Sorry, your time is up! No more tomorrows."

I can promise you that the Dharma works well if you use it well. I have a great deal of trust that the teachings of the awakened Buddha are extremely profound and precious. Their practice can solve our basic problem permanently and completely. All our confusion, all our emotional obscurations can be completely undone. Not only can we achieve liberation for ourselves personally, but we can expand our capacity to benefit others at a deep and true level, not just superficially. All these tools and insights are presented in the Buddha's teachings. To use them only for temporary, shallow purposes, as is often the case with therapy—approaching practice as a bit of self-improvement—degrades the Buddha's teachings to the level of a self-help book. There is no need for that. There are already more than enough of those—stacks of them, mountains of New Age self-help books suggesting this or that kind of therapy. If this is all we want out of Buddhism, we can turn to the easily understood self-help books that already exist. They are actually very useful. But if the future of the Buddhist tradition is no more than another self-help variation, I feel somewhat sad. Someone who simply wants a stronger ego to face the world, make more money, influence people, and become famous maybe doesn't need Buddhism.

This sort of Dharma talk was probably not heard in the past in Tibet. It wasn't necessary then, because the country was full of true practitioners. You just had to look up the mountainside and somebody was sitting there practicing. You could see the dwellings of hermits from wherever you were, scattered all over the sides of mountain ranges. At any given time throughout history, the Drukpa Kagyu tradition abounded with great practitioners who had given up all material concern. These people were happy to just get by on whatever came along, happy to let whatever happened happen; they were free of all emotional baggage and worry for themselves. Maybe they did worry somewhat in the beginning, let's say the first six months of practice, but then they went beyond petty worries. They did not spend their whole lives trying to deal with emotional issues. They dealt with them and went on to the real practice. They did not remain inside the cocoon of spiritual materialism. Wouldn't it be sad to die like that, wrapped up in selfish worry?

Particularly when we come to Vajrayana practice, we must also have a certain amount of courage, a certain kind of mental strength, and together with that, an openness and softness of heart. This quality does not mean we are spaced-out or preoccupied with one thought after another. Rather, we should have a willingness to understand how to practice, along with the open-mindedness. This quality of inner boldness is very important in Vajrayana: being bold not in an aggressive way, as when you're ready to fight whoever opposes you, but rather being ready to do whatever needs to be done. That is a very important quality.

To be a Vajrayana practitioner requires a certain degree of inner strength that grows out of confidence. This is not the aggressive strength of a fighter; it is more a preparedness that refuses to succumb to any obstacle or difficulty: "I am not going to give in, no matter how hard it is. I will just take whatever comes and use the practice to spontaneously liberate that state!" Be this way rather than timid and afraid, always shying away from difficult situations. It is very hard to be a Vajrayana practitioner with a timid, chicken-hearted attitude toward life.

The teachings I discuss here belong to the vehicle of Vajrayana. The Sanskrit word *vajra* literally means "diamond," which is the hardest of all substances. A diamond can cut any other substance, but it cannot itself be cut by anything else. The diamond's strength and impenetrability signify that when the true view of Vajrayana has dawned within our stream of being, we develop a quality of being unmoved or unshaken by obstacles and difficulties. Whatever kind of harm may present itself, whether it be a negative emotion or a physical pain, we have a certain quality of being unassailable, instead of immediately becoming lost and being defeated by that obstacle. The true practitioner of Vajrayana is unassailable in the face of difficulty.

We can succeed in really improving our motivation, and that would be wonderful, not only for ourselves, but also for being able to benefit others.

Salad Dressing

My style of teaching is not necessarily a style that belongs only to me personally, although it's one I often use. I lean toward an approach that emphasizes knowledge. Equally significant is the approach that emphasizes method, or means. Please understand that means and knowledge must always go hand in hand, that we should always practice them in combination. In other words, we need to combine the two accumulations of merit and wisdom. Another way to phrase this is to emphasize the need to combine the two levels of truth, relative and ultimate. This combination of means and knowledge, merit and wisdom, relative truth and ultimate truth is like a great eagle in flight, which needs two wings to fly. The eagle unfolds its wings and soars through the sky based on these twin supports. Shantideva said: "Unfold the two wings of means and knowledge and fly to the state of enlightenment, the realm of all buddhas." The point is that the two wings are equally important. Imagine a bird flying with one wing: it might manage to get off the ground, but it will soon plummet without having gotten very far.

There are plenty of other analogies for this. Doesn't a human being need two legs? When speaking, don't we need both the upper lip and the lower lip? When eating, don't we need both the upper and lower teeth in order to chew? And to determine a distance, don't we need both eyes? To ring a gong, don't we need both the mallet and the instrument to make the sound? In the same way, when practicing the Dharma, we need both means and knowledge, method and insight. This is not somebody's invention or bright idea; this is how reality is. It is a natural law in all cases and situations.

The best situation is to practice in a way in which mind essence is recognized in conjunction with the skillful Vajrayana methods. These methods include refuge, bodhichitta, the preliminary practices, the yidam deity, and so on. To practice these concurrently, excluding neither one nor the other, is the most profound way of perfecting the two accumulations. It is the way of bringing the ground into the path. This is a topic that we might want to reflect on a little bit more.

No matter what Buddhist practice we apply, we should always remember that the two accumulations must be perfected. This holds true from the beginning level of *shravaka* training all the way up to and including Ati Yoga. There are various ways to perfect the two accumulations; here, I will discuss an approach unique to Dzogchen.

The recognition of empty essence—in other words, the insight that realizes egolessness, the absence of an independent identity—is the state of original wakefulness itself. Training in this state perfects the accumulation of wisdom. During whatever formal practice you undertake, do not leave behind this accumulation of wisdom beyond reference point; rather, embrace the particular practice with the recognition of empty essence. Training in this perfects the accumulation of merit, and it does so without your having to hold on to any concepts or struggle to do so. In this way, by simply training in recognizing mind essence you can simultaneously perfect the two accumulations of merit and wisdom.

Through the profound methods of Vajrayana, the two accumulations can be perfected on a tremendous scale. By utilizing certain skillful means to further enhance the recognition of mind essence, we can develop even more quickly, reaching progressively deeper levels.

Let me mention some of these methods. The first entrance to the Buddhist path, which is taking refuge, involves regarding the Buddha as your teacher, the Dharma as your path, and the Sangha as your companions on the path and using all three of these as support, as a refuge. We take refuge in the Three Precious Ones, which are called the outer Three Jewels, in order to realize the state of complete enlightenment. In other words, you could say, "I place my trust in you, the outer Three Jewels, in order to recognize and actualize the inner Three Jewels."

It's not difficult to understand taking refuge once we realize that we already take refuge to a certain extent in various things in the outer world during the ordinary course of our lives. For example, as university students we are helped and supported by the educational setting. We respect it for what it is, that it enables us to get our degree. Here we are taking refuge in the university, and in that sense it is worthwhile. The secular tutoring we receive enables us to reach that full degree of education, of intellectual knowledge, which is similar to the Dharma teachings. Our fellow students and the faculty are the university sangha, whom we respect as helpers on our educational path. In Buddhist terms, there is the Buddha, who represents the ultimate state of enlightenment. There are the teachings that he gave, the Dharma; using them is the path to that state of enlightenment. Then there are the Sangha companions, our fellow practitioners, who provide the support and help for us to reach that destination. When we take refuge in this way, we accept the precept of giving up harming others as well as relinquishing the basic causes for harming others.

Generally speaking, reality has two aspects: the seeming and the real. We take refuge from the seeming aspect, which is the state of confusion, in order to realize the real. As long as we haven't realized how things actually are, there is a need to seek support in the objects of refuge. A certain beneficial influence arises though this, which, in old-fashioned terminology, is called blessings.

By taking refuge, we are actually requesting an influence. We *want* to be influenced by what the buddhas have experienced; we *want* to have their state of realization sway our minds. That is the real purpose of taking refuge. It is actually possible because the realized state of the buddhas is not a solid, material substance but something insubstantial. Since our minds are also not made of material substance, a connection can arise between these two—between our minds and the enlightened minds of the buddhas. Using material substances to influence our immaterial mind can have a certain effect, but it is superficial. True blessings can take place only through that which shares our mind's immaterial quality.

We could distort the act of taking of refuge by thinking of ourselves as lost, helpless, and worthless: "I can't do anything except surrender to the Buddha, Dharma, and Sangha." Then we wait there and expect that the buddhas will take us and throw us into an enlightened state, just like flinging a stone into a pond. I'm sorry, but this is not the way it works. This is not the right way to take refuge. Rather, regard taking refuge as being willing to realize the state of enlightenment so that we understand the fundamental indivisibility of the wisdom of the buddhas and the original wakefulness present in ourselves. That is the real refuge.

Once we have established the refuge attitude in ourselves in a realistic and effective way, the next step is to become a bodhisattva. Taking the bodhisattva vow essentially means we form the resolve to help other beings, and we actively work to create the basis for doing so. In other words, having taken the vow, we are counted among the bodhisattvas. This doesn't mean we become perfect bodhisattvas simply by taking the vow. Rather, it means that we are aiming in that direction; we are moving toward bodhisattva perfection. Taking the bodhisattva vow is like planting the seed of being a bodhisattva. We are creating the basis for helping and benefiting others.

Bodhichitta, the enlightened attitude, is like a moisturizer for our basic nature. It is like salad dressing on the salad of our basic state. Without this, we are just a little too dry. Our usual way of solidifying and fixating on experience causes us to be deluded, to move away from our basic nature. This pursuit makes us very dry, antsy and restless. We are always chasing after this and that, in a very limited and narrow-minded way. Both our perspective and aims must be opened up. We may not immediately be able to generate the true and perfected state of awakened mind, but we can at least begin to by forming a wish, a resolve: "I want to benefit all sentient beings, and for this reason I will practice the Dharma." It's possible for us to experience that opening, that starting point, right now, this very instant.

The real bodhichitta, which is awakened mind, is of course already present within us as our basic nature, but somehow it is covered up by our normal way of thinking, encased within the shell of deluded perceptions. It's not so easy to have it become visible immediately in a full-fledged way. It's as if we need to plagiarize awakened mind a little bit, by forming a thought as an imitation. There is really no way around this other than to make a facsimile of the awakened attitude. When a new gadget is invented in the United States, in China someone immediately makes a copy of it to sell. The real gadget is still in the USA, but the copies are being fabricated right and left. Similarly, we need to copy bodhichitta by forming the thought of compassion for all beings. There is nothing wrong with that. Bodhichitta is not copyrighted; no company manufactures it, so it's not as if we'll be sued. We simply want to imitate what we have heard so much about, the awakened state realized by the buddhas and masters of the past.

Now we may have heard in various Mahamudra and Dzogchen teachings that we should be totally free from artificial concepts, completely natural, and realize mind's original, natural state. And here I am saying, "Form the thought of wanting to benefit all sentient beings." We might think, "That's artificial. If I try to make up something that is not already present, then I'm corrupting the mind's natural state." We might even feel guilty and shy away from doing so and thus end up with nothing. Of course, it is wonderful if you have already realized the original wakefulness that is the awakened state of all buddhas; by all means, don't hold yourself back. There is no problem at all if it arises as an actuality in your own experience. But if it doesn't and you feel guilty about fabricating bodhisattva motivation, you simply end up without anything—without either the real thing or the copy. Many people stumble on this problem.

To make a copy, to fabricate a conceptual thought, is perfectly okay if it is helpful and useful. If a copy works like the original, what's the problem? The idea here is that if we don't have anything, if we don't have a natural orientation toward the bodhisattva's frame of mind, then it is fine to make a copy, because then you at least have something. As you improve upon it, it gets better and better, so that ultimately it may be perfectly splendid. There is nothing wrong with imitating the vow taken by all bodhisattvas; in fact, we should do so.

Refuge and bodhichitta are both included in the excellent method known as the preliminary practices of the four times 100,000. To undertake these preliminary practices, the *ngöndro*, is something very precious. We begin by taking refuge together with making prostrations, bowing down 100,000 times. Sometimes we form the bodhisattva resolve along with refuge and prostrations. The purpose of taking refuge, as I mentioned earlier, is to turn away from samsaric existence and aim in the direction of complete enlightenment. We do so by seeking help from the Three Precious Ones.

Next in the *ngöndro* comes the meditation and recitation on Vajrasattva. Vajrasattva is the buddha who embodies all other enlightened families. He is described as their natural form and as the buddha of purification. This practice removes all our negative karma and obscurations, all our faults and failings in the sense of broken promises, which prevent us from making progress on the path to enlightenment.

Next is the mandala offering. The purpose of this is to relinquish all kinds of ego-clinging and any form of conceptual attitude that holds on to something as being one's own. Giving away everything, by means of the outer, inner, and innermost mandala offerings, relinquishes all types of clinging. Automatically, at the same time, the accumulation of merit is perfected.

It's said that the first mandala offering was made after the Buddha attained complete enlightenment, when the kings of the gods, Brahma and Indra, requested him to teach the Dharma. Presenting the Buddha with a thousand-spoked golden wheel and a miraculous rare white conch shell that coiled clockwise, they requested him to begin teaching, to turn the wheel of the Dharma.

Later, when the Tibetan king Trisong Deutsen invited Padmasambhava to Tibet to establish the Buddha's teachings in his country, he composed four lines of verse to accompany his offering. As he made the mandala offering to Padmasambhava with the request to teach, he gave his entire kingdom, all three provinces of central Tibet, as an offering. While making the offering of his kingdom, he chanted these lines, which we still recite today:

> The earth is perfumed with scented water and strewn with
> flowers,
> Adorned with Mount Meru, the four continents, the sun, and
> the moon.
> Imagining this as the Buddha realm, I offer it
> So that all beings may enjoy that pure realm.[1]

I am told that it was due to the auspicious coincidence of the king making this mandala offering that the Vajrayana teachings were able to remain for such a long time in the country of Tibet, in a natural and very propitious way.

What is the substance of such an auspicious coincidence? It consists of a complete surrender of ego-clinging. That is essentially what our practice of the mandala offerings is about—laying down everything that could be clung to as being "me" and "mine." We could say that the king totally opened himself up. He turned over to Padmasambhava whatever he might cling to as being his, and in this way he rendered himself a genuinely suitable recipient for the Vajrayana teachings.

By completely surrendering ego-clinging, King Trisong Deutsen established an authentic basis for the Vajrayana teachings in Tibet. Not only was giving away his entire kingdom an incredibly courageous deed; it was also a way to temporarily make a gap in ego-clinging. Of course,

---

[1] Translated by Nalanda Translation Committee.

ego-clinging cannot be totally and permanently erased from one moment to the next. This is a process that happens through disciplined training. Still, the temporary suspension of ego-clinging is in itself something truly remarkable.

Some people might ask, "How can I offer Mount Meru, the four continents, the sun and the moon, and so on when they don't actually belong to me? How can I give them away? They didn't belong to King Trisong Deutsen either, so how could he give them away?" It's not necessary to be this nitpicky. As a matter of fact, our world does belong to us. Whatever we perceive through our five senses and whatever occurs in our mental field constitutes our world, our life, and as the contents of our own experience it is ours to give. Our personal experience doesn't belong to anybody else. Thus, we are able to give away whatever we perceive as our world.

One purpose of the mandala offering is to eliminate ego-clinging. Another is to perfect the accumulation of merit. Any act of giving is an offering, not just of the object being given but of the effort that went into creating that object. For example, when giving a single butter lamp you offer not only the act of lighting the wick, but also the work you put into obtaining the butter or the oil, creating the vessel, providing the metal that formed the vessel, and so forth. This principle applies to other types of offering as well. Basically, all that energy is what creates the merit.

Some people understand the concept of merit quite readily, while for others it's difficult to comprehend. Merit most definitely does exist. Like everything else in the world, it's formed through causes and conditions. All phenomena come about through causes and circumstance; there is no independent entity anywhere. Everything depends on causes and conditions. For instance, anything material is dependent on the four elements. Especially in the West, with its emphasis on materiality, matters are very dependent. Like everything else, merit is dependent on causes and conditions. Through the accumulation of merit, positive situations can be created. For example, meeting with the Dharma and receiving instructions on practice requires a certain amount of favorable circumstances to arise simultaneously. The occurrence of this requires merit.

Mandala offering is a very profound practice, which is why it is one of the preliminaries in the Tibetan tradition. I personally feel that all the preliminary practices are extremely important, but among them, the most profound are probably guru yoga and mandala offering. That doesn't mean the others are not profound, but rather that these are perhaps the most profound. People often come to me and say, "I understand the reason for doing the prostrations, taking refuge. I also understand the purification aspect of Vajrasattva practice. But I just don't get the point of making mandala offerings, and I don't understand guru yoga." This kind of statement shows how profound these practices actually are. Ego is not so willing to accept them. Ego is very clever and would like to create doubt for us about anything that undermines it, anything that might prove hazardous to its favorite practice, which is ego-clinging. This is really true—check it out for yourself. Whenever something is harmful to ego, ego will try to raise doubts about it. We need to recognize this trick from the beginning.

Prostrations are easy for people to understand. Some look at them as if they're good physical exercise. They think that they're good for the heart: "Oh, I understand. Prostrations strengthen my legs and back. If I sit for a long time in meditation and I get back pain, then I'll just do prostrations to correct this. I might feel drowsy or lazy, but prostrations will chop up the laziness. I think refuge is very important: whatever we do, we need a certain type of guidance. So we have the Buddha as our guide, Dharma as the path or technique, and friends as the Sangha. I completely understand taking refuge. And Vajrasattva is the natural form or the manifestation of compassionate emptiness. I get it. By chanting the mantra and visualizing this thing moving down through me, well, I don't exactly know what bad karma and obscurations are, but I feel less guilty. All this feeling bad about myself goes away, so that's great. Karma, all these things, well, I don't really know—but never mind, I certainly have some baggage, a few emotional patterns. I must clean these out; it makes sense.

But mandala offering I don't understand. Offering the whole world—it doesn't even belong to me. Mount Meru does not even exist, and what's this about the four continents, when there are actually seven? And why offer the moon and sun? It's ridiculous, crazy talk. Also that thing about blessings, I don't get it. And why do we have to supplicate the guru, who after all is somebody made of flesh and blood, just like us? What's the point of that?"

These doubts come up because we don't really understand what the "guru" in guru yoga really means. The guru is not just the particular person you met. The guru principle refers to a lot of things. There is the guru as *nirmanakaya, sambhogakaya,* and *dharmakaya,* and the essence body, the *svabhavikakaya.* There is the guru as living lineage master, as well as the guru who manifests as our life situations and the guru who is the scriptures we read. Then there is the guru who is our intrinsic nature. We should understand all of these aspects as being the guru. If you learn something from a tree, then that is the guru as symbolic experience. You could say, "All right, I'll take support from the tree; I learned something there." If your wife is giving you a hard time and you learn something from that, your wife is your guru in that situation.

The purpose of guru yoga is to receive the blessings of realization of the root and lineage masters. Recognition and stability in the self-knowing wakefulness of one's own nature doesn't take place without direct transmission by a living teacher. Therefore, connecting with a living master and practicing guru yoga is essential.

There is a very good reason the preliminary practices come before the main part of practice. Every single aspect of the preliminary practices is meant to be like a pestle to grind and smash your laziness. Imagine that you are making hot sauce, *achaar,* with a stone mortar and pestle. When making this Tibetan salsa, you successively add garlic, ginger, chili peppers, and spices, grinding them all together into a smooth sauce. It's the same with the preliminaries: you smash your laziness first with prostrations, then with Vajrasattva practice, then with mandala offerings and guru yoga, till all the laziness is gone. If you really go through these practices in an effective, thorough way, there is no room for being lazy, for hanging on to personal comfort—none at all.

After we do all the preliminary practices, we find we can sit for one hour, five hours, six hours in meditation, and it really feels like taking time off: "What I went through before was so hard, but this is nothing—I can easily sit and meditate for hours and hours." This is because the laziness has been totally vanquished.

You might think it would be enough to do only 10,000 repetitions, but our tradition is to do 100,000 of each. With this quantity, there's no way to be lazy. You'll never finish unless you really persevere, really push yourself and use a lot of effort. In this way, because you do 100,000 of each practice, the laziness does not dare return. It'll mutter to itself,

"I'm just getting a beating if I stay around here. If I dare to come back, I'll probably get 100,000 beatings again, so I'm not gonna hang around this guy any longer." I'm not joking here; it's really true.

For a practitioner who has already recognized self-knowing wakefulness, doing the preliminaries can totally obliterate all laziness so that none remains. At the same time, these practices also perfect the two accumulations and remove all hindrances. The essence of mind is further and further revealed by the steady process of removing that which obscures it. All this takes place through the practice of the preliminaries.

When we are about to begin Vajrasattva practice it is good to have received empowerment to Vajrayana. This empowers us to realize the three vajras—the fact that body, speech, and mind are by nature the innate three doors. There are four levels of empowerment in Vajrayana: the vase empowerment, the secret empowerment, the wisdom knowledge empowerment, and the precious word empowerment. Once we have received empowerment, utilizing skillful means is like squeezing our body, speech, and mind in such a way that they have no choice but to be realized as the three innate vajras, as the vajra body, speech, and mind. There is no alternative to this; it is inevitable.

There is much to learn in Vajrayana, and many skillful methods. For instance, the five negative emotions are by nature the five wisdoms. These five wisdoms are the buddhas of the five families—that is, if the vital essence of the emotions is recognized. Then it can be truly said that one doesn't have to suppress or reject the emotions. Rather, they can be realized as being the five types of original wakefulness, the five wisdoms. I will go into more detail about this later.

Vajrayana is something precious and rare. The methods of Secret Mantra are not often given. Of the thousand buddhas to appear during this world period, the Vajrayana teachings are available only during the reign of two of them: Buddha Shakyamuni and the last, who is a manifestation of Buddha Manjugosha. Other than that, Vajrayana doesn't really happen. Why is this? The methods of Vajrayana appear only during the right time, when emotions are visibly manifest in a very blatant and crude way. Our present era is one of these times.

When the emotions are very strong and rough, the potential intelligence within them is equally strong. Strong emotions create big problems. Whenever there are more problems and turmoil, there is an opportunity for strong insight to take place. This opportunity is available right now. Now is the time when the methods of Vajrayana can be utilized. Based on the very profound and swift methods of Vajrayana, it is possible to attain true and complete enlightenment within this very same body and lifetime. If we don't do this within this lifetime, it is said that it will occur within three, five, or at most sixteen lives; that is, if one doesn't break one's samaya and develop impure perception, turning against the teachings. Thus, Vajrayana practitioners are guaranteed to reach enlightenment within at most sixteen lifetimes.

The general teachings of the buddhas are more a matter of developing a placid, uncomplicated state of mind free of strong emotion. Precisely because of this emphasis, there is no presence of a strong intelligence. This doesn't provide the opportunity to realize the wisdoms and swiftly attain enlightenment. Using the general methods one must journey along the path for three incalculable eons, which is a very, very long time. This route offers a very gentle, steady journey toward enlightenment that is relatively uncomplicated and certainly safer than Vajrayana.

Right now, however, we have the opportunity, rather than suppressing negative emotions, to realize their natural purity. To apply this, and to truly understand Vajrayana, you must have a strong intelligence, otherwise you cannot pick up the methods. You need a very sharp innate intelligence in order to eliminate or break free of the conceptual frame of mind. Conceptual mind wants to make you stay within the boundaries of concepts.

Vajrayana practitioners should not belittle the emotions. Emotions are like smoke, and if there is smoke, there is also fire. In other words, when you look at somebody who has very strong emotions, that person may also have a lot of wisdom. Who knows? Such a person may perhaps, through skillful methods, be able to realize the original wakefulness within the emotions. Such a person may be able to make tremendous progress on the Vajrayana path. That doesn't mean that one should get caught up in the emotions, of course. When we are overtaken by emotions, we are exactly the same as an ordinary person: we are not progressing on the path.

Please don't misunderstand this point. What I just said is that in Vajrayana practice we appreciate the emotions. I don't mean that you necessarily have to *create* more emotions. Don't be thinking, "When I'm in front of my master, I should show some aggression; then maybe he'll teach me Vajrayana." Please don't go looking for trouble!

We don't have to create emotions at all. Rather, within the naturally arising emotions we find a certain strength, a certain intelligence. That strength can be realized as the fuel of original wakefulness. Imagine the opposite of that—someone who is never angry, never irritated, never depressed, and never delighted; who has no thought of wanting to hurt others and no thought of wanting to help others either. That type of personality is listless and complacent, content with being dull.

We don't have to worry about becoming like that, because it won't happen: right now we live in a time of very turbulent emotions. Perhaps in the future this type of emotional placidity will arise again. It's said that when Buddha Maitreya comes there will be a gradual absence of disease. The human life span will lengthen so that people will experience no worries about being sick or uncomfortable. There will be plenty of food, so that whenever one wants to eat one can just reach out and take some. There will be no need to apply effort to take care of oneself, so there will be no hope and fear about one's own existence. One can just sit back and relax without having to worry about a thing. Since there won't be many emotional disturbances, there will also not be anyone who is a suitable vessel for the Vajrayana teachings. Therefore, the Vajrayana teachings will not be given.

We are not at all in this situation nowadays, of course; we are in the opposite situation. Emotions are abundant. As we apply these skillful methods of Vajrayana to eliminate confusion, less and less confusion arises, especially through our having recognized the basic nature of original wakefulness. Some of these methods cut off the ears of confusion; some of them tear off the arms of confusion; some peel off the skin of confusion. Through the use of these methods, fewer and fewer moments of confusion will arise, until confusion is totally gone.

Please make a distinction between illusory experience and the belief that illusory experiences are real. These are two different points. Illusory experience has already happened; its scenery has already been produced. That's what we live in right now. We're not yet able to be free of illusion from one moment to the next. What we need to deal with, our point of critical action, is something other than that. We *can* turn away from and eliminate the belief that illusory experiences are real. It's as if we have already fallen asleep and are already dreaming. There is nothing to do about that. But within the dream, we can confront our belief that the dream is real. We are able to recognize that it is just a dream, that it's not real. And once we discover that the dream is just a dream while dreaming it, then it is possible to wake up. Do you understand this analogy? In the dream, you are dreaming. And if you know that what you are experiencing in the dream is just a dream, then you can look for a method to wake up. But you don't know how to wake up. You realize that it is the dream state, but you lack the method to wake up. So in the dream, you look around to seek the method. Seeking the method is also part of the dream. Then you might meet the dream master inside the dream. You request the method from that dream master, and the dream master teaches you. That teaching is also part of the dream. But because you apply the dream teaching, you arrive back into the original state. That is like having woken up. The dream teacher gives you a dream method to actually wake you up. So then you wake up. You are not *really* getting the awakened state from the dream teacher, because the dream teacher is also a dream. But you get the method from him, you utilize it, and then you wake up.

In a similar vein, the Buddha once said: "I never taught the Dharma. I am not teaching the Dharma now, and in the future I will never teach the Dharma either." As with many teachings, there are many levels of understanding this statement. There is the expedient level of meaning as well as the definitive meaning. We shouldn't necessarily cling to every single statement as being the ultimate truth.

Having recognized mind essence, we utilize various types of methods to perfect its strength. We need to progress by strengthening the insight aspect. Developing this strength is difficult, but we should not give up. Soccer players who want to participate in the World Cup train ceaselessly. They try to perfect their strength to qualify for the World Cup series. It's a basic requirement that you have to be a human being to be a World Cup player. You could train a monkey to be a World Cup champion, but he won't play because he is a monkey. A monkey will only perform his own activities. In the same way, you need first of all to recognize mind essence. And it is that recognition of mind essence, the strength of that, that needs to be perfected gradually through various methods.

The Vajrayana depiction of deities in union shows us that means and knowledge are both necessary. Unity is the nature of the deity—the unity of emptiness and experience. The experience aspect appears as the male, while the empty quality is the female. Not understanding the real significance of these deities in union, one may think, "Why are the deities always in union? Aren't they ever satisfied? It seems as if they're stuck together!" Actually, this symbol means that intrinsic to emptiness is a state that is totally untainted by any obscuration, which manifests as bliss indivisible from emptiness. That is the purpose of depicting the deities as naked. Their fully developed attributes of bliss symbolize that the deities of our aggregates, elements, and sense factors are totally revealed in their purest nature through the recognition of empty bliss.

There is the approach of attaining liberation by means of desire, attaining liberation through aggression, attaining liberation through dullness, and so forth. In this way there are many profound methods in Vajrayana. The Vajra Vehicle of Secret Mantra is extremely profound and extremely effective.

When you apply the Vajrayana teachings, do so with clarity, free from any misconceptions about what is what. We must know clearly the purpose and the significance of the symbolism, so that we don't form distortions about the profound nature of the Vajrayana teachings. It is very, very hard to find anything in this world more profound or more precious than the Vajrayana teachings. This is my personal opinion.

Why is this so? In order to overcome emotions, not to get caught up in them or be overtaken by them, there is no method more profound than recognizing mind essence. You may want to smash a painful emotion to bits, but you can't blow it up with a nuclear bomb. Even hundreds of thousands of nuclear bombs detonated at the same time will not stop dualistic mind from creating more emotions. If someone were to kill every single human being in this world, dualistic mind would still continue making emotions. Through the power of karma, all these minds would take rebirth in some other world and continue in the same way as before.

No matter what drug one takes, there is no way to stop dualistic mind from churning out selfish emotions. It's not like in the movie *The Matrix*, where you take a pill and wake up to reality. It doesn't happen this easily; there is really no way to do that. Of course there are pills to eat. There are pills to make you feel less, to make you unfeeling, or to make you feel nothing, to become totally oblivious—no emotions, no wakefulness, no nothing.

However, there are not any pills to make you genuinely more compassionate and less aggressive, to make you wiser and less caught up in negative emotions. There are no pills like that that I know of right now. In the future, who knows? But it certainly doesn't help to wait for that pill to come along someday. Much better to use the realistic approach of practice right now!

What we need first of all is to recognize mind essence and to develop the strength of that. As we continue to develop the strength of this recognition, one day we will attain stability.

Can I have a few questions now?

STUDENT: I don't want to question the Dharma, but I have some problems in combining the Dharma teachings with modern psychology.

RINPOCHE: I don't feel that there's any real conflict between the psychological method and the Buddhist method. The vital point is whether the method works or not. If it works, great; there is no conflict. If there's still a remnant of anger or resentment left behind, then it didn't really work and so it's not that good a method. The real test is whether the psychological method is truly effective

For example, one discovers there's a reason one feels aggressive again and again, and one starts to investigate: "Why am I getting so angry? There doesn't seem to be much reason in this. It's irrational." And then one finds out that it has some earlier cause, that something was done to *me* that wasn't really resolved from the past; maybe Mom and Dad mistreated me as a child, or somebody else abused me. Because of understanding this, one can step away from hating oneself. One understands oneself better; there is more self-knowledge. But still there is some resentment toward Mom and Dad or whoever the perpetrator was. That part of the problem hasn't really been resolved. One's anger at oneself has gone, but there is still some other anger remaining. This means that sort of therapy didn't really work that well in terms of eliminating anger altogether.

But let's say the therapy goes a little deeper, so that one is actually able to forgive the target of one's resentment and totally relinquish it. This means it worked: the anger is given up and resolved. In other words, when the method works, it's wonderful. One experiences a kind of liberation through that. One is free of that type of emotion. Then it is a genuine therapy, a real cure.

I must admit to having one criticism of a certain type of Western therapy. Even though it can solve a lot of problems for people, there is the tendency to blame Mom and Dad, or early childhood problems, for everything: "You're fine, there's nothing wrong with you, but you have problems because of how your father treated you. Therefore your father is no good." Temporarily there is a certain release in this, because you take the focus of the problem away from yourself. Also it's logical in its own way; there's some reason in it. But it creates the basis for another emotional problem, which is resentment toward one's own parents.

Buddhist psychology attempts to solve the whole issue from a different angle. You begin with accustoming yourself to thinking of all sentient beings, countless as they may be, as your own fathers and mothers. Other beings are the first objects of compassion. If you instead build up resentment toward your mother and father, there is no way you would want to regard all sentient beings as your own fathers and mothers. If you are trained in regarding Mom and Dad as your enemy and then are told to regard all sentient beings as Mom and Dad, basically this will mean, "All sentient beings are my enemies!"

The point here is that honestly, you don't have to blame anyone. You don't even have to blame yourself. Just understand this very important point: everything you experience is empty form, an unreal presence of empty form. Realizing emptiness solves every problem right there.

Buddhism has many methods. There are two major ones that can be applied in this situation: one is analytical, the other is just letting be. Analytical meditation involves trying to track down where the anger actually is, where it comes from, what it is made out of, and so forth. If one discovers—as one can also discover in psychological therapy—that there is actually no real anger to find anywhere, that it doesn't consist of anything, then this method actually solves the problem.

In the other method, called resting meditation, or "training in letting be," you simply drop all involvement in a conceptual frame of mind. This too can solve the problem from its very core. Sometimes analytical meditation is not enough, because a conceptual attitude still lingers on. That is why I usually emphasize the second method, the training in letting be. In Tibetan it's called jo-gom, literally, "release training."

In the analytical training, one may try to find the reason a situation happens and to resolve the problem by figuring it out. For example, I examine why I feel a certain way: "What made me feel this way? Was it Mom or Dad or some event in early childhood?" If the me is still held to be real, and the analyzing mind, the *me* who is trying to investigate, is still believed to truly be there, then it is hard to genuinely forgive, because the hurt was really done to *me*. No matter how much one tries to tell oneself, "They couldn't really help it; you can't really blame them because they were also caught up in what they were doing, so why not just let it go," it's difficult to actually do so. Because of the holding on to *me*, it's not so easy to let go of the one who received that hurt.

On the other hand, when we discover through the training in letting be that this *me* actually doesn't really exist, it can just be dropped. Then it's much easier to resolve the whole problem. The technique here is mainly to let go of this *me*. I understand it's not necessarily easy. But I also know that it can be very useful if we succeed. Please trust me on this.

Shamatha:
The Benefits

Well, here we all are in the Kathmandu Valley. There is pollution, life is difficult, and all our programs and plans are continually being interrupted. When people first fly in, they think, "What a pure land! I am arriving in a buddhafield! Whatever I planned I can carry out smoothly and neatly." But then what happens? As soon as you try to do something, you're told, "Not today, tomorrow. No problem ... it'll happen ... but not today." Even if you present someone with a difficult job, they will say, "No problem. I'll take care of it tomorrow." At some point you realize that this is not like the United States, where people just say no. Here they say, "Sure! Yes! No problem." And you think how wonderful it all is: "In two or three days I can do a lot!" Then you find out that "all right" actually means "not all right." I believe a lot of you residents are familiar with this.

Some people come to Nepal with particular plans and goals in mind. A Dharma practitioner may think, "Okay, I have six months here. I will meet this teacher first, next that teacher, then this third teacher. I will request such and such teachings and receive them; then I will go practice in this or that holy place. I will have such and such realization and go home."

If you are a foreign aid volunteer, you might think, "I'm going to carry out this particular project, which will be completed on such and such a date." If you are a mountaineer, you might think, "I am going to climb this mountain and go trekking in that area. If there is extra time, then I'll go to such and such a place." You may have all sorts of different plans, but at the end of the visit you'd be doing well to have accomplished even 20 percent of what you set out to do. There is nothing to be done about this particular situation; it's just an illustration of the habits of the planning mind. Meanwhile, the Nepalese people are quite content. They are easygoing and happy to smile and say, "All right, no problem. Tomorrow, no problem. Five o'clock, okay?" Then you wait until five o'clock, but nothing happens. They say, "Sorry, something came up. Tomorrow, two o'clock, no problem." Also the next day, nothing.

Foreigners in Nepal are faced with a confrontation between their habit of having everything on a fixed schedule and their consequent assumption that things will happen on time, and how it actually is here in reality. Things are much looser in Nepal, not so fixed. If we somehow manage during those six months to let go of our rigid expectations just a little bit, we may actually be happier people when we go home, even though we didn't accomplish much. But if we start to find fault and obsess about what didn't happen, we'll find only one thing after another that did not work out. That could make us unhappy. On the other hand, we have the opportunity to become happier by learning not to care so much.

What I would like to convey here is that if we aim to learn how to be at ease with ourselves and our surroundings in a way that is content, open, and free, then Nepal is a pretty good place to learn that. To be rigidly goal-oriented and want to nail everything down according to a certain schedule—"I want to achieve this now; I want to finish that on time"—only makes us more stressed here. To import our rigid Western scheduling mind-set and superimpose it on the chaotic reality of the East is an exercise in frustration. We must know this distinction. Here in the apparent chaos of Nepal, the illusion of this world seems more obvious. It is frustrating to try to make the illusion more concrete, because it is ultimately impossible. We cannot solidify an illusion; it is not its nature.

The basic quality of illusion is bewilderment. Illusion immediately becomes more workable when we acknowledge it as simply an illusion. The Western habit is to work against the grain and try to organize the illusory into something solid and structured. This approach is fundamentally problematic, because it is inherently futile. It seems that many people are fond of trying to frustrate themselves. In the stressful attempt to nail down the illusory nature of things, our chance to be at ease, spacious, awake, and free, which already exists within ourselves, gets lost. We lose track of it.

I would like us to discover that there is a way in which we don't get totally caught up in obsessing with objects—a way to be in our own nature. Not only being able to be free and easy in ourselves, but also not lose that while moving about in our daily activities. Moreover, there is a certain radiance that could come forth from being in this natural state. This radiance can manifest as compassion.

A lot of people talk about compassion in this world. It's a word that's on many people's lips, and certainly it is very important. If we truly succeed in being a real bodhisattva, someone who has the enlightened frame of mind, that is wonderful. But for this to actually happen, many factors have to be lined up. The first stumbling block to bodhichitta being genuinely present in our minds is our tendency to be preoccupied with objects we perceive, in the sense of our attention focusing in a more rigid way on "me getting that." There is no real rest from this obsession. We are constantly fixating on objects and becoming tired from this effort. Our experience is a mixture of fixing our mind on different things, one after another, and being worn out by doing so. Because we are almost incessantly preoccupied with this, that, and the next thing, there is hardly any free time to be there for others and care for them. True compassion gets no room in one's mind. That is the first obstacle: preoccupation with personal gain.

What does a novice bodhisattva, someone who is trying to be a bodhisattva, do in this situation? First, realize that it is necessary to calm down this busyness, this constant preoccupation with one object after the other. Allow this to relax a bit, so that the qualities of shamatha have a chance to emerge in your mind. These qualities are generally termed *bliss, clarity*, and *nonthought*. Through training, they become more present in your mind. Perhaps "being at ease" fits better than "bliss" in this context. The more we are at ease, the more we are willing to open up a bit. When our attitude is not oriented exclusively around "me," we experience a greater readiness to share. There is a sense of wanting all our friends to be at ease that gradually expands to encompass the whole population around us, the whole region.

First, a calming down is required, followed by the mind training in wishing others well and caring about their well-being. All this grows from being at ease with ourselves—in other words, being free of suffering and not feeling so needy ourselves. Only when we are no longer so needy can we can start to care. In order for bodhichitta to be genuine, we need a basic sense of calm and ease before the possibility of training our minds to care for others becomes feasible.

It seems to me that the process follows this sequence: If we are not calmed down, it means we are still busy. This busyness pervades our whole system, including the channels and the energies that move through the channels. These become speedy and restless, drying up our vital essences. Without calming down, there is no sense of being at ease. The calmer we are, the more we begin to relax and settle. This makes room for the energies to circulate more freely and our essences to saturate our system more. As this occurs, we feel a natural delight that can turn into compassion. This being at ease with ourselves, accepting or having a certain affection for our own state of being, can be steadily expanded to include others. This is the true beginning of meditation practice.

The genuine warmth that grows out of being at ease with oneself is a little different from the *idea* of being a bodhisattva. The formula for the latter is the thought "I want to bring all sentient beings to the state of enlightenment."

That idea is one aspect. Another is the actuality of how we really feel while we practice. There can seem to be quite a large disparity between the two! By relaxing and feeling a little bit at ease, are we truly establishing all beings in the state of enlightenment? This seems somewhat presumptuous, if not a bit outrageous. Still, we have to start somewhere in order for it to come true. We believe, "I am benefiting all sentient beings right now," but it is not really true. Realistically speaking, all that we *can* do is start somewhere, be relaxed, have a sense of delight, and expand it to become compassion that can then gradually become all-encompassing.

To start cultivating some empathy for yourself, begin with your right arm: "What a nice little arm. Cute little fingers too. It used to look better, though, when I was younger. Ah, poor little fingers—what to do? They're there; this is the way they are." Then you have a left arm, legs, a body, and so on. All of these are okay; they are all there. Inside too—lungs, heart, inner organs—all okay. But before, you did not seem to give much love and care to those parts. This is not the same as body-building or trying to be something other than what you actually are at this moment. Rather, it's more the sense of appreciating the hard work that, say, your kidneys have been doing all this time: "Sitting in front of the computer, oh, you must be tired now. I will give you a little rest.

You have been working very hard. I'll let you relax a bit now." Also—especially!—feel some empathy for this poor brain. We have been constricting it by concentrating so hard. Now let's give it a break.

We can begin with ourselves in this practice, trying to relax enough to finally be at ease within ourselves. Then we extend this feeling to other sentient beings who are also troubled by various difficulties: "May they all be free of suffering." We can gradually expand from there to cover greater and greater numbers of beings, until our compassion becomes infinite.

Because it is so important for practice to be based on a relaxed mind and a carefree, easygoing attitude, the Buddha began with the teaching of shamatha. The Buddha gave two types of teachings: one for the intellect, or the brain if you prefer, and the other for experiencing an aspect you can call the heart. Thus, we have heart teachings and brain teachings. As a matter of fact, the Tibetan word for compassion has the word "heart" in it; *nying* is heart, and the word *nyingje* is compassion. *Je* means "the most eminent." The eminent heart is compassion.

People are often more interested in Buddhism's brain teachings than its heart teachings. If you focus exclusively on brain teachings, however, you start to look like this. [*Rinpoche hunches over, furrows his brow, and squints his eyes*] You start off like that, and it only gets worse. You're just about to break, just about to snap, because of trying to hold on to, catch, keep, and grasp more facts, more details, more concepts. Similarly, if you focus only on the heart teachings, it can be like this [*in a singsong voice*]: "Luuuuv, be kind. This feels so good. Aaaah, it's so nice. La-la. Kiss-kiss …" That could also get a little weird.

The Buddha's teachings actually aim for a balance between heart teachings and brain teachings. In fact, we need the brain teachings to improve the heart experience and vice versa. There needs to be some balanced connection between both the heart and brain.

So how about some teamwork between the two aspects of heart and brain? We can make a connection between the brain's understanding of the teachings and the heart's feelings, so that we understand both the reasons for compassionate kindness and the experience of its application. Combining heart and brain is actually the ideal solution.

Getting back to the original point—without calmness of mind, it is very hard to have a sense of delight. Without this sense of delight, there is no genuine compassion. If we are totally preoccupied with our own experience—how *I* feel, what *my* problem is, and so forth—there is no chance at all for us to care about how others feel. There is simply no room for compassion. Therefore the Buddha said, "First, train in shamatha."

We may first want to study in order to get an idea of the Buddhist teachings. But in order to become real bodhisattvas, practically speaking, we must first calm down and then generate bodhichitta out of that. If you only want the *idea* of being a bodhisattva, rather than the actual experience, it is enough to merely think, "May I establish all beings in enlightenment," and it is done. Chant it a few times in the morning. In fact, do not even bother thinking about what it means, just chant it.

Imagine that this mind of ours is like a big bank, and in our account we have invested many thoughts, concepts, and inclinations. Now we are earning interest on a daily basis, nonstop, in the form of further thoughts and concepts that arise incessantly. This bank account is high-yielding! Even when we try to relax, thoughts keep popping up about this and that. We don't have to *try* to think of them—somehow they just come. They occupy us, and we give them time. Other times we get advertisements, or reminders that our credit limit is running out or our account is overdrawn. Something is always coming up, even when we sleep. Even while we're dreaming, thoughts are coming up continuously. Right now, those of us who are middle-aged have already made substantial investments in this account. We're drawing quite a bit of interest by now. We start earning major interest around the age of forty-five. Before that, we get a certain amount of interest, but mainly we're busy investing and reinvesting. You understand?

Isn't it true that the moment you lean back and relax, you naturally start to think of something? An object comes into your field of thought. Even if you don't want to think, it happens. This is the interest from your previous investment coming into your mind. Even if we decide, "I don't want that to happen! I'm closing this bank account!" it still happens. Thoughts continue to arise, because this is the natural course of things. We are totally and completely caught up in the cogs of this thinking machinery right now. If we want to stop this process, we must blow up the whole bank. There is no other way. Where exactly is this bank? It is located in a place called the *alaya*, the all-ground, and the name of the bank is *concepts*. Call it Conceptual First Bank. The interest that is paid out at such a generous rate is called *thoughts and emotions*.

What can we do about this situation? The bank is already there; we've already made considerable investments on which we are receiving enormous interest, and we don't know how to blow up the bank. Most people just suffer through this situation, thinking each thought as it comes, feeling each emotion as it wells up. In practical terms, how do we deal with this? This is where Dharma practice comes in. It is another sort of investment. It begins with investing in shamatha, then vipashyana and bodhichitta, and continues with following the course of the spiritual path.

In our present situation a constant feedback of thoughts and emotions arises. We try to play deaf and dumb; we act as if it isn't happening. We try to hide, but this doesn't work. We need to try something else. In truth, we are not at the point where everything is spontaneously liberated. We have to start somewhere, and that starting point is shamatha. The first step in shamatha is to stay put: in other words, relax and stay present. In order for this mind, this attention, to stay put, shamatha has two methods: one with support and another without any support. People differ, though; some practice a lot of shamatha, some not so much. Please understand that the situation differs according to the individual.

If you want to know whether you need to practice shamatha, just take a look in the mirror one morning. If your eyes are staring into the distance, your forehead is wrinkled, your cheeks are drawn, and you look tense, nervous, and unsettled, then you can say, "Hmmm, this person needs a little settling down; she needs a little shamatha." At this point, you don't need to worry too much about what color lipstick to put on, about whether a little extra facial cream is necessary, or whether you need to shave. You're looking for something else here. Rather than wondering, "Are my lips a bit dry?" instead you ask, "Are these eyes somewhat rigid? Do they look almost dry?" No water in the eyes, no moisturizer on the face—even if you put cream on, it still looks dry. If you feel your face is very far from being able to simply smile, and if smiling feels artificial, then try to say the words "content ... relaxed ... wonderful ..." If it's very difficult to say them and you feel, "That is definitely not my nature right now," this is a clear sign that you need some shamatha. If you feel like you're making fun of yourself, that the moment the smile is relaxed your face immediately hardens again into a humorless mask, well, maybe some shamatha is required.

We can notice this simply by being a little mindful. With a little presence of mind we can give this face a little daily checkup. We don't have to wait through the hard-driving ages of our twenties, thirties, and forties and then wake up and say, "Wow, I'm forty-five—I need to go relax up in the mountains; I need to go somewhere else." That is a bit late in the show. We do not have to wait that long. Could anybody reading this possibly be forty-five?

If we look absentminded but are completely occupied by thoughts and don't even know it, then we definitely need some shamatha in the sense of relaxing. Whatever we are sitting and thinking about, obsessing about, just let it go and relax. There's a definite need for shamatha here.

The basis for bodhichitta is relaxation. Without relaxing or settling down, there is no sense of ease. Without a sense of ease, there is no delight. Without delight, bodhichitta is not possible. Do you understand this?

As we get more relaxed, more free and easy, our minds become more malleable and it becomes possible to truly take in and understand the brain teachings of Buddhism. We better understand the wonderful qualities of bodhichitta and the benefits of giving rise to the bodhisattva spirit, as well as the harm of failing to do so. Through practice, these teachings can fuse with how we feel, with our actual experience. At this point, something can really happen.

There is a time in our practice and in our lives when we can put the teachings of bodhichitta to use for real. What Shantideva taught in *The Way of the Bodhisattva* and other teachings, what the Kadampa masters and others taught, can actually become something real in our own experience. Once we are at ease with ourselves, a certain delight and joy arises. At this point we have something to share. The *tonglen* practice of sending our well-being to others and taking their suffering upon ourselves can now be actualized, because we really do have some happiness to share. Before that, if we're ill at ease and confused, what happiness is there to give to others? Really, there isn't any—it's just words. After engaging in shamatha practice, we can use the resulting sense of delight to make this wish: "May this delight be experienced by everyone; may everyone else have it too." One can also pay attention to others and care for them with the thought "How horrible that they have to suffer like this! I wish they did not. May they be relieved of their pain; may I take all their suffering upon myself." In this way, the tonglen practice of sending and taking can become a real practice—not an intellectual process but an actual experience.

Let's do some shamatha practice to feel more at ease in our whole body. In your heart, leave room for love. Wherever you feel tension, loosen and release it, whether it is in a muscle, in your emotions, or in your thoughts. If your energy is up in your head too much, let it settle. If your love is a little tight, let it spread out a bit. Mentally let your mind smile, an inner smile that is not necessarily on your face. Let the juice of that feeling saturate you. Sit with your body straight—don't slump like a sack. The shoulders are straight. There's a certain sense of being grounded in your belly, with a centered area rising up through your body like a central channel. Your mind is not trying to make anything happen: simply be at peace.

If you want an object to hold in mind, notice the breath. It is good to keep the eyes open here. Open your eyes, open everything. It is all right. You do not have to completely sink into the feeling of being relaxed. You can be relaxed and yet alert. You notice everything—sounds, sights, how it feels. The "feeler" here is relaxed, and yet it feels.

When you notice that you are relaxed and at ease and that there is some sense of delight, slowly let this delight expand to embrace everything and everyone else—the whole world, including those people and circumstances you don't particularly like. Include your friends, Mom and Dad, everyone. Feel very loose, like there is no tightness anywhere and you're not mentally holding back anything.

When you feel some sense of delight and ease, some feeling of empathy, love, or bodhichitta, don't cling to it. We need to be loving and yet not keep hold of that either. To think, "Wow! Now I'm doing well. Now bodhichitta is being born in me. Wow! I must be a bodhisattva now" is not productive. In fact, bodhichitta is diminished if we claim possession of it and try to own it. It is not something for us to own. It does not belong to us at all.

Whatever helps bodhichitta to arise is good. A frame of mind that is gentle and at peace is good. This is how it should be. A spiritual practitioner should become softer and softer from the inside. If we instead notice that our "practice" seems to be making us harder, that we are becoming tighter inside, then we should take a break. Take a holiday from Buddhism. Go to the beach in Thailand or Goa and sleep.

STUDENT: What is the point of shamatha?

RINPOCHE: As I explained earlier, this mind does not really know itself at all. When we are totally unaware of ourselves, completely preoccupied and busy with external matters, then shamatha has a point. The mind can get very busy, very caught up in its own affairs. It can feel like it cannot relax in itself for even one instant. The attention does not stay with anything in a sustained way, not with a simple cup, not even with a cup's lid, much less you and your feelings! Mind does not even truly know what feelings and sensations are. This is where the training known as the fourfold application of mindfulness comes in: mindfulness of body, mindfulness of sensations, mindfulness of mind, and mindfulness of samadhi. This is a very good teaching.

Especially for people whose thoughts are in turmoil, who completely lose track of themselves. Maybe you forget about whether you have a leg or a heart or a lung, because you're so busy looking in this one place: "Oh, maybe I have a neck." But mostly it's a very cold leg, a cold hand, a cold heart. You are completely out there, and it's very scary—no trust. The fourfold application of mindfulness is the best way to connect with yourself. With this, you notice you do have legs, you have lips, feet, warmth: "Warmth, there is warmth around my heart. I love my heart. Oh, heart, relax." This is the application of the mindfulness of body. "Oh, I love my neck pain. I know you need space. You want some space from me. I can give you a little space. I can give you my love. Relax." Give it time—why not? Those parts are asking for space, for love from you, so you can provide that. Noticing different sensations and feelings—a dry sensation, an ugly sensation—allow the feelings and sensations to be felt and accommodated and settle down. Hug and kiss the feelings: "I am here for you." No problem, really. You have squeezed yourself so much—like a toothpaste tube. Everyone has squeezed themselves so much, you squeeze and squeeze until very little comes out. You have become completely dry, and no juice comes out, no juice at all. Relax, breathe in. Relax the feelings and sensations. This is necessary in order to relax, to be aware of how we are.

Then there is mindfulness of mind. Realizing that mind is everywhere, we respond to it with warmth: "Oh, poor mind! I love you too. Don't get jealous because I love feelings and body—I love you too. You also work so hard. I'm always squeezing my brain, my mind." So give warmth to your mind, hug, kiss, relax your mind. Any thought that comes is okay. If anger comes, it's okay. "Whether I am happy or angry, I welcome it into my mind." Give space to anger. Don't look at anger and think, "Oh, anger, you are so bad!" That means you are giving your anger a bad time and bad thoughts. Whether a good thought comes or a bad thought comes, just give room to any thought. Anything that comes in your mind, just make space, and mind settles down. Good thought, bad thought—you are aware of that. You treat them the same; give them equal rights. This tolerance toward all kinds of thoughts actually makes it easier for them to dissolve naturally later.

People who have low self-esteem and feel bad about themselves—if another person just praises them and comforts them a little bit, they really appreciate it and are helped by it. Their own thoughts have nagged them, saying, "You are bad, you are bad, you are bad." So when someone comes along and says, "You are okay," they really like it, and why not? Mind has "emotional rights." Anything can come into the mind—happy, unhappy, good thought, bad thought. There is no law that says some thoughts should have restricted access while others should be allowed to move freely in and out of the mind. There is no such law! You can allow anything to come. But whether you cling to it or not is *your* right. The rights of the emotions are to come in as they please. *Your* right is to decide not to follow. So, you cannot disturb their business and say, "If you are emotional, then you cannot come in!" That thought should not happen here, because it will create problems. Mind is creative; anything can come to the mind. That is mind's beauty. Whatever comes, comes. When it comes, your only responsibility is whether you cling to it or not, whether you go with it or not. You have a right in this regard. We need to learn that.

To learn how to allow thoughts to move freely while not clinging is the mindfulness of mind. In this way, we become skilled in dealing with thoughts. We become more aware, more present. A mindful presence develops so that we know what the body actually feels like, how the sensations truly are, how thoughts and feelings really are. Through training in this way, we become more and more mindful.

The fourth application is sometimes called the application of mindfulness of samadhi. This means that the awareness of everything else needs to be allowed to remain as it naturally is. It settles into itself. It is aware, undistracted. While being allowed to be that way, it notices the body, the sensations, and the mental activity. All of that is being hosted by the mindfulness of samadhi. We can call this mental stability. There is complete harmony between all the different events here, between body, sensations, and mental events. We are simply letting everything be, and as this awareness becomes increasingly settled, subtle, and refined, it can grow further. That is the point. If all goes well, then it can be rigpa—the possibility is there. For that to happen, however, the attachment or clinging to meditation must be relinquished. This is called "undistracted while not meditating."

STUDENT: How do we not get carried away?

RINPOCHE: The main problem in most cases is not the lack of theory about how to do things, either on the material level or the mental level. Rather, it is that one forgets how to deal with a particular problem the moment it arises. Our sense of being mindful and alert is forgotten; it gets lost. Due to habit, we lose it; we somehow lose control. We are no longer in charge of the emotions in which we are involved, and at that point the real problem begins.

Centuries ago, many human problems had causes consisting in a lack of expertise—curing diseases, for example. There was not much education in human society, and not many proper laws. Also, there was not much understanding of human psychology. The situation now is different, of course. Our current problems are due to a scarcity of the ability to not be carried away by our own tendencies. It is almost involuntary. We almost seem to be enslaved by the habit of being carried away.

Actually, I think we have more problems than people did six hundred years ago, although our problems are not due to a lack of education. We are very well educated—you could say we are almost too well educated. We have the wrong way of being educated. It is an incomplete education, because there is no inner education.

This problem happens a lot. Circumstances arise, and somehow the intelligence seems to get switched off and one loses control of oneself. It is like being a smoker. You know smoking is no good for your health, but, being addicted, you just cannot give it up. If you didn't know that smoking was bad for health, then it would be a different matter, but that is not the case. Nowadays you're educated about the hazards of smoking—that all the black stuff goes into your lungs, that your teeth get yellow and your fingertips discolored, that you have bad breath all the time. When you try to kiss your girlfriend or boyfriend, they are disgusted. And if you don't have a boyfriend or girlfriend, it makes it more difficult to get one. You know all this, and still you continue smoking many cigarettes.

It is precisely this addicted attitude that we deal with through meditation practice. Meditation practice is simply about how to release habitual attitudes; it's not about anything else. And this is done through shamatha and vipashyana. Really, there is no other way to address this problem than by learning how to naturally release or liberate the addicted conceptual attitude.

Shamatha without support is a superb way to exactly identify my particular addiction. "What is it that carries my attention away repeatedly? When a certain thought or emotion comes, I am sucked into it right away. Now I notice, I see exactly what is going on." That is the function or the effect of training in shamatha without support. And it is the vipashyana, free of concepts, that actually cures it, like taking the medicine that heals that problem. If you don't know your particular health problem, it doesn't help to take just any kind of medicine. Once you diagnose the disease, you can obtain the exact cure and be free of it.

If the problem is a mental addiction, then no material substance can really cure it. Likewise, nobody's help from outside can "do it for you." Rather, this addicted mental attitude needs to cure itself through knowing how. Certain physical substances can cure a material problem like a physical disorder. This is because material substance can influence material substance. But that which is immaterial or insubstantial—which mind surely is—cannot really be influenced by material substance. *The mind needs to cure itself.* This is a very important point. Through the practice of shamatha without support, we become aware of exactly what our problem is.

Imagine that a wild elephant is to be tamed by an elephant tamer, but the elephant tamer is also a little wild and also needs to be tamed. In fact, you need to be a little wild to even *want* to deal with a wild elephant, or you may get stepped on and squashed. But what happens if this wild, slightly too energetic elephant tamer gets into your home and starts to move things around? Maybe he'll smash things; maybe he will rob you or beat you up. He needs some taming as well. Shamatha is the method of taming the conceptual mind; it is the elephant tamer. But who will tame the elephant tamer?

That method is called vipashyana, egoless vipashyana. Within the method of egoless vipashyana you find Mahamudra, you find Dzogchen, and you find the great Middle Way.

The wild elephant is our rampant emotions, our tendency to get attached, get angry, get closed-minded. The elephant tamer is our ability to be mindful and alert, to tell ourselves, "I'm not going to get involved in these strong emotions. I'm going to be quiet and calm; I will stay collected; I'm going to be mindful; I'm going to be alert. Now I'm quiet; now I'm peaceful; now I'm at ease." That is the tamer.

But this tamer himself also needs to tamed. What can do that? The elephant tamer continues thinking in a dualistic way: "I must remain mindful; I shouldn't be distracted. Who knows, maybe the elephant will get wild again. I'd better watch out. I must be mindful, I must be alert," and so on. If this attentiveness of the elephant tamer is not allowed to be naturally liberated, dissolved, then one is still stuck in that dualistic way. The watcher has not dissolved. He is still watching.

Shamatha:
The Training

The previous chapter was a prelude, a warm-up. Here I will teach about shamatha, or calm abiding, in detail. First, I want to address the issue of conceptual mind—the state of mind in which experience is divided into or held as having two parts, subject and object. This holding of duality is what fuels the whole play, the whole drama. (Conceptual mind in Tibetan is called *lo;* dualistic thinking mind is *sem.*)

The view held during shamatha practice is a conceptual view. There are a few types of shamatha. One I call "stupidity training," a training in being dull and absentminded. It is actually not a formal meditation practice, but people do use it, so it needs to be mentioned. As a matter of fact, many people mistake their stupidity training for real shamatha. The genuine training is traditionally described as being of two types: one is supported shamatha with object, while the other is unsupported shamatha without object.

The idea of meditation started to become popular in the West in the sixties. People began to associate a certain mental state with that word. Sometimes it is used to refer to a kind of shutting off, a process of remaining uninvolved and going into your own space, an altered state where you don't notice anything happening in the outside world. To practice in this way means to distance yourself from experiencing through the senses. You go into a state of oblivion, absentminded and totally dim, just like animals do in hibernation. This process of shutting off from anything and trying to stay like that was sometimes called deep relaxation and even meditation. Many people still do this. One can slip into this when training in shamatha, and many people are in fact fond of it. They like it because it's peaceful, and it feels like taking a break. Someone who trains like that for years and years will become progressively duller and more stupid. His eyes will become very cloudy. This type of "progress" is dangerous. Please watch out! There's a big risk in mistaking that state of stupidity training for the training in shamatha.

Just as an experiment, let's rest in stupidity training for five minutes. We should be familiar with it so that we can identify what it is. Close your eyes. Do not think of anything. It's just like when you lean back in the sauna after working out—there's no attempt to know anything. You may even drool. You completely close down but are somewhat relaxed. Mentally there is no activity. Do you recognize this state?

First-class stupidity training for even five minutes will surely put you to sleep. There is a strong link between this state and sleep. Falling asleep is caused by dullness, and to train in shutting down like that pulls us into the absentminded state of sleep

Shamatha is definitely unlike that. It should have a certain brightness. During shamatha, you are well aware of what is happening all around you. Your attention is focused on nowness, and yet at the same time you are able to notice what is going on around you, both right and left.

Let's do another five minutes of stupidity training. Do not keep hold of anything; just forget all your worries. Totally shut off into a state of dullness. Don't try to figure out anything. This is not the time for realization. We are not trying to attain anything from this. Do not maintain any particular thought activity; simply withdraw inside.

Those of you who have gone to the beach know this state. Those of you who have gone trekking in the mountains know this state. It is not something new. You go to the beach, you swim around, then you lie on your back with a towel over your face and do stupidity training. You just kind of pass out there on the beach. After about twenty minutes, you think, "How relaxing!" But that sort of training does not brighten your intelligence; it brings no insight. Without insight, there is nothing to wipe out the seeds for further samsaric existence. So, right now, close your eyes. You have to close your eyes for this practice, but still sit with a straight back.

[A few minutes of stupidity training]

Enough. This is risky. You may fall asleep. The other danger is that tomorrow you might want to repeat this practice. Stupidity training is no good. It may feel cozy, but it's not Buddhist meditation practice. It is not shamatha and it's surely not vipashyana. It's in no way a noble practice.

Shamatha, calm abiding, is completely unlike stupidity training. It is found at many levels of Buddhist practice, as well as in many other spiritual traditions—for instance, the Hindu schools and probably other places as well—but its origin was in the teachings of the Buddha. The Buddha taught meditation as shamatha and vipashyana. Buddhist shamatha has two types: one with support and one without support.

The purpose of shamatha is to improve our presence of mind. We all have an innate ability to pay attention, to know. To improve upon this presence, to make it steady instead of being scattered and distracted, we try to remain attentive in a stable way.

In stupidity training, there's no sense of nowness. The sense of nowness is allowed to fade away. Stupidity training has no sense of being present. We hold nothing in mind, but we are just about to fall asleep. We are dull, absentminded. In shamatha, we focus on nowness, on being here, right now. There is a sense of knowing, of being mindful: that I am here, that all the objects are here, that everything is taking place and I'm aware of this. There is a certain brightness in this state. The brightness is the quality of knowing what is taking place, even though it may not be a state of liberation.

You can say the brightness is liberated when there is a sense of knowing what it is in itself in the present. That happens at the time of vipashyana, or at the time of the view of the Great Perfection, of Dzogchen. Right now, during the straight and honest shamatha of dwelling in nowness, this quality of freedom is not yet there; it is missing. Nevertheless, we need to begin with the type of nowness that is mindful of the present. In order to be here now, we need a certain amount of support to not let the attention drift off or slip away to this and that.

Shamatha has three components: being mindful, alert, and settled. Imagine a shepherd at work. When the sheep are tethered, they remain settled. They have a rope tied around their necks to prevent them from walking too far away. That rope is mindfulness. But there is also the shepherd supervising the whole affair, not paying too much attention to each individual sheep, but looking to see if everything is okay, keeping an eye out in case something goes wrong. Some really stupid sheep may get tangled up in their rope, and if there's no shepherd there to undo it immediately, they can strangle themselves. Then the shepherd walks over and undoes the rope so the sheep can again roam and graze. That is alertness.

That was the analogy; here comes the meaning. When this attention of ours, this mind, is not following the past and not planning the future but just remaining in nowness, that's a sense of settling, of staying put. Next, something extra is needed to keep the attention on the present, to prevent the attention from going astray into thinking about the past or the future. The sheep feels a tension at its throat if it walks a little too far away, so it moves back to make the rope more slack. That is the analogy for mindfulness, the method for keeping the attention tethered to the present moment, remaining settled in the present. Third and most important is the sense of alertness, the supervising quality that stays alert to whether this attention remains present or not. Without this, how would one know whether one is being distracted? How would one know whether this mind actually remains settled in nowness? Thus, the most important quality is this sense of overall alertness, the sense of being awake to the whole situation.

This alertness sees the whole picture. In midst of the entire panorama of shamatha, there is something that knows very clearly that you remain settled. You know you are settled, while at the same time you know you are not distracted. You are there together with the sense of abiding, and this knowing also is aware. This whole atmosphere is needed in shamatha practice. Slowly and gradually, the alertness will become more alert, more alert, more alert.

The correct practice of shamatha further and further strengthens this alert quality. It transforms into an increasing sense of being awake. Meanwhile, the mindful quality becomes more and more mindful, so that it requires less and less effort. You are just naturally mindful, naturally present. And the sense of being settled, of dwelling in the nowness, becomes more and more of the same identity as the alertness, until finally the alertness pulls this state into something that is no longer just shamatha: it has become vipashyana, the state of seeing clearly.

The Mahamudra teachings say that when the division between stillness and thought occurrence falls away, this is the recognition of one-pointedness. This one-pointedness is actually shamatha. At the beginning, there was a very strong division in one's mind between being quiet and thinking. However, when this alertness, in Tibetan called *shezhin*, becomes a sense of wakefulness that grows stronger and stronger, then at a certain point there is no longer any wall between stillness and thinking—the boundary falls apart. Everything is just one continuity of being alert and awake. And this alertness or awake quality is completely settled, without your having to try to settle it.

Please understand that Buddhist meditation training from A to Z, from beginning to end, has one central quality: this sense of knowing, this sense of being awake. It comes and goes again and again, but it is always identical in essence. This quality is given many names—alertness, wakefulness, *shunyata*, insight, omniscient wisdom—but it is the same basic quality that goes all the way through. And if, at any point during Buddhist meditation training, this quality goes missing, then that is definitely not the path to complete enlightenment. Please understand this point very clearly. Even at the very beginning, in shamatha practice, this sense of knowing is that which keeps alert to the existence of subject and object, that which stays aware, although in a dualistic sense. As it becomes the vipashyana quality, it is aware of nonduality, the absence of subject and object. The knowing quality that extends all the way through these various practices is identical in essence, though the subject of its knowing may change. There are different levels of practice, but you always need this basic knowing, this sense of awareness.

Actually, stupidity training does have some purpose. It is useful when you are very agitated, when you cannot sleep, and if you want to get a stupid rebirth. Otherwise, it's not much use. Though one could mistake stupidity training for shamatha practice, most people don't. Instead, they go astray when introduced to Mahamudra and Dzogchen. In Mahamudra and Dzogchen it is said, "Do not concentrate, do not fixate, do not meditate, do not hold anything in mind, don't do anything at all." Some people might think, "All right, I don't need to do anything, so I'll just relax," and then they go into that state of stupidity. It does happen. This is why many meditators go to sleep as soon as they meditate, especially Tibetans and other Asians. Westerners are a little different.

It's also very important to have open eyes during meditation, even though many people say it's hard to sit with open eyes. It may be difficult at the beginning, but the real difficulty lies in the way of looking— in knowing how to place the eyes, how to gaze. We have the habit, whenever our eyes are open, of spearing one object after the other with the eye consciousness. Therefore, when we try to just leave the gaze free it feels funny; it feels like we can't stay that way. Many people ask, "Where do I need to look? In which direction am I supposed to look?" You don't have to focus, but that doesn't mean looking in an unfocused way. Wherever you look, just look in that way. You do not have to look at a particular spot.

I think you know the difference between these two styles of meditation, between stupidity training and shamatha with support. One is to withdraw the knowing quality, and the other is to focus outwardly. The real meditation state is not withdrawn, nor is it focused outwardly, nor is it the maintenance of a certain state in between these two. It does not dwell on anything at all, but rather is totally free and pervasive. Do you understand this? The real meditation state is like space. Space does not dwell on anything, but at the same time it is all-pervasive. This is how shamatha without support should be.

Shamatha with support focuses the attention on an object like the breath and uses this focus as a way of abiding. Shamatha without support doesn't focus on any particular object but simply abides in nowness. Either way, however, shamatha is still a way of confining your mind. Among the possibilities of arising, dwelling, and ceasing, shamatha is a way of ceasing, of confining yourself to nowness. Did you get that? In shamatha practice you are occupying yourself. In addition, it contains hope and fear.

Shamatha has an object held in mind, and the object is nowness. It's a way of occupying oneself with nowness. Instead of being occupied with attachment, anger, stupidity, jealousy, and pride, one is occupied with nowness. Unfortunately, at the same time, there is also no devotion, no compassion, and no omniscient wakefulness. None of these is present, only a sense of nowness.

It's like when you're in the toilet on an airplane, the OCCUPIED sign is lit up. For as long as you're occupying that space, you are unable to meet the people on the other side of the door. Even if the Buddha comes onto the plane, you won't meet him. The Buddha comes and sees the sign: "Oh, occupied, I'm not going to enter." So you do not have a chance to meet the Buddha. Next, an obstacle demon comes and says, "Oh, it's occupied, I won't go in." Inside the cubicle, you still have hope and fear—especially when you are returning from Kathmandu to your own country, because your stomach is not feeling so good. You have the sincere hope to stay in there and rest and make sure everything is fine, but you also have fear because people are waiting outside, maybe knocking on the door. Shamatha is a little bit like that. You are occupied with the present moment, and thus unavailable to whatever may happen to pass by. Anger comes and you are occupied; a positive emotion comes and you are occupied. You are present, practicing correctly, having a nice time in the toilet. Shamatha with support is something like that.

Shamatha is indeed a skillful method. Without it, your attention is so wild, all over the place, like a whirlwind. If you submit to whatever this movement is and go wherever it takes you, there is the risk of going nuts. It's better to shut yourself up inside the toilet for a while and take a little rest.

Next is unsupported shamatha, in which your attention makes use of no support. Unsupported shamatha keeps no real object in mind. We're simply allowing the aware quality of mind to be as it is, without doing anything to it. It seems as if there is no support. This is true, but only relatively speaking, within the context of shamatha itself. When viewed from higher levels of practice, some support is still apparent. This support, this object that is held in mind, is the feeling of being present: "This nowness, all of this is *right now*, moment by moment; it is vividly present." Nowness is the object, and the subject is the knowing of that, acknowledging the nowness. Unsupported shamatha is simply remaining undistracted from nowness. Generally speaking, for a beginner there is the danger of mistaking stupidity training for shamatha. But for a practitioner, the real danger lies in mistaking unsupported shamatha for vipashyana. Please understand this point.

To get a taste of this teaching, let's first do a short session of shamatha with support. Right now, you should not close your eyes. Just use any support in front of you—but not the neck of the guy in front of you, because when he moves you get distracted. Just relax and remain very quietly, with your attention simply resting on something, without being distracted by anything else. At the same time, allow everything else to be present as well. Nothing is blocked out, but your attention is directed only at your support.

Don't close your eyes, because if you close your eyes now you risk falling back into stupidity training. While it is perfectly all right to use the movement of breath as the support, in our tradition we still do not close our eyes. As a matter of fact, do not close any of your sense organs.

Do not close any doors. Simply pay attention. When exhaling, notice that your breathing is moving out. When inhaling, notice that your breath is coming into you; just that, nothing else.

Or, as an alternative to using the breath as the support, pay attention to the picture of the Buddha on the wall or a flower on the shrine or the crown on the Karmapa's statue. Pick something ten or fifteen feet in front of you. Anything will do. You can just let your breathing flow freely, without being concerned with it at all.

Together with that focused attention, there should be a certain feeling of being unblocked. You are not concentrating, not trying to grab hold of something tightly. That's not what is meant by focused. Rather, you're just staying with the object of your attention.

Don't do anything weird with your eyes; just leave them as they are. Look in the same way you usually look at something. Normally, when you walk around you don't stare; you just allow things to be seen. Some people may seem as if they are trying to twist their eyes around while meditating, so that one eye is up and the other is down. That is not necessary. Imagine that you have a basin of water and two glass spheres—you just put them into the water and leave them there. That is how you should leave your eyes.

Do not twist your eyes or move them in two different directions. If you do, your eyes will start hurting. You might as well be natural. When you listen to a sound, you do not have to sit like this either, in order to hear. [*Rinpoche crooks his neck*] You can just allow the sound to be heard. It's the same with any sensory input—we can be totally natural about how that sensory input is being received. So right now, let's be relaxed and comfortable. Happy mind. Choose your object.

[*Practice session*]

RINPOCHE: All right. Now, what is the difference in the feeling of this state compared to the previous one? Any difference?

STUDENT: Brighter.

RINPOCHE: How about feeling? Which one felt nicer, the first time or the second?

STUDENT: The second.

RINPOCHE: I disagree. I prefer the first one, it feels better. Now, what's the main difference?

STUDENT: More wakeful.

STUDENT 2: There's no sense of "I" in the first one.

RINPOCHE: During the session, there was somebody beating a drum over there. Did you all hear this?

STUDENT: Yes.

RINPOCHE: Very good. What else did you notice?

STUDENT: The light dimmed.

RINPOCHE: Wasn't that being distracted?

STUDENT: No.

RINPOCHE: How do you know that? How do you know the difference between being distracted and noticing that the light is dimming or that someone is beating a drum? Could it be that the moment the light dims, you switch your focus from the support of your attention over to the electric light?

STUDENT: Well, no, maybe not, because being able to perceive that object depends on the light, because it could be dark. [Laughter]

RINPOCHE: Is it possible to be open and yet at the same time notice that someone is beating a drum?

STUDENT: Yes.

RINPOCHE: I said open, yes. But I did not say undistracted. Wide open. Now, what is it we call "the present"? Is it the presence of the electric light, the presence of what you were using as the support, or what? Right now, in the context of shamatha with support, you pay attention to one spot. Is it possible to pay attention to more than one thing at the same time, without being distracted from the first one and then moving over to the second?

STUDENT: I would have to be totally blocked off to not notice what took place. I acknowledged it, but quickly returned to the stillness practice.

RINPOCHE: Shamatha with support is similar to what you are saying. You pay attention to the object with 80 percent attention. Twenty percent is still allowed to register everything else. That is the best way. Otherwise, if we pay 100 percent attention to the object of focus, there is a risk of getting stuck in that and becoming absorbed. So what you said is actually very good.

Now, for the second type of shamatha, do not worry about the breathing, and don't worry about using an object as support. Just leave the attention as it is, right now. Let whatever happens happen, but do not get caught up in it. Do not hold any special object in mind. At some point a thought will form. When that happens, do not follow it. Just remain in the present.

Do you understand what is meant by "the present"? Not following the past, not planning the future, not holding an object in mind right now. Just leave your attention totally relaxed, and remain like that. Remain in *nowness*. Following thoughts is not good enough. Trying to stop thinking is not good enough. Shamatha without support remains in the nowness without getting caught up in thought.

Did you understand what I said? Is it clear? What did I say?

STUDENT: Remain in the nowness without getting caught up in thought. *[Laughter]*

RINPOCHE: Please explain what that means.

STUDENT: When a thought comes up, you just let it go rather than following it.

RINPOCHE: But still remaining in the present. You need to stay in the nowness. The main focus here is presence of mind, knowing whatever *is*. Keep to that. In this context as well, you keep your eyes open. A lot of you seem to like to close your eyes. That is not a good habit. If you close your eyes today, then tomorrow you might be closing your ears. You will bring along your earplugs. Then you will want to close your nostrils too, so you don't have to smell anything. Let's not get into attitudes like that. You're allowed to notice whatever takes place. It's okay. If you train with closed eyes, then later on when you leave here and you have to carry the practice with you in daily life, how will you be able to function walking around with closed eyes? Wouldn't it be better to be capable, to have open eyes right from the start? The purpose of our present meditation training is to become capable of dealing with any emotional state that is triggered while we walk, talk, eat, or lie down, rather than being overwhelmed. When the emotions well up, do you always have time to sit down and close your eyes in order to deal with it?

Some people seem to regard meditation training as a little holiday, the equivalent to taking a break, a dietary supplement, or a vitamin pill in the hope of regaining their energy. A person with that attitude has no need for the Dzogchen teachings. He doesn't need shamatha or vipashyana either: stupidity training is perfectly fine. Just train in that. When you get up from that practice, your muscles are more relaxed, you don't have so many thoughts, and as you train further for a couple of months, you'll have even fewer thoughts. You will worry less, and you will know less. It is very nice. It is perfectly good enough.

Our present practice of shamatha is certainly unlike that. We have not come here to learn stupidity training or a practice to get peace for just ourselves, to feel good for ourselves alone. We have come here to learn how to cut through the very root of ego-oriented emotions and the very root cause of all of samsaric existence, and to discover the basic nature of emptiness that is free of ego. We are not going to remain in a peaceful state for ourselves. Rather, we will allow compassion to manifest out of emptiness for the benefit of all sentient beings. Since emptiness and compassion are not separate, this compassion is not limited in any way or in any direction. That is the purpose of Vajrayana training. It is not only to gain a little personal peace. Is that clear?

To summarize: the training in shamatha without object, without support, is to keep all your senses open and alert, without being blocked off in any way. Don't shut down your five senses at all; rather, allow whatever takes place to be present. When something takes place, do not catch on to it deliberately; don't grab it with your attention. Don't get caught up in forming thoughts about it. Just remain; be present in this nowness. Keep your attention on nowness.

Ready? Now! [*Rinpoche chimes small hand cymbals*]

Again, let go into nowness. [*He chimes the cymbals again*]

[*Practice session ends*]

RINPOCHE: Among these three types of meditation I have taught here—stupidity training and shamatha with and without support—which is the easiest, the most simple?

STUDENT: The first.

STUDENT 2: The second.

STUDENT 3: The first two are easier.

RINPOCHE: Very good. Well said; it is true. The first two are easier. Most people think the third is easier, because there is nothing to do, nothing to hold in mind, no object, but it is actually more difficult. Tomorrow and the day after, something even more difficult will be presented. When you hear it, at first it sounds extremely easy. But honestly, when you get down to it, it is much more difficult than the third type here. So here's a question: What is the difference between the first and the third?

STUDENT: The third feels like there's more of a focus on the present, like I can feel the nowness, while in the first I am almost asleep.

RINPOCHE: The third type, unsupported shamatha, requires some effort to keep our attention in the present. In the first type, stupidity training, you have no care about anything, no need for effort. You merely let yourself get swept away. If there is daydreaming, let there be daydreaming. If you're dull, just feel dull—there is no need to do anything about it. What you said is good; you understood. Most of you are quite clever—until now. How clever you will be as the days go by, we will just have to see. Until now it's been okay! Next, during the third type of meditation, which we just did, we're supposed to be aware of whatever is taking place—a dog barking or any other kind of occurrence. But were you aware of that? Did it happen?

STUDENT: Sometimes you get caught up in that awareness and you start attaching labels; then your mind starts running around.

RINPOCHE: I wanted to bring that up myself, but now you've said it. When something happens—either a thought just comes, or there is some sound or occurrence that triggers a thought—it's best if we don't get involved in following that thought in the second moment, the third moment, the fourth moment, and so forth. Immediately return to being present, unoccupied. However, if we do start to get caught up in what we are thinking of and form a second thought about it and then a third thought and a fourth and a fifth and a sixth and a seventh, then we are definitely already distracted. We've wandered off from unsupported shamatha. Are you clear about when you are distracted and when you are not? In this context of shamatha, just the hearing of the sound, the noticing of something, is not called distraction. In fact, from the Dzogchen point of view, shamatha itself is already a state of being distracted. Then there is not much to say, is there? It means the whole shamatha setup is deluded when seen from the Dzogchen perspective. But we will get to that in the coming days. Right now, we are proceeding very nicely. We must know this difference very clearly, so that later when we progress we will know what is what. If we make the mistake from the beginning of accepting shamatha as the ultimate training, then after five or six years of having trained in a deluded state, we find there is no progress. Then what?

We'd just be fooling ourselves. "I came all the way up to Nagi Gompa—boy, was it cold, sleeping in a tiny tent. When the wind blew at night it felt like we were being blown down the hill, but still I stayed on." All that effort will be wasted if we are not really clear about the difference between the ultimately right and wrong meditation.

STUDENT: When training in shamatha without focus, without support, how do we maintain mindfulness?

RINPOCHE: During the third type of practice, are you aware of when you get distracted? Do you notice it?

STUDENT: Yes.

RINPOCHE: After you become distracted, or during it?

STUDENT: I find it very hard to pinpoint the starting point; I just know I am distracted now.

RINPOCHE: During the shamatha practice without support, is it that you're already aware of it just when you're about to be distracted, or is it that after five minutes of daydreaming, you look back and say "Oh, I was distracted." Which of the two is it?

STUDENT: Of those two, it's closer to the first one. I do not get to thought number twenty-two before I realize I am there. I think I realize it a little before that.

TRANSLATOR: So it does not take five minutes?

RINPOCHE: Maybe ten minutes? [Laughter] Actually, both of these things happen to you. You may not notice, but actually they both happen. There is an alternation. Sometimes one notices being distracted right away, and sometimes it takes a while before regaining one's senses and returning to the practice. Both can happen.

What exactly makes the third practice superior to the other two? It is two qualities: one is the sense of being settled, of remaining, and the other is the sense of being *aware* of being settled, of being undistracted. Both of these are necessary aspects of unsupported shamatha. When the settled steadiness weakens and is only aware, then it turns into thinking. At that point one has begun to think, and that is distraction. Similarly, when there is only steadiness and the awake quality of knowing gets lost, you are back in the absentmindedness of stupidity training. At this point you're either dull, daydreaming, or falling asleep. When the awareness itself is lost, then it is supported shamatha. Unsupported shamatha distinguishes itself by having the two qualities of steadiness and an awareness of being steady.

The moment you notice that you got distracted, you're supposed to return to the practice. In other words, return to acknowledging a state of just remaining. There is a certain strength in that; there is some sturdiness or steadiness in simply being that way. It is your acknowledging this steadiness that naturally cuts off or interrupts the distraction. The practice of unsupported shamatha definitely is dualistic mind. It is an artificial and not a natural way of being, a constant attempt to keep a particular state from slipping into old habit. This training maintains a sense of steadiness instead of distraction, and an aware presence rather than dullness. When everything gets a little too loose, when there is too much slipping away, we bring our attention back. We start to slide, and we bring ourselves back.

All of this is very contrived. Subject and object are being constantly maintained, so this practice is dualistic. In the next few days, we will be introduced to a way of practicing that is not based on dualistic mind at all. If at that time we sit and train in constantly trying to create an altered state of "settled presence," then it is totally artificial, and it's not the right way. You should be clear about this.

Right now, unsupported shamatha is dualistic, but among all kinds of dualistic states, it is one of the best. There is a certain relationship going on between unsupported shamatha, which is a dualistic state of mind, and the true vipashyana, which will be introduced later. You could say that if vipashyana has a friend in dualistic mind, then the state of unsupported shamatha is its best friend. Anger is not the friend of vipashyana; attachment is not the friend of vipashyana; but unsupported shamatha is a close friend, and from time to time the two do have a conversation. In the context of Dzogchen practice, however, you can sometimes say that even angry, attached, or dull states can be a friend of the Dzogchen training. We'll get to that point later.

I'd like to hear a question from someone who has not yet asked any questions. Those of you who are staying quietly not saying anything, here is your chance.

STUDENT: Could you please explain a bit more about shamatha without focus?

RINPOCHE: The terms that we use are "shamatha with support" and "shamatha without support." In both of these cases, there is a focus. To quickly review what I have said, mind is supposed to be itself, naturally abiding in itself without clinging to objects, totally open. This is how our mind is supposed to be. Unfortunately, mind has this nasty habit that goes way back of clinging to whatever comes along. Because of our previous investments in the concept bank, the interest keeps accumulating. Objects keep appearing. Due to this habit, the moment an object arrives there is immediately a thought. The thinking mind instantly connects with the object and holds on to it. The next moment, there is a thought about how that feels, and that gets added to the previous investment to receive further interest. This process goes on and on, endlessly. This is samsara.

Since it is unlikely that dualistic mind will spontaneously be able to let be and be free, at the beginning a substitute is used as a support. It is a weaning process, so to speak. That is why shamatha is first practiced with support—for instance, paying attention to the movement of the breath and remaining with that. This is the first of the three aspects: settling the attention so that it remains. The second is to keep mindful of the breathing. The third aspect is being alert to whatever else happens. Sometimes one may become distracted, but still, one is able to notice that. This alertness is more like an overall supervisory awareness. These three aspects of being settled, mindful, and alert are necessary at the beginning.

In shamatha without support, there is no specific object held in mind, neither the breath nor a visual image like a *tangka* or statue. However, something is still held in mind: there is still a focus on the present moment. Unsupported shamatha is to be in the nowness, to be continuously aware and mindful and remaining in that. While there is no concrete support, there is still a focus, and one settles in that.

You could say that practicing shamatha is like being a doorman. When you go into a five-star hotel, there's someone who opens the door for you, says "Welcome!" and lets you through. That is his job. The mindful presence during unsupported shamatha needs to be like this doorman, simply opening up and allowing everything to come into your mind. You should be aware of whatever happens inside your mind, but try not to follow it. The doorman does not hug people when they arrive; he only says, "Namaste!" Nor does he follow people in or out. Similarly you're neither particularly trying to keep something nor trying to reject anything. The main point is to be aware and to stay with the present moment, undistracted. Shamatha with support would be like placing something in the door to keep it closed. The door is shut, so there is no desire, no anger, no stupidity. Nobody can go in or out, but there is also no compassion, no sense of trust, no bodhichitta, nothing. There is merely one object alone, no other distraction.

In the case of shamatha without support, the doorman is busy opening the door and saying hello. He doesn't block the door, but sometimes he misses some people coming in or going out. He tries to be very alert, but sometimes he dozes off or becomes dull or gets carried away because such a beautiful object goes by that he wants to go after it. Sometimes very ugly, smelly people show up and he wants to close the door. Sometimes he runs after someone and ends up following him or her into the toilet. And sometimes very strange people arrive—let's say a huge, strong guy comes along, thick-necked, his head half-shaven, with dragon tattoos on his bulging, muscled arms. In this kind of situation, the doorman does not have the power to block him! He tries to say, "I'll let you go, I'll let you go." But the other guy does not let *him* go. Sometimes you letting go is not enough. You need vipashyana to let go of strong emotions or habits. The strong guy, the strong thought, can grab you because you're meditating. If you keep hold of something, you also risk losing it. Shamatha is an act of meditating, so it can be lost, while vipashyana—in the sense of Mahamudra or Dzogchen—is *not* an act of meditating on something, so there is no risk of it getting lost.

Our mind always has open doors, so sense impressions are constantly arriving. You can close the door with stupidity training and lock it, not allowing anything in. You could also block the door with supported shamatha. Just as in the example of controlling the door with a doorman when too many visitors come in, you next train in shamatha without support in order to be capable of remaining firm. The sights we see, the sounds, smells, tastes, textures, and thoughts are now like the guests arriving at the hotel. There is a noticing that they are happening. This mindful presence, which is our mind knowing, can stay put, be mindful, and have the panoramic overview of alertness. A well-trained, skilled doorman has these three qualities: to be alert, mindful, and settled.

Practicing shamatha, first with and then without support, is like training a doorman to be excellent. Whoever comes and goes, he is on full alert. All the details are noticed, but he neither follows any particular guest nor closes the door on anyone. Deep relaxation could be like closing the door in that it can be very uptight, a training in dullness. Eyes are closed, everything is closed, mouth wide open—the face also looks unintelligent, if not downright stupid. If you have a Polaroid camera and manage to take pictures of yourself when meditating, afterward when you look at your photos you can see: "That's stupid meditation. That is shamatha with support. That is without support. Oh, this is loving-kindness, compassion, juicy meditation, moisturized, very open, all smiling, happy, no tension, relaxed but not drunk, nor sinking into the juice because alertness is there also, very alert." We should check the photo for all these qualities.

The doorman I just mentioned can be simple-minded during the practice of shamatha with support. It's fine to be a little stupid, because it's merely a matter of staying put with the object. You don't have to understand much, and you don't have to be distracted. You just keep in mind whatever you are supposed to keep in mind, keep your attention on it. However, in shamatha without support more presence is required because you need to notice when something is coming so that you can open the door while still staying put. The always-open door is not so good, as it's very noisy in Kathmandu. Nothing comes, door closed; something comes, not necessary to close. It is not good to always leave the door open and space out.

After shamatha comes the practice of vipashyana. This is where Mahamudra and Dzogchen come in: they belong under vipashyana. At this point, the doorman is no longer needed because the automatic laser sensor is there. It senses when someone is present and the doors open automatically. Likewise, when you go out, the door closes. It does not matter how many people are going in or out—the door automatically opens and closes. When someone has mastered the training of Mahamudra and Dzogchen—like Dilgo Khyentse Rinpoche, Tulku Urgyen, Nyoshul Khen, or Chatral Rinpoche—there is no longer any busy meditator there, keeping hold of being present, mindful, and undistracted. Anything can take place: it does not matter how many guests come in or out. It is not at all overwhelming because there is no meditator to be overwhelmed.

The inexperienced doorman, meaning shamatha with support, sometimes gets into trouble. Let's say sixty Indian tourists come to the door.

Indians can be very big, very tall. The doorman is Nepali and very short. Many things can happen in this situation. Maybe he is overwhelmed by all the Indian tourists, and he can no longer function as a doorman. It's like when we have rush-hour thoughts: so much is happening in our minds at the same time that our mindfulness and alertness is overwhelmed. When that happens, we need to upgrade the practice. Sometimes a thought comes onto the scene that's particularly big and tough, like a strong fighter. One big thought comes up to the doorman, with his muscles rippling and glistening. Half his hair is spiked up like a knife blade, and he's coming up to you at the door and trying to catch you. But you are alert: "Oh my, the distraction is back, I must meditate." You try to pray, you try to watch your breathing, you do shamatha, and you remember all those things, but you still cannot cope because the emotion is too assertive. Sometimes, due to the force of habit, we get so involved, so engrossed in a forceful thought that even if we try to just follow the breath or remember to try to be present and mindful and pray to the Buddha, Dharma, and Sangha, no matter what we do it just doesn't help and we get carried away.

I feel that shamatha with and without support can probably solve 60 or 70 percent of our problems, but that means there is still 30 or 40 percent left. In order to address this, we must remove the doorman and still function as if he were there. This is the state of nonmeditation. But that is not the topic for right now. It belongs under the main course, and I will get to it later.

PART TWO

MAIN COURSE

GROUND, PATH, FRUITION

Although I discussed the topic of ground, path, and fruition in detail in *Carefree Dignity*, I will quickly review it here. There are various ways of explaining what is meant by ground, but simply put, ground is the natural state of mind. You can call it the nature of things. It is your basic state, endowed with certain qualities and found already within yourself. These qualities are present as a mere seed or potential right now. Because the ground is present, we can apply the path, and through practicing the path, we can realize the fruition. To understand the ground means to understand what is basically present in oneself. As we understand our basis, our ground, and understand what qualities are potentially present, then we are also able to realize these qualities through practicing a method. But if we are not clear about our nature, then it's very hard to realize it or to distinguish between being mistaken and unmistaken about it.

Here's a basic illustration of ground, path, and fruition. Say that the piece of white paper here is the ground. The path, which is the stage of delusion, of confusion, is like covering the white paper with the yellow paper. The fruition is what happens after the yellow paper has been removed, revealing the ground, the white paper. *The ground has become the fruition.*

When speaking of the ground, we are speaking of the white paper, our basic state. The path means the period of being deluded. Path is like explaining why the yellow paper exists, as well as how to remove it. If the yellow paper were identical with the white, meaning indivisible with it—if ground and path were indivisible—then there would be no point in our practicing the Dharma. If this were true, it would be meaningless to apply a view, a meditation training, and a conduct during the path stage. All the effort we go to in maintaining the meditation posture—

our back aches, our throat gets dry, our eyes hurt—would be pointless. It would be like trying to wash a lump of coal white. No matter how much soap and water you use, it does not help; coal will never become white.

Therefore, if our basic nature were delusion, ignorance, and there were a real individual ego-identity—if this were really true—then there would be no reason whatsoever to practice. We might just as well give up practicing a path, drink beer or wine, and enjoy ourselves! Go to the beach and try our best to find some pleasure in this world. That is supposing that this world were an enjoyable place and we were actually able to enjoy it. If we could somehow do this, then that would be fine. But, in trying to find pleasure in the world, we attempt to organize the perceived objects we find pleasant. As soon as the pleasurable experience is over, we try to find another one, and then another. It becomes a habit. We always need a perceived object in order to make ourselves, the perceiver, happy. We become conditioned in this way. Some people spend their entire lives like that.

Someone else, a little more intelligent, thinks, "What is the use of continuously chasing after one thing and then another? It makes me dependent upon always having *something* to make me happy. I've lost my freedom in this way. There must be a better way, something more profound than this. I must find it." After investigating what is really happening here, this person discovers that the pleasure and the pain are not actually dependent upon the object. Rather, they are dependent upon the chase—the success or failure at finding an object to feed on. This type of person becomes interested in finding another way of being and seeks a spiritual path. But it's also possible to get so used to the pattern—whether it is because the objects are too seductive or the habit is too deeply ingrained—that one gets carried away helplessly, again and again, and thereby continues to suffer. In this way, one misses the opportunity for personal freedom. The mind gets so extroverted that it loses track of its home.

This kind of confusion is like a string of conceptual moments that cover-up the basic nature. We must find out whether the confusion about our basic state, the ground, can be cleared up. Can the mess be cleaned up or not? Is our basic nature like charcoal, which no matter how much you wash it will never become white? Or is it like gold that has some tarnish on the surface that can be removed through a deliberate process and is then revealed to be pure gold? Our basic nature is actually like gold. Confusion prevents us from knowing our basic state, and this confusion is temporary; it can be cleared away.

Our ground—our basic state, which is like our source, the origin that is the basis from which everything arises—has three qualities: it is empty, it is cognizant, and it is an indivisible unity. Emptiness is considered an extremely important word in Buddhism. And the next word, "cognizant," meaning "able to know," is also of utmost importance. The third word, that these two are an indivisible unity, is likewise extremely important. Please remember these three words.

Our ground is empty. In this context, what is meant by empty? It means empty of being either permanent or nothing. "Permanent" means unchanging, whereas "nothing" means it never happened, it is not even there. Our ground is neither of these; rather, it is empty, and because of being empty, it is possible for it to be cognizant. Unless our basic state was one of being empty, it would be impossible to be cognizant, able to know, because the ground would be stuck in being either something permanent or nothing at all.

This empty quality is like the mother of everything, in that it allows everything to unfold. But this empty quality is not a concrete, material entity. It is neither permanent nor nothing. It is because of this emptiness that all of you are able to be here today in this world. And it is because of this emptiness that I am able to be here. Because of emptiness, you can say that Lerab Ling exists. Because of emptiness, the sun and the moon and everything else in the universe is able to unfold. And also it is because of emptiness that the state of no delusion, the buddhafields of all buddhas, and the states of delusion, the different types of experiences of the six classes of sentient beings, are able to unfold.

Now if our basic nature were truly nothing, it would be impossible for anything to happen in the first place. If the basic nature were permanent, there could be no change; it would be like that forever—or, if something did occur, it would be frozen right there and never shift into anything else.

If the basic state were one of permanence, you would be really stuck. Whatever posture you might have succeeded in taking, whatever movement of your leg you might be lucky enough to effect, would simply stay like that forever. The very fact that we are here, that we experience, is the evidence that our nature—what we basically are—is neither permanent nor nothing. If we were permanent, we could not even come into this world in the first place. And we are obviously not nothing— look, we can see each other. Therefore, our basic nature is one of neither permanence nor nothingness. This is the meaning of emptiness in the context of ground. It is because of emptiness that there is experience. Based on emptiness, the experiences unfold in dependent origination. And it is because of experience that everything takes place—the environment, the body, and the sensory objects.

Said in a slightly more detailed way, our basic state has three qualities: *empty essence, cognizant nature,* and *unconfined capacity.* The first is that it is empty in itself. The second is that by nature it has a quality of being cognizant, able to know. The third is how it operates, which is not confined and not limited. The second quality, cognizant nature, is our natural way of knowing—knowing while empty in essence. These two qualities, being empty and being cognizant, are indivisible. This indivisibility is something like the space that's here all around us right now this afternoon; it is infused with light from the sun, and this sunlight cannot be separated from the space itself. The lucidity and the space cannot be separated into two different entities. Light and space are indivisible, a unity.

The cognizant nature of mind refers to the empty essence's knowing quality. In other words, as far as empty essence pervades, cognizant nature extends just as far, with no center, no edge, no end or limit in any direction. Wherever the empty essence permeates, cognizant nature is indivisible from that. The very fact that one cannot separate being empty and being cognizant into two different entities means that they are a unity that cannot be taken apart. They are indivisible. This indivisibility is the third of the three qualities, the unconfined capacity.

We must recognize these three qualities, acknowledge them. In this moment of recognizing them, conceptual mind is almost gone. Conceptual mind cannot really grasp the fact that empty essence is beyond arising, dwelling, or ceasing and that cognitive nature also transcends arising, dwelling, or ceasing. It has to give up. Ego cannot cope with the groundlessness of the ground. It simply cannot face that. Overwhelmed, it just has to give up. In this kind of showdown, ego cannot compete any longer. Empty essence always wins.

The superiority of the Dzogchen teachings compared to other view-points does not consist in only recognizing empty essence or in only recognizing cognizant nature. That is just not good enough to be the Dzogchen view. We must recognize in actuality the indivisible identity of essence, nature, and capacity in a way that is totally free of any clinging to the concept of being empty and any attachment to the concept of being cognizant. That is called *recognizing rigpa*. When this recognition is totally free of any conceptual attitude—when it is totally pure and authentic—this is said to be equal to beholding the countenance of a thousand buddhas. Actually, it is superior to meeting a thousand buddhas, because the state of rigpa is itself the real buddha.

This mind essence is not something new that we must get our hands on. We recognize our essence as already present, something we already have. If it were a new thing that we needed to achieve by means of the path, then every attempt to achieve it would become an act of artifice, something contrived through deliberate effort. Such a practice could never be called "sustaining the natural state." Also, if we somehow achieve a state that first was not, then only later is, it becomes something formed, a product. Therefore it is also impermanent. The viewpoint of fruition as something we achieve, rather than discovering what is already present as the ground, is incorrect and can be faulted in many ways.

To reiterate, we must recognize the ground as being empty essence, cognizant nature, and unconfined capacity. We do so at the time of the path. There is no new ground being practiced at the time of the path. We need to accept that what is recognized as the essence of mind is the ground that is already present. The practice of the path is a matter of acknowledging this ground that already is, rather than producing something new. Some method is necessary to facilitate this. At first we should know the method, but later we must be free of the method.

The indivisibility of these three qualities—empty, cognizant and their indivisible unity—means they are not confined to being just one or the other; they are totally unconfined. When these three qualities are not appreciated as their actuality—meaning what is real, how they really are—they are misconstrued as being something other. Through our clinging with notions, the empty essence gets confused into being body. The cognizant nature, that which allows for communication of meaning, is confused into being speech. And their indivisible unity, the un-confined capacity, is confused into being dualistic mind.

This is a difficult topic, and the reason for the difficulty in understanding it lies in the fact that it is not a visible entity. It is hidden, and it is difficult to understand something hidden. But even though it is difficult, it's good to at least try to understand. We do not have to shut off our understanding just because something seems difficult, thinking, "I don't understand it, therefore it is unnecessary to understand." When we get to meditation training, to actual experience, then there is a certain connection between the description of the ground and our own experience. At that time we can then appreciate what is what; it rings a bell, and we say "Oh, yeah, that's how it is." That is the reason for getting the idea of the ground in the first place.

Our ground is empty in essence and cognizant by nature, and these two qualities are indivisible. However, we confuse them into being body, speech, and mind. Please understand that essence, nature, and capacity are not in themselves the causes of this confusion. Rather, the cause of confusion is the failure to recognize the ground as being what it is. In short, confusion happens. Confusion means failing to recognize what is as being what it is, and therefore perceiving it as something other.

The empty quality offers the freedom to be either unconfused or confused. It accommodates both. Confusion occurs through the cognizant quality. The unmistaken pure experiences of the kayas, wisdoms, buddhafields, and so forth all come about through the cognizant quality. And the confused experiences, the deluded perceptions of the six classes of sentient beings, also come about through the cognizant quality. Why does that happen? Why does deluded experience occur? Through our failing to recognize that emptiness and experience are indivisible. Whenever experience occurs, we fail to recognize that it is indivisible from emptiness. Instead, we cling to it as being solid, and we do this to such an extent that experiences are not allowed to be seen as simply expressions or displays of emptiness itself.

The heart of the matter is that we all have the capacity to be buddhas. We have the basic stuff, so to speak, of essence, nature, and capacity, and so the possibility is always at hand. But because we fail to recognize the actuality of this, there is bewilderment; there is a quality of being confused and deluded. And that prevents being enlightened. This confusion obscures the ground, and therefore the path stage is one of confusion. When we succeed in removing the confusion, when it is cleared up, then we are enlightened. Among ground, path, and fruition, we are presently at the stage of path.

You have to understand buddha nature as something beyond being permanent or impermanent. Our problem as a human being is that our conceptual attitude refuses to accept that anything could defy those two categories. It seems unacceptable to the rational mind, which is used to seeing everything as either permanent or impermanent. The trait of being deluded is that whatever you experience, when you inquire as to what it really is, you never find it; everything is basically *unfindable*. While it is unfindable, we still experience everything as being real. That is how it is to live in delusion. If "our world" were not a delusion, then we would always be able to find any given thing when we inquired intelligently into what it is we perceive—because we should have perceived it correctly in the first place. Since this is not the case, we can conclude that we are deluded.

There are so many issues for which we find no answer, for which there is no possible answer to be found. That is another hint of delusion. There are many questions even scientists cannot answer. No matter how educated scholars may be, much remains unanswerable. If everything could be answered, then they would not have been mistaken in the first place!

When we investigate where our present perceptions come from, we fail to find any real sources. They are only scenery that occurs because of confusion, just like the scenery in a dream. Don't worry about that; it is nothing to be depressed about. Some people feel immediately depressed when they hear that everything is like last night's dream. But as a matter of fact, discovering the real situation is actually something to rejoice in.

"All of this magical display of illusion is unreal, but I, the perceiver, I am real." That attitude doesn't help; it only intensifies our suffering. It is much better to think, "Just as everything perceived is illusory, so I, the perceiver of the illusion, am also an illusion." Tsoknyi Rinpoche seems to be sitting on the throne here right in front of you, but if you really investigate that which you call Tsoknyi Rinpoche, there is no entity to really find.

Unfindable when we look, yet things are seemingly there: that is the definition of illusion. It's like a mirage on a freeway on a hot day. It looks as if there is water ahead; you drive toward it and expect to drive through that water, but you never get there. Illusion is like that. While there is no "I," it seems as if there is an "I"; while there is no ego, no owner, it seems as if there is. It is all a magic show.

You could say that our state of illusion is like a Hollywood movie. A two-hour movie can show a person's entire life, but in reality it's only a series of individual frames spliced together. In the same way, the instances of believing that there is a *me* where there is not, and the belief that there is an owner where there is not, are pieced together frame by frame, so to speak. These pieces make one fascinating and seemingly complete movie.

We go to the movie theater, we sit there and watch the screen, and it provokes all the different emotions. Watching a movie, we see something that seems to be there but really is not. It looks as if something is there to be perceived, but when we look closely, there is no *thing* there at all. Not only Hollywood movies are like that; our own "life movie" is like that.

Movies are a very good analogy for how the whole spectacle of life is put together out of instances of deluded moments, creating the illusion that our life is one continuity. In truth, it is all like a movie. We could regard life as a drama, a magical play. You simply are one of the actors in the drama, a participant. To have the attitude that everything, including yourself, is a display of magical illusion means you are not really caught up in it. Otherwise, if you fail to acknowledge that this is really how it is, it would be like taking a movie to be real and suffering because of that, even though it's just a movie.

Our whole life situation is like that. It is not real, but at the same time, we do not always see it like that. We need to acknowledge this lack of knowing, this lack of understanding of how things actually are, and then deal with it. To understand that, it is necessary to practice; we must train in being undeluded, to systematically make our way out of the delusion.

The situation we are in is one of being in it from two sides, from two angles. We appreciate to some extent that everything is an illusion, like a movie we are part of. At the same time, we do not really realize it all the time. It is not enough to form the concept "everything is illusion," because we get caught up again and again. The film cassettes are already recorded; they are about to be played on the screen of our life. While we cannot deny that this happens, we can work with it and gradually become more and more undeluded.

To deal with the state of being confused, three points are necessary: view, meditation, and conduct. With the help of these, confusion is brought close to our own experience; it is brought into real life and no longer is just a story. Up till now it has been more like telling a story about what's going on. What was the story of our ground? If there is confusion, why did that happen; what is going on?

Watching the movie, there seems to be some purpose; you get entertained. There is a certain type of movie you can walk out of when it is over and then you are rid of it. That's the movie that plays the same old themes of birth, old age, sickness, death, love, violence, and all that stuff. That's not the best kind, however. There is another type of movie, the movie of the buddhafields, where you do not have to walk out. But that's not the movie we are in right now.

You could say that there are six movies for the six kinds of beings. Our feature presentation in the human realm is titled *Birth, Old Age, Sickness, and Death*. Hungry ghosts watch a movie of being really thirsty and hungry, of having stomachs so big and necks so tiny that they have a hard time moving around.

Each movie has its own producer and director. The director's name is Group Karma. He employs all the actors that belong to the same movie, bringing them all into one place. The director is very clever: he does not mix up the participants for the different movies. The humans do not act in the hell movies, and the hell beings don't appear in the human movies. The best solution would be to kill the director, because then no movie would be made. If you're not clever enough to do this, you'll only try to destroy the screens, the theaters where the movie is being shown. But if you do not catch the producer/director team, then they will just prepare to make another movie in some other place.

If you really want to get out of samsara, out of the movie theater altogether, you need to be free of that which controls the director, Karma. That is the producer, Mr. Ignorance. It is Mr. Ignorance, the unknowing, who sponsors the director. The director may have the skill, but without the money, the support, he cannot make the movie. Ignorance is the producer.

Any questions?

STUDENT: Your title for this movie is *Birth, Old Age, Sickness, and Death*. It sounds like a horror movie. I do not want to stay and watch it. But maybe it's another movie. Maybe it's a history movie, about the history of our universe. Maybe it's a very interesting movie from some point of view. How do you know that the movie is about suffering? Is that the whole issue?

RINPOCHE: This is true, the movie depends on the watcher. You choose your own channel, don't you? There are many ways of watching as well. You can watch as if you are just viewing the illusion. Or you can watch while getting personally involved and becoming really caught up in the illusion. Both are possible, and I will explain that next.

The opposite of this is the movie *Buddha Story*. It was quite a successful screenplay. The person in that movie started to realize: "Hey, what is happening here? To go on in this normal way brings nothing but pain. There is a reason for why it goes like that, why it always becomes painful. It is possible to stop; there is a way out. And the way is to stop creating the causes."

There is definitely a way that leads to another type of movie altogether. The Buddha discovered this. It was through watching and acting in the movie *Birth, Old Age, Sickness, and Death* that the Buddha discovered the Four Noble Truths. So please, right now, while acting in your own movies, use the Buddha's screenplay. Imitate the Buddha. Acknowledge that there is suffering. Give up its causes. Practice the path and realize the cessation of suffering.

ILLUSION

The method for realizing how confused experience is devoid of true existence involves teachings on *view, meditation,* and *conduct.* The task of these three has to do with clarifying confused experience. Confused experience has already happened; it is going on right now for us. There is a holding of this confusion that is continually being regenerated by our conceptual attitude, and this is not foreign to us. It is a very normal encounter. The whole point of view, meditation, and conduct is to release our clinging to that conceptual attitude.

The best situation would be if we had never strayed into the deluded way of perceiving to begin with. But somehow it seems that we missed the opportunity to be primordially enlightened, and now we are deep in confusion. That is not necessarily something we should be depressed about, because all the while our essence has remained originally free and pure. We need to deal with the expression of this essence that presently takes the form of conceptual thinking, a conceptual attitude that constantly clings to or holds on to deluded perceptions as being real. We simply need to learn how to release that clinging. Even though we missed the chance to be primordially enlightened—"pre-enlightened," if you will—we can still attain stability in the natural freedom of our essence and become "re-enlightened."

The issue of whether there is confusion or no confusion, whether one is deluded or not, does not belong to our essence. Essence is not subject to being either confused or liberated. Being confused or not confused has to do with its expression, with whether or not this expression takes the form of thinking. That expression can be either liberated or entangled. From the essence the expression arises, and this manifestation turns into thought. Confusion happens from this thinking. Again, being confused or not does not relate to the essence; it relates to the expression.

Let's begin with examining the view so that we clearly understand what is meant by conceptual attitude. There are two types of view: the view with conceptual attitude and the view that is totally free of any conceptual attitude whatsoever.

What is meant by conceptual attitude? Conceptual implies there is a dualistic holding of subject and object. Sometimes it is simply called "mind" or "dualistic mind." Sometimes it is called "thinking" or "thought," as in "conceptual thought," *namtok* in Tibetan. It is vital to understand what that state of mind is. Clinging to subject and object creates a duality, and that creates a way in which mind behaves in terms of either being attached to something, being against it, or being closed-minded regarding it.

Take any object, for example, a thought of the past. Here the past memory is the object, while the present thought is the subject. Or the object could be something that I need to do tomorrow. There is no real tomorrow, but there is the present thinking about tomorrow. In this case the future plan is the object, while the thinking of it right now is the subject. This is the way a conceptual attitude maintains subject and object in the present moment. Whether the object is something we label "'past thought" or "future thought" or "present thought," in truth, at any given time the past has vanished, the future has not yet arrived, and there is only the present moment. Therefore it is only a present thought that makes the assumption that a past existed or exists; and it is only a present thought that makes the assumption that there is a future. Whether it's a memory of the past or a plan about the future, all these thoughts exist only in the present moment.

This thinking of something in the present in terms of subject and object is a conceptual attitude, in Tibetan, *lo*. Whenever any thought activity takes place, whether the object has to do with the past, the present, or the future, the thought itself takes place in the present. That sort of thinking is a conceptual attitude. There is also a type of knowing that is not tied up in this kind of dualistic thought of subject and object. This way of knowing is original wakefulness, *yeshe* in Tibetan.

Whether it is lo or yeshe, in both cases there is a sense of knowing. The difference lies in how the knowing is. In the case of lo, conceptual attitude, the knowing takes place in terms of holding a duality of subject and object. In yeshe, or original wakefulness, there is no holding on to subject and object. It is a way of being without any attachment, anger, or closed-mindedness, a way in which the knowing is in itself naturally free. Please remember this well! From the very moment you enter the gateway of Buddhist practice, all the way until you arrive at complete and perfect enlightenment, that quality of knowing is very important, very precious.

In these two ways of knowing, the first one means that there is a feeling of *me* knowing. You can call it ego's way of knowing. Attention is paid to "something there," an object where mind or attention can get caught up in perceiving "something over there".

Let's illustrate lo. *[Rinpoche holds up a flower]* Here is a flower. It's a beautiful flower, and it smells so sweet. The moment you see it, it delights you. If you're feeling a little bored, it invigorates you; if you're feeling a little chilly, it makes you warm. The moment you look at it, the first thought is: "There is a flower." Next, you know it to be a nice flower. The third moment: "I want that flower. I must possess it; it should belong to me." In other words, ego enters. Simply knowing "There is a flower" does not involve ego.

Someone might say that it's not possible for there to be any knowing without ego. That is a big mistake, a serious false assumption. Knowing is not a function of ego but rather a natural quality of mind, in the same way that a flame is hot or water is naturally wet. Mind's natural ability is to know. For the most part, ego steps in and takes over the knowing. It takes charge and then claims ownership, trying to make the knowing belong to itself. Therefore it might seem as if every instance of knowing is the ego's way of knowing. In almost 99 percent of all cases, this is in fact true.

Rather than simply allowing the first moment of perceiving to be as it is, ego wants to claim this knowing, to be in charge. In the moment of seeing the flower, to want to possess it is attachment. Or one could react with aversion: "I don't like having a flower here, it will smell up the room. Let's get rid of it. Don't even put it on the table; throw it outside." This way of being is not quite anger; it's more dislike, a source out of which anger can grow. Or, if one does not really care to know whether it's a flower or not a flower, but just shuts off from it, that is closed-mindedness or stupidity. These three poisons are ego's constant companions.

Ego knows no moderation. And it doesn't stop with just claiming 20 percent ownership of experience—it wants to go all the way. For ego, this going all the way is endless. There is no stopping anywhere. If we could just remain with simply knowing whatever takes place, that would be fine; there is no problem with that. But ego is not happy with just that, it goes on and on: one thought, the next thought, and the third thought: "I want it. How can I get it?" Then it wants to get involved in more and more activity. It becomes a habit, and that habit can be end-less. That is the problem. When a habit is reinforced by being used again and again, it's like we lose our freedom; every moment of per-ceiving seems an involuntary involvement. We get caught up all the time until we feel totally lost.

I have noticed that most people I meet are to some extent afraid of themselves. Often they say something like, "Well, maybe I can handle it, maybe I cannot. Maybe I should listen to him, maybe I shouldn't. Maybe I cannot take it." All this doubt, all this reluctance, is based on fear, *fear of not being able to take it.* "If I do this, if I end up in that situation, maybe I couldn't stand it. Maybe I don't know how to deal with it, maybe it will be too much. I'd better not." There is a certain timidity in that fear, and this feeling of dread is a way of imprisoning oneself inside a lack of confidence. Once we confine ourselves to that prison of timid-ity, ego will take the key, lock the door, and put the key in its pocket. We become the prisoners of ego.

Ego always needs the support of the knowing quality, otherwise ego is nothing. Without the tool of the knowing quality, there is nothing it can do. When you dread doing a certain job, you are actually not afraid of the job, you are afraid of your emotions. There is never anything wrong with doing a job. It's more the fear of not being able to deal with the emotions that come up during the job, the emotions that are pro-voked by being involved in a certain sort of job. What happens is we blame the job at hand, because we feel incapable of handling our own emotions that might arise while doing the job. But honestly, without knowing how to handle our own emotions, it doesn't matter what job it is; we'll always have that feeling of being inadequate, which creates fear. And this fear makes us not want to do anything. We become closed in; we refuse to be involved in anything, which is a distorted form of re-nunciation.

This is not renunciation in the true Buddhist sense. It's a little sliver of renunciation. Such a circumstance could bring you to true renuncia-tion. Some people have so much difficulty in dealing with emotions, such pain, that they may want to learn how to solve their problem through meditation training. That is good; there is nothing bad in wanting to solve the problem through meditation training.

Maintaining the notion of *me* refers to separating oneself from others. It's as if one is holding on for dear life, being utterly concerned about *me* and pushing aside that which is other. All this is called ego-clinging. This is not the same as simply taking care of your business, making sure that the body is fed and able to experience and perceive. This basic process of taking care of oneself is not called ego, not at all.

Some people ask me, "If I'm free of ego, how can I eat, how can I walk, how can I do anything?" But simply eating or simply walking doesn't necessarily mean that there is ego-clinging. There could be, but it doesn't have to be that way. According to Buddhism, it is possible to function while being free of ego-clinging. In other words, when the body has to be fed, feed it; when it needs to be washed, give it a shower. But when something unfamiliar happens, it doesn't mean you have to claim ownership of it and make it your problem. If you always do that, collect problematic issues as if they were your own, then it's very hard to feel free in life. You're always collecting baggage, carrying a burden.

The Tibetan word for ego literally means "owner," as in claiming ownership or clinging to being the owner. This indicates that ego is something extra added into the situation. This is how to understand ego or self in the Buddhist context. It doesn't mean that being free of ego is like being switched off, like all the doors and windows are shut and there is no experience of anything ever again. In order to understand the actuality of "no owner," no self, we need to understand two levels of reality: the seeming and the real—also called the relative and the ulti-mate. Really and ultimately, we don't own anything, because really and ultimately there are no things to own. Everything is impermanent and everything is devoid of any independent, true existence. There really are no entities to claim as one's own. This is a very important point.

Nevertheless, the seeming level of reality also comes about because of not realizing how things actually are, ultimately. We need to respect that level as well, so that we can work with how things seemingly are experienced.

Here's an example. Let's say that your daddy has given enough money to a hotel so that your bills are covered for your entire life, no matter how long you stay or what you eat or how much you spend. You move in and stay for a month or two. It is very nice, and you enjoy yourself a lot. You don't own the hotel, but you are allowed to stay there. Still, you respect the hotel. Something in your suite may break or get a little crack, but this doesn't really depress you; you don't fall into despair about it, because after all it's not really yours. Still, you notice when something breaks, and you take care that it gets repaired. It doesn't mean that you have to think, "This is not mine, I don't care, let it break. In fact, I'll even help a little to break it!" and so you kick the toilet and tear the curtains into pieces. That's not necessary at all. Just because you don't own it doesn't mean that it has to be destroyed. You don't have to disturb anything. When you act in this way, both levels are present.

Because of respecting the relative level, you are careful about things breaking. Also, when you move to another room, it doesn't mean you pocket any of the articles. You don't have to be that way. But because you don't have the sense of being the owner, because you don't have the ego-feeling in your relationship to the room, you don't worry too much if something breaks. It's not really your problem, although you still take care of it and make sure it gets fixed. My main point here is that it's possible to live like one is staying in this hotel—in a way that is respectful but doesn't assume an extra degree of ownership. Your life is something like a hotel room. You don't own it forever. You might own it for sixty or seventy years, but it's not a permanent situation. You are staying as an honest, respectful guest in a hotel.

As long as we keep putting up walls and barriers, freedom in the Buddhist sense will never happen. Ego-clinging in the Buddhist context refers mainly to the way we add something extra on top, beyond what is necessary to function. The word "ego" here is not the same as the modern psychological use of the term; that's not the way ego is used in the Buddhist sense. Go back to the original sense of the word, which just means "me." We need to clean up that word a little bit, wash off the modern connotation. If you really look into it for what it is, every single time you say "me," what is the "me" you refer to? It is only this sense of knowing—there is nothing else behind it. What can you really pinpoint?

When you look for this "me," for this "I" or ego, you find that it is mind. It is this knowing quality that you call "me". In fact, there is no "me" to find anywhere other than the knowing quality. You can't pinpoint anything other than the knowing quality. When that knowing quality is misconstrued, it is given the name "me." If it is understood as just being what it is, then it is called intelligence.

Samsara is like a magical illusion, magical in that it seemingly exists without actually existing. For example, right now it seems like Tsoknyi Rinpoche is here. There is somebody with a name, doing his thing, but at the same time it is also possible that there is no entity whatsoever. Yet at the same time he is here. It is very strange; it is magical. If there in actual fact were a real, truly existing Tsoknyi Rinpoche, then that truly existing Tsoknyi Rinpoche couldn't be cut into pieces and pulverized no matter what kind of machinery you used.

Without truly existing, things still seem to exist, and these two aspects of experience occur at the same time. This is the magical way that everything is. Everything unfolds in this magical way. The two main reasons for this magic are these two qualities: empty essence and cognizant nature.

Actually, the biggest blame for the situation falls on empty essence, because it is a little too lenient, a little too permissive in just allowing everything to take place. Empty essence has a completely laissez-faire attitude. There is no restriction on anything: if a state of mind wants to be confused and delude itself, it is free to do so; if it wants to be enlightened and manifest the buddhafields, it is equally free to do so.

Everything is allowed, completely free; that is the quality of empty essence. It is a little too permissive. As a matter of fact, it might be better if there were restrictions, like: "Hey, you are just about to become confused here. It's not allowed; stop right there!" Unfortunately, it is not like that. Everything is possible, both delusion and enlightenment. And this quality of unlimited possibilities is exactly what characterizes the three realms of samsara. Anything happens, anything goes.

Here comes another bad example: In America, people are allowed to own guns. Why? It is to demonstrate their freedom. If they were not allowed to bear arms, they would not be free, or at least that's the argument. In America the Republicans and the Democrats argue back and forth about whether this freedom of having a gun should be allowed. The argument is: "If I am prohibited from having a gun, then my basic American freedoms and rights are being violated." Therefore, as it stands right now, there is still the right to bear arms in the United States. "Otherwise," they say, "we would be like Singapore where they're not allowed to do this and not allowed to do that; everything is totally restricted. We refuse to be that way. We want to have a gun if and when we want it."

In the same way, let's say there's an argument between empty essence and cognizant nature. Empty essence would say to cognizant nature: "If you want to go to hell, the path is free and clear to experience what it's like there. If you want to be enlightened and experience how that is, you are free to do that as well. Everything is free and open." In one way, having guns can be a big problem: people die. But in another way, it shows basic freedom. When you are deluded, the delusion is painful, but it also shows that your basic nature is freedom. Because your basis is freedom, there is the possibility of being deluded; otherwise it couldn't happen. That is the openness that describes empty essence. It is because of this freedom that all our experiences can happen. Selfish emotions are free to happen; but original wakefulness is also free to happen.

To give an example that some of you may have already heard: A simple-minded guy went to New York, to Times Square. He'd been told that space at Times Square was very expensive, so he took out a little glass bottle he had with him, opened the lid, and let some of the space of Times Square in. Then he screwed the lid on very tightly, zipped it up in a Ziploc bag, tied two other bags around it and put it in his suitcase. Then he got on an airplane, flew across the Pacific, and arrived back in Nepal, where space is not that expensive. Now, my question is: as he was flying through the sky above the Pacific, and then when he landed in Nepal, at these stages of the path, what did he have inside that jar? Was it the space from Times Square? Was it the space above the Pacific, or was it the space in Nepal? That's a question for you. And I'm not talking about the *air* in Times Square, the polluted air.

STUDENT: It is the same air.

RINPOCHE: How is that possible, when he was flying for seventeen hours? How could it possibly be the same space? For it to be the same, you'd have to remain at Times Square.

STUDENT: He did not have all space, he had only a little piece in a bottle.

RINPOCHE: Somebody else, please.

STUDENT 2: It was left behind in New York?

STUDENT 3: He carried the space from New York to Nepal and then opened the bottle.

RINPOCHE: But there was some space, right? There was some space that didn't go anywhere. Why am I giving this example? Did I go nuts? Is there any connection between empty essence and some space in New York City?

STUDENT: It accommodates everything.

TRANSLATOR: The space in New York?

STUDENT: The space accommodates, whether it's in New York or in Nepal. It's space.

RINPOCHE: Then why do you say it's New York space?

STUDENT: Habit.

RINPOCHE: So what's the connection between the concepts here? Space in New York, New York and space.

STUDENT: New York and space, what's the connection?

RINPOCHE: If space is just space, then there's absolutely no reason to say something like "I have no space, my room is too small."

STUDENT: Because New York has a very vast habit of mind, thinking that space is the center, it's confining, and that's like our dualistic mind, but space is like mind essence, the nonconceptual or empty, you know, cognizant.

RINPOCHE: The problem is actually New York, not the space.

STUDENT: Right.

RINPOCHE: We must do something about New York. The ceiling and floor here, up and down. These concepts of up and down, why are they being used? Based on what? Why talk about space as having an upper and lower part? Why?

STUDENT: Because we couldn't communicate.

RINPOCHE: Why not?

STUDENT: We wouldn't be able to talk, to cognize, to be able to look, to know up or down.

RINPOCHE: So it's only to communicate; it's actually not true that there's an upper or lower part to space?

STUDENT: Okay, yes.

RINPOCHE: So if something is not true, why speak of it?

STUDENT: Because we're confused.

RINPOCHE: Very good.

STUDENT: Rinpoche has rooms upstairs.

RINPOCHE: I also have a room downstairs.

STUDENT: There is up and down, but only relatively speaking.

RINPOCHE: There is up and down; but not really; but there still is. Why? What do you mean by relative? What is the source of all relative concepts? It is based on a center being here, which is "me." Everything is defined based on that, based on this "I." Based on that comes the thinking that "I am here right now, therefore I was before, yesterday, and I will be later on, tomorrow," and so on. It *seems* to be that way, and because it seems to, we take it as if it were real. It is a nonexistence that *seems* to exist. Do you understand this? It's like when you start constructing a house. You start in one spot, then you take the rope and start outlining the shape of the building. But you have to put the peg down somewhere to start with. You can't put the rope in midair. Isn't that true?

So in the same way, the original yardstick for samsara, that which everything is measured from, is *me here now*. It's not a *me* in the past or the future, but rather the moment-to-moment, right-now feeling that *I am*. Everything is measured from that. Above me, below me, to my right, to my left, and so forth. It's in the present. But if we look into that present, what is it? We don't find anything.

The present is actually egoless. We should think well about this to understand it correctly, otherwise we can have the feeling that all this is meaningless: "This is very weird, what's the point?" It seems like falling apart. It feels awkward, uncomfortable. We need to continue training in order to deepen this and make it an experience, so that our clinging to things as being real and our clinging to ego as something that truly exists is about to fall totally apart. But just as it's about to fall apart, ego starts spewing out more pollution. It rallies its forces again. In that moment, one feels scared: "Hey, this is too much." People get afraid of the feeling that everything is falling apart. Actually things don't really fall apart. It's just that there's a sense of timelessness, being beyond time, which can be scary.

Samsaric experience is based on the present thought "I am." Everything actually has to be brought into the present moment. In Buddhist practice, bring everything, whatever it is, from all directions, into the present moment, then drop the present. Then time vanishes.

Timelessness in Buddhism has to do with the dissolving of conceptual mind, letting go of concepts. In the moment of letting go of concepts, you are already in timelessness. The Buddhist worldview holds that billions of worlds exist simultaneously, not just this one, and that life didn't originate on one particular planet. "Life" here is in the sense of mind. Mind did not begin at any point. As a matter of fact, we say that there is no particular sequence between matter and mind. It's more like a simultaneous occurrence, if you want to speak of an occurrence. However, it's not that first there was matter, and that mind appeared out of matter at some later point. It's definitely not like that.

We often use the analogy of a dream. You can say that the dream world occurs simultaneously with the dreaming. And in this dream world, there is a guy called Einstein who starts to wonder, "Where did all this come from?" It's like that. "Well, let me think," this person in the dream ponders. "First, there was this world of solid stone, of matter. Then slowly, slowly, life began, and *then* mind came." But really, there's no guarantee that that dream is true. Actually, there's no guarantee at all. Everything is a state of delusion to begin with.

In the same way there is also what could be called *timeless time*, which is not necessarily what we usually call the past, present, and future. Without timeless time, nothing could unfold. This timeless quality, like the space from Times Square that we thought we could bring from one place to another, is a pervasive spaciousness that is already there, independently. We cannot put a finger on it; it is not something that first happens, remains at a particular place and then vanishes. Rather, we allow our cognizant nature to simply be indivisible from that spaciousness, and we acknowledge that this is how it actually is. That is the timelessness of rigpa, the basic dimension of rigpa. Got it?

STUDENT: I do not understand that there is no present moment, that it does not exist. I am having difficulty understanding this.

RINPOCHE: Anything that we call the present moment is not really the present, because a fraction of an instant after we label it, it is already old. It is not the present; it is not fresh any longer. As a matter of fact, just two moments after labeling it, it is really old and out of date. Another point is that it is just a projection, and one second after the projection it is no longer the present; it is old. So it is old, old, old, old. In the real present, as a matter of fact, you cannot find anything more present or more fresh than the openness of space that does not arise or cease. It never grows old because it is not a concrete article that could go out of date.

When we discuss the real present, it can only be rigpa, the spaciousness of rigpa, not a projection of thought that labels something "the present moment." The label "the present moment" can never be the present; it is already out of date. For example, if you try to define one second, one instant, you can easily cut it up into sixty or a hundred pieces. Which of these is the present? You can carry on doing so, on and on. It is therefore impossible to nail down "the present" aside from it being your own invented label. It cannot be found; it does not exist. The only real nowness is therefore emptiness. There is no other possibility.

STUDENT: It seems to me that as soon as we try to think about the present moment or put any thought on it or even experience it, it is already in the past, as I understand. However, just because we can't think about it or pinpoint it, does not mean that it does not exist. There is lots of stuff that we can't think about but does exist.

TRANSLATOR: Doesn't that sound like an inverted proof?

STUDENT: I am not making a proof; I am simply saying I don't understand. If we can't pinpoint it, if it gets smaller and smaller and smaller down to an infinitely small fragment of time, that doesn't mean that it does not exist.

RINPOCHE: Then there's nothing to do, huh? In trying to determine how something is, we can either reflect upon it and dissect it, or we can observe it directly. Trying to establish the existence of something outside of these two options becomes very problematic to verify. But if there does exist *a something* separate from your knowing of it, the question is obviously: how do you know?

According to Buddhist philosophy, it is impossible to prove the existence of any phenomenon separate from the knowing mind. If there were to be anything that could be said to exist apart from your knowing of it, then that would mean that that object would have an independent existence. It would be totally independent of the knowing mind. That would mean that there was no connection, relationship, or link between your mind and that object. If that were the case, then the mind could become enlightened but the object would still linger on somewhere out there. That would mean that the totality could never be enlightened in your experience; that you would be enlightened but there would still be a remnant hanging around unknown. In such a case it is quite questionable whether total enlightenment is possible.

In the same way, speaking about time, we may train in the meditation state, but if real, concrete time were still hanging around in some other place, independently, then we again run into this same problem.

Let's use the example of the dream state, in which the totality of the dream phenomena does not exist in any possible way apart from the dreaming mind. When an ordinary person dreams, the empty spaciousness is ignored and instead the cognizant quality, the *experiencing*, is taken to be real and solid. That is how the confusion of the dream state takes place.

Let's say there are fifteen elephants in your dream. Fourteen of them are just dream phenomena, but the fifteenth is a real, solid elephant that exists outside of your dream. If this were really true, then it would not matter how hard you tried to wake up from that dream. You could liberate fourteen of the fifteen elephants, but one would still remain, a huge elephant inside your tiny room. What I am trying to say is that it certainly wouldn't; that fifteenth elephant is not there either.

This could be a difficult topic. Actually it's not difficult, but it could seem so. There could be a doubt here: "Am I dreaming of that, or is that coming into my dream? Am I in his dream or is he in my dream?"

Some spiritual systems claim we are all figures in somebody else's dream, in "the big guy's" dream. Could that be true? Buddhist philosophy says that dream phenomena unfold because of karma: they are *karmic phenomena*. There are two types of karmic phenomena: individual and shared. Shared karmic phenomena are evident and perceived by beings in common, while individual karmic phenomena are felt by oneself but hidden from others. There is so much we can experience individually but others cannot, or vice versa. We are like people meeting in a dream.

In this sense we are all born into some sort of group dream; we are group dreaming. At the same time, there is also individual dreaming going on. Just because one person's dream ends doesn't mean that other people's dreams cease. Individual dreaming and group dreaming take place at the same time. Even if I wake up, the other guys are still dreaming. This is one important basis for compassion. Who are you to disturb other people's dreams? You have to respect their dreams. To fully respect them is to be compassionate. To disrespect this and have no empathy for other people's dreams, because obviously they are just dreaming, is to stray into spiritual conceit, which is surely a wrong track. Many practitioners steer onto that distorted path.

There are six major types of group karma or group dreaming: hell beings, hungry ghosts, animals, human beings, demigods, and gods. According to Buddhist teachings, the hell realms do not really exist, but on the other hand they certainly do. What does it mean to say that the hells do not really exist? It means that there is no real hell to be found separate from the karmic phenomena in the minds of sentient beings. There is no architect and engineer who constructed the hells.

Let's say that all sentient beings become enlightened simultaneously. Do the Lord of Death and his henchmen now stay unemployed in the hells? Are they just sitting there waiting, or do they retire and go somewhere else? This illustrates the interconnectedness of all types of phenomena. This is how it is when things unfold, and in the middle when things remain. At the end of any experience, the interconnectedness makes it so that when it ends, the whole affair is no more; it just dissolves. It is not that the Lord of Death just sits there in the hell realms, unemployed, and worries about where to go in his retirement. It is not like that at all. When the interconnectedness of everything runs out, the whole infernal setup no longer exists; it is simply like that. Where does the darkness go when the sun rises in the morning? In which direction does it flee? Where does the darkness come from when the sunlight disappears? Hell is like that. It is the condition of sunlight that makes it so that there is no darkness, and the absence of sunlight that allows there to be darkness. Similarly, hell realms are dependent upon the deluded experience of sentient beings; and dependent upon the absence of the deluded experience of sentient beings, there are no longer any hells. The Buddhist statement that there are no hells means that there are no *permanent, concrete* hells. It also means that there is no separate maker of hell. The creator of the hells is simply the individual karmic experience of sentient beings. It is not that someone arrives on the scene with a construction crew and iron plates, then heats them up and bangs them together to build the hell realm.

This is actually an extraordinarily important point. Let's say that I have just died. The particular type of group dreaming I shall now join— whether it is a hell group or a hungry ghost group or a group of celestial beings—is entirely dependent upon the karmic phenomena that I have created earlier. Pushed in that direction by karma, I join one of the six groups. Once that happens, the karma begins ripening. I start to experience that type of scenery, and at that point, even if I change my mind and think, "I don't want to be here any longer," it would be very difficult to shift dreams. Why? Because it is ripening; it is happening. Before this happens, before the karma begins to ripen, there may possibly be a choice if we have the ability to choose.

Without understanding this important point, you may be uncertain as to what those realms actually are. Dependent origination and karmic experience are very central to the reality of what we are, and they are interconnected. I hope that based on these principles you are able to understand the entire picture of the Buddhist teachings. Without that you may come to Tsoknyi Rinpoche's retreat, hear some teachings about ground, path, and fruition, and then try to feel as if all karmic phenomena have been kicked out. You grab hold of one piece of the teachings, like grabbing a vajra around the middle and ignoring the top and bottom. Then later, when you get upset in your life and it doesn't feel very enjoyable, you may think, "I should use the teachings of the Great Perfection now so I'll feel better." When you do, you feel better: "My problem is not really so huge. Didn't he say it's all like a dream, an illusion? I think I will try the view now in order to feel good, so that I won't feel guilty. Okay, it's all like a dream, like an illusion."

If that is how you apply the Dzogchen teachings it is fine by me. If there is just a tiny flicker of benefit for one sentient being, then there is some value; I am happy. But merely using the Dzogchen teachings once in a while in your daily life to feel good when you're not feeling too well is a partial solution. It may solve the day's immediate problem, but the next day there will be another problem. For this reason it is good to get the big picture, a vaster view and perspective. In Tibet people were quite uneducated, but they understood certain important points very well. They had almost too much intellectual understanding at times, enough to become a problem. The Buddhist tradition teaches that true insight requires a meritorious attitude, or simply merit, and provides certain ways to go about generating merit. So people set out to create a lot of merit, and at a certain point the practice of creating merit could simply turn into a cultural system.

We must understand that deluded experience, the dreaming, has two aspects: group karma and individual karma. The evolution of karmic phenomena has to do with how karma is created, both negative karma and positive karma. Negative karma is brought to a halt by means of creating merit. This is how it works.

Our ultimate aim, therefore, should be to change deluded experience, not to eliminate experiencing itself. We can never get rid of experience, but we can change deluded experience into undeluded experience. Buddhafields are also a type of pure experience. As a matter of fact, buddhafields are not the making of one particular person; they are not made up. We may hear that the pure land of Sukhavati was conjured up by means of Buddha Amitabha's former aspirations, but this is not exactly true. Rather, once you happen to join that "enlightened" group, there is a certain experience that unfolds. You can remain within that; it is possible.

STUDENT: Rinpoche, could you say something about the difference between having a preference for something and ego-clinging? To use your example of a hotel, how does preferring a sunny room differ from clinging to it? Or really wanting something or just preferring it, as a human being?

RINPOCHE: Even though they are not that pronounced, having preferences still belongs under ego-clinging. It is still taking the five aggregates seriously as belonging to someone, to me. Once we fully realize that the five aggregates are naturally empty, we are not really subject to the craving connected to choosing one situation over another. That means everything is completely liberated. Therefore, because of this liberation through realizing emptiness, there is no longer any sense of one situation being better *for me* than another. And the whole question of preference doesn't come in any longer. It's all freed.

Nevertheless, as long as one hasn't reached that insight, one should respect relative reality, relative truth—the responsibility of taking care of this body being fed, well dressed, cleaned, and so forth. Of course it's based on ego-clinging, because while we take care of this it's still *mine*, subtly. But it belongs under respecting relative reality. There is no choice really, because you have five aggregates; they still exist. So you have to take care of them, but not excessive care.

Let's say you dream that a guy comes in with a machine gun. He is about to shoot you, and you feel afraid of what may happen once the bullets hit you, right? So you try to dodge, even though the shooting is not really happening. And because you succeed in evading the bullets, your fear during the dream vanishes. Taking care of relative reality is like that. It seems necessary to do so, to take care of one's relative situation, because we haven't fully realized that the five aggregates are just a magical show. We haven't fully realized this yet.

We must respect both levels—relative and ultimate, the seeming and the real—and we should certainly understand the real. Unless someone gives us the message that the five aggregates are a magical illusion, we may never realize it. At the same time, we must respect the illusion to a certain degree. Let's say that during the dream someone tells you, "Oh, you're just dreaming. It's not real." Once you understand that it's just a dream, you'll stop being afraid even if somebody is shooting. Isn't that true?

These two levels, relative and ultimate, are very important. The best understanding, of course, is to realize that all this is insubstantial and like a magical illusion. As long as we don't realize this, however, we must respect our lack of realizing it and make sure that we move toward realizing it.

Failing to understand the importance of these two levels of truth could make the Dharma practitioner go a little wild. Intellectually one may understand, "Nothing is real, nothing matters; this is all insubstantial, so I don't care about anything." You become frivolous and uninhibited. The other extreme is that of an ordinary person who thinks of everything as totally real and solid and gets caught up in it, becoming imprisoned by that belief. These are the two extremes: the practitioner is in danger of becoming careless about everything, while the ordinary person is in danger of being too serious and uptight. You should know the in-between state, the balance between these two. Again, it's important to understand both levels of truth.

Everything is like a magical illusion. We should understand these two levels: the seeming and the real. As spiritual practitioners we need to relate to everything very correctly, very nicely, until we attain the level of Drukpa Kunlek. Many of you may know the story of Drukpa Kunlek, a Tibetan yogi. At first glance it looked as if everything he did was totally crazy, as if he was insane. But if you look closely, everything he did was a teaching, and whoever he influenced or touched in his crazy manner became his disciple. And the disciples themselves didn't go crazy. If Drukpa Kunlek perceived that someone could actually go mad, he wouldn't behave like that toward that person. But when someone became his disciple, then he would teach in the proper way: first the introductory teachings, then the ngöndro, then the rest of the path.

STUDENT: Rinpoche, I was interested in what you were saying, and maybe we could hear a little more about it, about fear giving rise to a somewhat distorted renunciation. We have this Western idea of mixing Dharma and therapy, and we try to heal ourselves in any way possible. In one way, maybe we're increasing our suffering; we're trying to heal our illusion, our ego. So what's the difference and how do we really use the suffering to progress?

RINPOCHE: My honest view is that you must know a few key points of Buddhism, especially of Vajrayana Buddhism. You should understand that everything is part of emptiness and that whatever you perceive is an illusion. When I say illusion, I'm not saying bad. I'm saying what it is. If you understand that all phenomena are illusion, they are already softened. The clinging to them is already 20 or 30 percent relaxed. The problem is you usually don't think that way when faced with difficulties. You believe that outside, inside, everything is some kind of absolute entity—that the problem exists and that you also exist. It becomes a very solid idea.

To turn this around, Buddhism teaches at the very beginning that everything arises from emptiness, like a dream or illusion. This doesn't mean that everything is bad; don't be upset. Simply acknowledge illusion to be illusion, and then be happy because you know the nature of your phenomena, your life. The word in Tibetan for existence literally means "possibility." Anything can happen in your mind. Don't get caught up by what happens. Learn the key points in order to be able to deal with every type of experience. That's what the view and training is all about.

The United States, for instance, is a prosperous country: there's plenty of work for everyone, food is abundant, there is good housing, and people from other countries like India or Indonesia long to go there. Once they do, they feel they've arrived in a buddhafield. Their job may be lousy and low-paying, but they are so happy that they finally made it. Now look at the Americans themselves. One out of five takes antidepressant medication. I saw that in a newspaper the other day. Many people suffer in the United States, and not from going hungry. It's not the suffering of being without a job. It is *mental* suffering, which can often come from not taking charge of oneself, one's own experience. So much pain is created by letting ourselves get lost in whatever happens. You project a thought, then the second thought believes the first one. The third, fourth, and fifth thoughts are projected. The first thought is by this point already a reality, and then the tenth thought believes that the fifth thought has always been an actuality. And on and on, with more thoughts and more validating. That's how delusion is perpetuated. First an illusion is created in our mind, then a second thought takes the illusion to be true, and it goes on like that. It's possible to sit for fifteen or twenty minutes and believe that what we are thinking about is real. A key message in Buddhism is that all of this stuff is merely concepts created by our own minds. What we call "world," "time," "place," and so forth are all mentally created concepts.

The fickleness of fashion is another proof that the whole affair is an illusion. What was stylish ten years ago is laughed at today. What one attaches reality to is never fixed. Our emotions are like that. We tend to trust whatever comes to mind as if it were factual. Instead, we must gain certainty that the very nature of all this is emptiness.

How do we do this? We need to distinguish between two aspects: dualistic mind, *sem* in Tibetan, and mind essence. According to the Dzogchen teachings, the view is mind essence free of conceptual attitude. The view is not dualistic mind. Dualistic mind is when the attention gets caught up in a perceived object and fails to recognize its own nature. It is taught that while we are caught up in dualistic mind, confusion takes over and samsara continues. You can say that samsara is the magical display of dualistic mind. From another angle, it is stated that the pure experience, the buddhafields like Akanishtha and so forth, is the magical display of mind essence. I will explain more about mind and mind essence later.

Some masters teach that both samsara and nirvana are the magical display of mind, in that the magical display of dualistic mind includes the whole of samsara, while the magical display of mind essence, its natural expression, includes all the kayas and wisdoms, all the buddhafields, and so forth. Dualistic mind is full of shortcomings and has an abundance of faults. As long as one is caught up in being that way, there is no steadiness, since dualistic mind is impermanent. One is like a feather blown in a hurricane. There's no peace, only suffering. Dualistic mind's inherent instability is the basis for all suffering. Why is this? Because dualistic mind is unreal and insubstantial, like foam or a bubble on water. It immediately gets overtaken by whatever happens, whatever the circumstance is. It's like a hungry street dog in Nepal: if you throw it something to eat, it will immediately give chase. This example doesn't work in America, where dogs are well fed! Dualistic mind is like a hungry Nepali street dog. It always feels, "I must eat, I must drink, I must take charge, be in control." And it always gets caught up in the moment, no matter what it is. A hungry dog may sometimes bite its owner; worse than that, when starving it may even try to eat itself. If we give free rein to the habit of conceptual mind, all sorts of terrible things can happen.

These are the negative traits of dualistic mind. Its function is to constantly grasp at and chase after objects. It pays attention to something, then another thing, then a third, and so on—always reaching out toward something other, thereby getting farther and farther away from its own nature. Dualistic mind's way of grasping is a hopeful, longing attitude, a wanting to take hold of something, of an object, and trying to get at it somehow by grasping again and again. But since all objects are impermanent and by nature insubstantial, there is ultimately nothing to grasp at. Therefore dualistic mind always ends up at a loss, disappointed in some way and not knowing how to come back to itself. One ends up completely homeless.

By pursuing and pursuing and pursuing in this way, chasing after one object after the other, sooner or later one discovers that objects are futile to pursue; that there is nothing there to get. We learn that the attitude of chasing something meaningless is futile as well. At this point one is at a loss, like a lost child without a mother. This is why masters' songs often express pity for that frame of mind.

Mind is fickle and objects are seductive, it is said. The Buddha told us not to be that way. Don't chase after one object, then another, then a third. That pursuit is not your real home, your real mother. This futile pursuit is steered by, influenced by, and affected by circumstances. Whenever something feels unpleasant, one gets disturbed by it; if it's pleasant, one gets caught up in it. Throughout this course of events, we are so unstable, so unsteady. Sometimes the obsession becomes so intense that one can lose one's own life. This way of being creates incredible anxiety. One experiences fear, worry, feeling lost, feeling uncared for: "Nobody loves me, nobody takes care of me, nobody worries about me." This lonely frame of mind is because of being unstable, being steered by objects, being oversensitive in a wrong way.

Instead of this relentless chasing about, we ought to take a break.

MIND AND MIND ESSENCE

Now we get to the nonconceptual view, the view free of conceptual mind. To understand this, we must distinguish between thinking mind and mind essence. As I mentioned earlier, sem is the state of mind that gets caught up with, stuck to, or absorbed in perceived objects—all the sights, sounds, smells, tastes, and textures, all the plans and the memories. First, an instance of attention gets caught up in an instance of perceiving an object. This is followed by a second instance of getting caught up in what is perceived, and then a third one, a fourth one, and so on. Completely losing track of oneself, being lost in the experience—that is called sem.

Dualistic mind is remarkable in that it constantly validates itself. Once you believe your previous thought, it becomes part of your life. The tapestry of all these deluded thoughts is what makes up our superficial reality. The reason this deluded experience is so believable to *me* is not the first or the second thought by itself. It's the cumulative force of all these thoughts that after a while helps one to convince oneself that the previous thought was true; it was real. And then one gives reality to whatever one happens to think of. This is how this world, *my world*, my personal experience, becomes a solid reality.

We thoroughly exhaust ourselves this way. After being tossed about on the waves of the ocean of samsara, blown here and there, east and west by the wind of karma, the little rigpa child needs to take a break.

Something is surely amiss. We feel incomplete; we are defeated because we don't know how to let dualistic mind be at ease in itself. We lack basic stability. Our normal state of mind is so easily influenced, so easily seduced. Because of one's own sense of wanting, one gets sucked in again and again and believes that whatever happens is real. One convinces oneself again and once more gets lost.

But you already know this. You're experts at this. This is our daily experience. The Buddha said, "Don't be like that." Instead, he said, "Recognize your natural state. That outward chasing is not your natural state."

I would phrase it like this: you have gotten lost from your mother's home. You've gone out, out, out, a hundred kilometers away. All your attention is directed outward, chasing after phenomena in whatever scenery unfolds. You move outward, believing that this experience is surely a meaningful object. Being impermanent, these experiences will fail you sooner or later. By repeatedly trusting in a misperceived reality, you have established the wrong habit, and you don't know how to come back home. We can see this habit in people's eyes, in their faces: their spirit is directed outward, with no juice at all. Some people take drugs when they have this problem; some become violent. People try so many ways to come home.

In short, the problem is being caught up in sem, in dualistic mind. This failure to recognize your mother's house, your basic state, creates a lot of pain. There are so many distractions in this world, so many enticing possibilities being presented in order to suck in dualistic mind. If you succumb to that, you lose your independence, your freedom.

The Buddha told us to distinguish between the relative and the ultimate, the seeming and the real. Distinguishing is very important in the Dzogchen teachings as well. Here we distinguish between sem—dualistic mind, the attention being caught up in the objects and not knowing itself—and mind essence, the nature of mind recognizing itself. This doesn't mean recognizing the deluded state and just acknowledging it as being deluded. No, it means recognizing the *nature* of this deluded state—mind essence itself.

The Buddha said, "Child, come home. Stay in your mother's lap." How is this home? What are the amenities at home? Is there hot water or not? Is there central heating or not? Is it possible to warm it up when it gets cold; is it possible to turn on the air conditioning when it gets hot? Is there an attached bathroom in the master bedroom? We look at how our home is equipped: are we able to deal with the guest Mr. Attachment? Are we able to invite the guest Closed-Mindedness? Are we able to be hospitable and accommodating when Mr. Anger arrives as a guest? We must prepare for these events right now. This home is our mind essence, the nature of mind.

The nature of mind has three qualities that can be described with terminology similar to that used in explaining the ground. There is still a difference. This home, the nature of mind, is empty in essence. That means it is accommodating enough to fit in everything. All buddhas, all sentient beings, everything fits. Attachment, anger, closed-mindedness, as well as all-accomplishing wisdom, discriminating wisdom, the wisdom of equality, and so forth—all of these are able to fit within empty essence. Cognizant nature is like the mother, in the sense that not only can all these emotional states fit, they can also be dealt with, taken care of quite nicely. And all these things that fit do so in an unconfined, unhampered way.

The identity of mind essence is to be empty. Its nature is to be cognizant, able to know. And its function is to be unconfined. These are the three primary qualities: empty in essence, cognizant by nature, and unconfined in capacity. We're still involved in describing the map here.

This basic openness of our minds is like a highway. You could call it a freeway for the five emotions. Our mind's state is not like a nice big American highway, but rather like a Nepali highway. The roads are very narrow, so that two cars can barely squeeze by each other. Three cars come and there's a traffic jam. We have a lot of cars moving about, five of them in particular—attachment, anger, closed-mindedness, pride, and jealousy. As a matter of fact, we have 84,000 cars on this narrow highway.

Right now, *empty essence* describes the way our natural state is. This quality is not made up. Without this empty essence it would be impossible for any phenomena to appear. *Cognizant nature* is your present mind, your sense of being awake, right now, while knowing that its essence is empty; otherwise the cognizance is dualistic consciousness. That's the fundamental difference between dualistic consciousness and original wakefulness. The dualistic way of perceiving is being unaware that this awake quality is empty in essence. Original wakefulness is recognizing that it is empty in essence.

That covers empty essence and cognizant nature. So far, the unconfined capacity hasn't worked out so well. Why not? In our present state you could call it "confined incapacity," since it is not particularly capable and is also confined or limited. This is how dualistic mind is right now: confined either to being empty or to thinking. When these are a unity, being both empty and cognizant, that is the third quality, the unconfined capacity. We need to recognize this. Otherwise people may claim, "This empty quality is how it is; there isn't anything, there's nothing." That's the nihilistic view. Or they may assert the other aspect and maintain that there is a permanent "something," which is the eternalistic point of view. It seems impossible for people even to conceive of an option other than those two extremes.

Dualistic mind is what's going on right now. We're talking about our present mind, right here, right now. Your ability to experience, right in this very moment, is original wakefulness when it knows its own empty essence. Otherwise, it's dualistic mind. Therefore, when our present wakefulness, right now, comes to know its own empty essence, that is sufficient for us to realize the unconfined capacity—in other words, the unity of experience and emptiness. From one side it's actually very simple. Cognizant nature is not something we have to somehow pull off or make up; it is this knowing that is happening right now. We're not required to dissolve this present, awake quality into an empty state—not at all. Rather, the empty quality is allowed to be acknowledged *while being* awake. We don't need to stop being awake.

People often make a mistake here in thinking that the training consists of an attempt to dissolve this knowing quality into emptiness. They try to make nothingness, rather than just leaving this consciousness, this knowing mind, to itself. All you actually need is to let this knowing and awake atmosphere be permeated with emptiness, like allowing the moisture to slowly seep in. It's not that you have to deliberately dunk your napkin into the water, to just sit there spaced out and not know anything. Rather, it's more a sense of releasing the conscious quality, *loosely*. Then, all by itself, the moisture permeates. Our present cognizant quality—just let it be, and then slowly let the empty quality be evident. Speaking from experience, the masters describe this as simply opening up in a very gentle way.

First you let the napkin be; that's shamatha. And then slowly, a little vipashyana, a little Dzogchen wets the napkin, permeating it. As far as empty essence reaches, cognizant nature permeates to the same extent, until finally we are omniscient. Right now the question is, how do we wet the napkin? How do we recognize? How do we give birth to mind essence while in dualistic mind? How do we get to mind essence from dualistic mind? I will explain this a little later.

Let's use another analogy for the difference between dualistic mind and mind essence: ice and water. Their identity is the same, but they function differently. Dualistic mind is like being frozen, while mind essence is liquid, like unfrozen water. Most of us have mainly dualistic, frozen states of mind. Dualistic mind has three modes: unvirtuous, virtuous, and neutral. That's where we spend most of the time, in one or another of these three.

Whenever we get involved in being attached, aggressive, or closed-minded, that activity belongs to the unvirtuous type of dualistic mind. When we try to practice the Dharma, when we try to meditate, when we do something that is good, like circumambulations and other kinds of spiritual practice, that sort of activity belongs to virtuous dualistic mind. And then there's a lot of time in between when we're not involved in anything in particular; we're just indifferent to what is going on. That is the third type, the neutral. Dualistic mind is therefore either virtuous, unvirtuous, or neutral. It can also be described in terms of different mental states, such as the twenty-one subsidiary negative emotions, the eight types of cognition or consciousnesses, and so forth. Most of these states accompany us every day.

Dualistic mind means a way of being in which mind holds on to subject and object and ties itself up in the process. Mind thinks one thought and then another and then another, like beads on a string. One thought after another, again and again and again and again. Each moment of dualistic mind is a thought that thinks of something. This happens over and over again. We get wrapped up in experiencing that way. This process of spinning in a circle is called samsara. As long as one is caught up in that, occupied in this circle, there is no liberation. It is taught, however, that even though this seeming circle seems to spin endlessly, there are always gaps between the moments of thought. The mind spinning in this circle does not notice the gaps.

"Empty essence" certainly is a traditional Buddhist phrase. Experientially, it is a feeling of being wide open in all directions, without any barrier anywhere—open to the front, the sides, and the back. In discussing emptiness experientially, it's all right to use the word "openness." Please understand that openness here is not a mentally fabricated openness. If it were, it would be forgotten and lost as soon as something else happened. Real emptiness, first of all, does not come into being; second, it does not remain anywhere; and third, it does not cease, not at all. It's just like the way in which the space in a room does not arise, does not remain anywhere, and does not cease. Because of this emptiness, beings can move about, can fly in airplanes, can do all sorts of different jobs; they can make pollution or clean it up. All of this is possible only because of this open emptiness.

Attachment, aggression, and closed-mindedness are in themselves not the problem. It's rather that these three emotions don't have enough space: they're constricted and clash with each other. Emotions in themselves are also not necessarily painful. There is something together with the emotion that restricts, confines, or imprisons it. Empty essence, on the other hand, is already wide open, meaning there is no wall, no barrier, no limitation in any way. It's a way of being totally open. This emptiness is not something made by our ideas, and it doesn't really help much to try to figure it out. We must know experientially how to just *let be* in that openness. A lot more could be said about empty essence, and as a matter of fact, the *Prajnaparamita* scriptures—known as Transcendent Knowledge, the great mother of all buddhas—explain empty essence in great detail.

Let's take the sun as an example. Empty essence refers to the sun itself, which remains as its own identity. What is the sun's nature? It is hot, it shines, it illuminates. What is the sun's capacity? By giving warmth, it helps everything grow, it causes water to evaporate, and so on. That is its function. Similarly, the identity of mind essence is to be empty. That is simply what it is. Its nature is lucid in the sense that it can cognize; it can know. And what is its capacity? It is unconfined in the sense that it is not confined to being either only empty or only conscious. Rather, these two qualities are indivisible, and this unity allows any knowledge to unfold. Sometimes we hear that the unconfined capacity refers to the indivisibility of these three qualities. Recognizing rigpa is when the meditator acknowledges these three qualities simultaneously, and this rigpa is part of the ground.

How does this mind know itself? In a way that is without perceiver and perceived. The Dharma terminology for this is *rigpa that is the fourth part devoid of three*. In other words, time beyond the three times. Conceptual mind is connected to time. To be free of concepts is also to be free of time. In other words, rigpa means not to cherish a memory of a past state, nor to anticipate the coming moment, the future. Rigpa is also not analyzing or forming a concept or some kind of judgment about the present moment. You could say that being totally free of the concept of the three times is a clear, lucid state that is rigpa. In terms of time, you can say rigpa is the fourth time, beyond past, present, and future. This is timelessness. Without this, time would always fall within dualistic mind, which is always operating within one of the three times.

The yardstick for whether our experience is authentically rigpa has to do with whether these three qualities—essence, nature, and capacity— can be checked off as completely present. This is not always the case. To simply remain in a vacant state is to be "confined to voidness," staying in a state of nothing. This can turn into the nihilistic view of deciding, "This state is definitely free of cause and effect. Nothing is going to happen here; it cannot happen, it is blocked." Then no qualities will unfold—no devotion, no compassion, no love, nor any other spiritual qualities. The empty essence should be *unconfined* so that the open, unconfined quality allows all enlightened qualities to manifest.

Where do the enlightened qualities come from? Out of the cognizant nature. Where do the samsaric qualities come from? They also come out of the cognizant nature. So what defines the difference between samsara and nirvana? The enlightened qualities unfold when there is a clear knowing of no identity, of egolessness. This is how the inherent qualities can freely manifest. The samsaric drama unfolds when an imaginary ego is apprehended in the mind, as opposed to knowing that there is no personal identity. Samsaric mind unfolds out of ignorance and confusion, and the duality that is then held becomes the platform for all the samsaric states of mind to appear. So cognizant nature, the second of the three aspects of rigpa, is very important; indeed, it is vital. Everything depends on whether the cognizant nature becomes frozen into dualistic states of mind or unfrozen into realization of the essence.

How do you know whether your cognizant nature is frozen? Spaciousness—a purity, an absence of perceiver and perceived—is it there or not? Is there something being held by someone holding? Or is there knowing but the perceiver is unblocked, so to speak? In the unfrozen mode, there is perceiving, there is knowing, but it is not kept hold of in any way. The phrase is this: *not confined to being empty, not clinging while perceiving.* It is empty, but it is not restricted to only being that. While perceiving, there is no keeping hold of perceiving.

Please listen: you could say the exact opposite about right now, about how we normally perceive. Somehow the perceiving, the experiencing quality, seems to get confined to being "not empty." Isn't it true that we experience everything as solid, real, and concrete? Somehow the empty, spacious quality within experience is ignored or left out. Simply recognize that while experiencing, while perceiving, it is actually very spacious at the same time, and this frozen tendency melts, dissolves. That *unfrozenness* is the third of rigpa's qualities: the unconfined capacity. Being empty while perceiving, perceiving while being empty—this is the unity of appearance and emptiness.

We call the moment these three are simultaneously acknowledged "seeing mind essence." What is mind essence? In the specific terminology of the Great Perfection, it is called rigpa. What is rigpa? What is mind essence? It is empty in essence, cognizant by nature, and unconfined in its capacity. The key point here is to know these three simultaneously.

Sometimes we feel totally empty in a way that is blocked, because it is confined to being empty. This is a certain experience that happens sometimes in meditation. It is to be nothing, frozen within a void state, without a flexible, open quality, not juicy, not relaxed at all. Even if you wanted to think, you couldn't. Even if you wanted to be distracted, you'd be prevented from that as well. As a matter of fact, at this point emptiness has become a big distraction for you. Even if you wanted to say hello, you couldn't, because it is frozen there. But there is no other thought: no anger, attachment, jealousy, pride—nothing. There is only blank space. Being empty occupies you entirely. The cognizant nature here is frozen into blank emptiness. Some people may think this is rigpa. Well, it is not! Rigpa is a sense of being awake, present, lucid, bright, alive. This alive state of being awake is not made up; it is not our creation. It is simply the nature of our mind.

How many kilometers are there between dualistic mind and mind essence? What is the distance between the two? The Buddha said there are five kilometers. Is that true? Could it be true? Or maybe six, one kilometer for each of the six classes of sentient beings? No! It is said that samsara and nirvana are as far from each other as the front and back of your own hand. How far apart are these two? There is a certain distance, true, but at the line where they touch you almost cannot say whether it is front or back. At the dividing line, how far apart are they from each other, really? They are touching, right? Yes? No? Where do they touch?

Now let's talk about dualistic mind and mind essence: where do they touch? What is the dividing line?

Cognizant nature is the pivotal point here. Whether you turn into dualistic mind or into rigpa depends on how cognizant nature is. Does it cling to an object over there? Then it becomes dualistic mind. Does cognizant nature know itself without clinging to its own essence? Then within that state there is a knowing both of itself as well as of everything else. That, in Buddhist terminology, is sublime knowledge, which is what a buddha has. You've heard about buddha wisdom, right? Where does that come from? The basis for buddha wisdom is this cognizant nature.

Please do not misunderstand. We have to use the word "knowing"; there is no way around this, because there is no other word. However, this is not the usual way we use the word "knowing," in terms of a subject knowing an object. You can also use the phrase "aware but without clinging," if you like that better. The point is that this mind has a natural quality of knowing, of being cognizant or aware. That is just how this mind is. Its nature is like that. This natural knowing can be polluted by notions of *me* and *that*. These can grow larger and larger until this becomes the samsaric way of experiencing. We must reconnect with the natural way of knowing. That is one important point.

Where exactly is rigpa? Where does rigpa live? Rigpa lives with each and every thought we have. There is no thought that escapes being saturated by rigpa at the same time. Why? Because in each and every thought there is also cognizant nature. Right? This nature is the meeting point between the thoughts in samsaric mind and rigpa. Take the example of my *mala*. Wherever the mala is, at every point throughout it there is also a cord. Isn't that true? If the string inside weren't there, the mala couldn't keep its shape. It's the same with buddha nature. Wherever a thought moves, wherever there is experience or feeling, there is this ground of the Great Perfection at the same time.

Some people hear the word "ground" and abstract it, thinking that there is a fundamental *something*, a foundation somewhere, like the foundation upon which a house is constructed. You are welcome to use another word for ground, like base or foundation. The Tibetan word is *zhi* and there is nothing you can do about that. It is pretty precise. Just like the string inside the mala, basic buddha nature is present in any type of state, any thought state we have. So what is buddha nature? What is ground? I told you already. So what is this ground like? Empty essence, cognizant nature, unconfined capacity. This is how the ground is.

As I mentioned earlier, there are said to be 84,000 different emotions, one arising after the other in an endless stream. Sometimes they get jammed up like a traffic jam, or one of them gets accentuated, like anger or desire. If they are well organized, there is not much of a problem, but sometimes they get jammed up and we feel confused. We don't know how to carry on properly, how to run properly. The energy needs to be released, so anger or feeling upset pops up the middle of our experience. There does not seem to be enough space for all the emotions at the same time, but still they move, one after the other, in a procession. There are all different kinds of emotions, from the more blatant thought states to the more subtle and the very subtle, the undercurrent of thoughts. These emotions and thought states are not rigpa. Some are peaceful, some are wrathful; they can be gentle, wild, helpful, not helpful. There are all kinds streaming by, just like the seconds on a watch: tick, tick, tick, one right after the other. This stream of thought states needs to be interrupted. Like Milarepa said: "In the gap between the past thought and the subsequent thought, thought-free wakefulness continuously dawns." Past thought has ceased, future thought has not arisen; right now, don't cling.

Imagine punching holes in a sheet of paper with a needle. In the same way, the needle of discriminating intelligence that reveals the state of egolessness is able to perforate dualistic mind. The light of the ground that is always present as essence, nature, and capacity begins to shine through; there is a little ray of light. Then the strong habit of conceptualizing covers it up again. But then you punch another hole, and again there's some light. It's not the complete illumination from the ground, just a little ray of light coming through a little hole. You could say that a fragment or a portion or a little part of the ground shines through as a tiny ray of light. Training in mind essence is like punching one hole after the other. Samsara's deluded perception gets more and more perforated, so that it's not so solid any more. At a certain point, it just falls apart.

The gaps between thoughts reveal basic wakefulness. Our training is to allow more and more gaps. Allow the needle to puncture deluded perceptions, again and again. In the beginning these openings don't last that long, only short moments, like pinpricks from the needle. We need to perforate the paper very persistently, making more and more holes.

Another analogy can be found in the movie *The Terminator*, in the scene where the hero is shooting the robot. In the beginning it doesn't seem to help, but as he shoots again and again, finally it collapses. In the beginning, one shot, nothing happens; the robot is still coming on. The hero shoots again and again, and the robot keeps coming. He shoots more, then, slowly ... *[Rinpoche demonstrates the robot collapsing]*. In the same way, in dealing with the deluded state, we need to recognize mind essence again and again and again, making gaps in the delusion, until finally ego-clinging and confusion completely fall apart.

LOOKING, SEEING,
LETTING BE, AND BEING
FREE

"How do I experience rigpa?" This question is really about how dualistic mind and mind essence actually are. When I teach, usually I first give the story of mind essence, offering a theory about how mind essence is so that you can get the idea intellectually. But it is quite possible that someone has already experienced the actuality of mind essence before hearing it explained intellectually; let's not rule out that possibility. Traditionally, first the theory is given, then the way or method of experiencing mind essence in actuality is taught. I haven't gotten to that point yet; we are still working on the intellectual picture.

When I give this explanation, it's easy to make the mistake of thinking that mind essence is an entity somewhere *inside* dualistic mind. If we do this, we may gain some understanding of how mind essence is, but this understanding is within a dualistic framework—like the idea that within dualistic mind *there is* an empty essence, the idea that within dualistic mind *we have* a cognizant nature, and so forth. This is a conceptual understanding of the mind essence beyond concepts.

Right now, from within our state of dualistic mind, we must actually experience how mind essence consists of essence, nature, and capacity. We try to approach how that mind essence actually is as an experience. That experience takes place by means of the pith instructions given by a master.

Right here is the point where a qualified master would give the pointing-out instruction, directly pointing out the nature of mind. I myself have to use words; otherwise there does not seem to be any way. Hearing those words, we may apply them in our own experience, and then it is possible that someone may recognize mind essence through these words. Let's say that most of us now have an idea about what mind essence is. Getting the experience of it rather than just the idea has to take place in a way that is free of concepts. Bringing theory into experience requires the pointing-out instruction.

Traditionally, when the pointing-out instruction is about to be given, the students or disciples have already thoroughly prepared themselves. They will make heartfelt and sincere supplications to the lineage masters and to their root guru. The master who is about to impart the pointing-out instruction will bring forth the strength of the unconditioned original wakefulness, be inspired with great compassion, and be in that state himself or herself. At that point, the pointing-out instruction is given. But this is not the way it is going to be here right now; I am not going to do that. In the future, when you meet a great master and are able to connect deeply with such a person, you should definitely request the pointing-out instruction. There are still many such "antique" masters who hold the lineage, so slowly, slowly, and when the right time comes, please request and receive the pointing-out instruction.

Right now, as I mentioned earlier, dualistic mind is extroverted, getting caught up in one object after the other. Dualistic mind now needs to know its own essence. It needs to recognize its own identity. When we recognize mind essence, we experience it as being naturally present, not as something fabricated through our ideas. It is simply something that is by itself. Along with being naturally present as empty essence, there is also a sense of being awake. This may not last long; it may be quite short, but mind essence is naturally empty and cognizant. In Dharma terminology, this is called "the nonarising essence whose radiance is unobstructed so that its expression can manifest as myriad experiences."

Right now, we are like a movie character you see up on the screen in handcuffs, with tape over his mouth and rope bound around his body. The moment of recognizing mind nature is like the moment this character becomes untied, completely unfettered. The sudden disappearance of these confinements gives a feeling of deep release. In our case it is not physical release, like the disappearance of all those ropes, handcuffs, and tape. Rather, it is a mental release. The knots of conceptual attitude are untied, released, set free, so that our state of mind feels completely unrestrained; it opens up and remains so. The physical knots in the channels are also released and relaxed. That very moment has a sense of empty essence in this way of being wide open; at the same time, it is seen by cognizant nature in a way that is beyond seer and seen, just wide open.

This short moment of recognizing can surely be called mind essence. You can also name it natural mind or ordinary mind, although natural mind is better in this case. It might be a little too early to call it the rigpa of the Great Perfection. But as this state gets more clarified—you could say more refined—and becomes the authentic state of rigpa according to Dzogchen teachings, then at that point it will deserve its name. On the other hand, it is also possible that someone might recognize the state of rigpa from the very beginning.

The term *rigpa*, in the authentic Dzogchen sense, is not to be used lightly. It is defined in a very particular way as the *fourth part devoid of three.* This description is in terms of time, and time always has the connotation of conceptual attitude. As I explained in detail earlier, time *is* conceptual attitude, and so the fourth part means timelessness without the three concepts of past, present, or future. In other words, rigpa is totally free of conceptual attitude. As long as there is a notion of being in the present or thinking of the past or future, that state of mind is not really rigpa but is still mixed with conceptual attitude. Rigpa is totally free of that.

Rigpa is completely beyond conceptual mind. As we grow more and more used to training in a way that is beyond seer and seen, beyond meditator and meditation object, we are wide open and cognizant at the same time. The actuality of this becomes simpler. The "dirt in the soup" begins to clear, which is exactly what should happen. At a certain point, our experience really deserves the name *rangjung rigpa*, self-existing awareness. Before that point, though, it is somewhat hidden from oneself, like a natural secret. Once the secret door is opened up by means of knowing and applying the key point, we realize that rigpa is right there, completely accessible and present—which of course it was all the while.

This self-existing awareness or original wakefulness was never really away from you. It has been there in the background all the time. The moment it is fully revealed and you feel 100 percent confident about it, you might jokingly tell rigpa, "Hey, you were here all the time! I've been looking and looking for you all over the place. I spent so much money trying to find you, buying all these airplane tickets and flying here and there, doing all this searching. And you've been right here all the while! What's the matter with you?" This is what rigpa's secret is like. It is not actually secret; rather, it is hidden from you by yourself, not by anyone else. It is not that Buddha Samantabhadra somehow hid rigpa from sentient beings. Nor is it that your guru has been hiding it from you. You have been hiding it from yourself all the while.

To go along with this joke, rigpa could reply, "I didn't go anywhere, and I wasn't trying to hide from you either. You can blame me, but I'm not really to blame. What am I supposed to do if you are always so busy searching elsewhere? I was always with you. From the moment you were born, from the very beginning, I've been right here with you. You just didn't notice. You were always preoccupied, paying attention to something else."

Then conceptual attitude might ask, "If you've really been here all this time, why didn't I see you before?" And rigpa would reply, "You always wanted two; you were fixated on duality, wanting something other. Because of wanting two, there arose a third, a fourth, a fifth, a sixth, and so on, endlessly. Wanting to find something other than me, you never seemed to notice me. You were searching and searching and searching. Then you got tired and you wanted to go home, to your own house. Maybe your master helped you a little at this point, when he said, 'Poor you, you must be tired from all this running around. Now take it easy.' Then your teacher gave you a method to apply. It is because you did this, and because you were also more intelligent by this time, that you see me right now."

Rigpa goes on talking: "Seeing me is no big deal. Anyway, I am not an article that could have been lost. Neither am I something you could ever find or obtain. I am like a naked person, completely naked, without anything on. You always wanted to find the rich guy, the one dressed in fancy clothes. You were looking for the wealth, chasing after that. That doesn't mean I am not wealthy, but I have a different type of wealth. I have the wealth that ends samsara. I have the splendor that lets you cut through negative emotions. That kind of wealth didn't seem to awaken your interest or whet your appetite. You were wanting to sink your teeth in something other all the time, like chewing on a nice juicy lamb chop, chasing after sights, sounds, smells, tastes, and textures." People who are fond of meat prefer their steak to have some resistance when they sink their teeth in, so that it isn't like chewing butter. If the meat's too soft, afterward they miss the feeling of having actually chewed something.

Honestly, this whole issue is extremely simple. It's very, very easy. This way of practicing is also something very simple and easy. To discover this ease we need to train. Through training it also becomes easier and easier to release negative emotions. We very naturally and simply draw closer and closer to simply being in the natural state.

The pointing-out instruction points out the view. This is not possible to do in a book. Students must receive it in person from a realized master. The sketchy explanation I have given here is meant to create a certain initiative in you to receive personally this instruction and to receive the blessings of the lineage. It's through the blessings of the lineage that we can ready ourselves to recognize mind essence.

Among the two types of view, with and without conceptual attitude, this was a brief explanation of the view without conceptual attitude. My father, Tulku Urgyen Rinpoche, usually offered three steps in realizing the nonconceptual view. I have expanded upon this by giving four steps: *looking, seeing, letting be,* and *being free.* Looking is the method. The seeing is the natural state itself, in which seeing is not a dualistic subject seeing an object but rather a *self-seeing* in terms of a naturally knowing self-cognizance. The looking before seeing is of course an attitude of wanting to see something, a trying to see. That is its function, its task, its responsibility: to try to see. Normally this attitude doesn't just give up. Once you try to see, you keep on trying to see. It doesn't just let go of itself; it doesn't say goodbye. Therefore, you have to drop the looking at a certain point. On the other hand, there is no way to see in the beginning unless you make use of looking in the first place.

Just as the Dzogchen view is not a conceptual state, meditation is not a conceptual act. It is not a *doing.* And the view and meditation are not two separate things: whatever the perspective is, that must be the training as well. When the view is free of conceptual attitude, so is the meditation. Please do not forget what was meant by nonconceptual.

Here, *meditation* means to allow the continuity of the view to be. That is also called *letting be,* which is the third of the four points: looking, seeing, letting be, and being free. What is it that we should let be? Whatever is seen as being the view is simply allowed to be. This is not an act of meditating, since you are not "meditating" on the view. You simply see the view, a seeing free of subject and object, a seeing without any ownership. You simply let be in a state in which there is no mental doing. That is called continuity, a very precious word—not losing the continuity of samadhi. And in this context, samadhi is a synonym for the nature of mind. The nature of mind in Dzogchen terminology is also called rigpa. Rigpa is empty in essence, cognizant by nature, and unconfined in capacity. Simultaneously seeing these three is named rigpa. Rigpa is the simultaneous seeing of these three, not a sequential seeing that acknowledges them one after the other as either empty or cognizant. In this case, you do not have the unity, because they are already separate. Simultaneously, they are seen by your simply looking. Simply seeing, we need to let be.

Let's say that we have now seen the view. We may or may not have at this point, but for the sake of teaching let's keep this moving along. At this point of seeing the view, something more than seeing is necessary: we must know how to let be. Unless we know how to let be, we will start to entertain ideas about the view: "This mind essence is good. I must keep it; I must maintain it. I must make sure it doesn't get lost. If I could just see it all the time! It's so nice. Exactly like Tsoknyi Rinpoche said, that's how I want it. Now I saw it. Oh, no! Now it's slipping away. What am I to do? I must hold on tight so it doesn't get lost."

Letting be here means knowing how to be in a way that is free of hope and fear. In other words, when recognizing, we simply let the view *be*, without trying to modify or correct it. To know exactly how to let be in the right way and to then train in that is called meditation, which is the second among view, meditation, and conduct. Meditation here is to sustain the continuity of the view. Its purpose is to maintain the view.

To reiterate, the view is the simultaneous knowing of essence, nature, and capacity, which is recognized by merely looking. When one sets free one's basic state, it is empty, cognizant, and unconfined. In the same moment, all three qualities are present. That view needs to be allowed to continue, and this continuing is called meditation. In this context, several words could be used: natural continuity, natural mindfulness, intrinsic mindfulness. In other words, what is seen in the first moment needs to be allowed to continue. What is recognized should be allowed to be like that continuously—like this sound. *[Rinpoche strikes the gong]*

The gong's sound carries on and on; there's a continuity to it. After the gong is hit once, you don't do anything else. At this point, you don't have any choice as to whether the sound that comes out is good or not. Often people hit the gong, then try to improve on the sound afterward, which only spoils it. To improve the sound after striking it once involves use of the intellect. And if you do that [*Rinpoche touches the gong, and the sound stops*], the sound is spoiled. If you try to improve the view, you are already in dualistic mind, not mind essence. Just like striking the gong, you have to go about it in a very natural way: use the mallet to strike once, then stop using it. In the same way, recognize and then let go. Just relax there until you're distracted, as you would with the gong until the sound is all gone.

There are two important words that may sound a little crazy, but I want you to listen carefully to them: *undistracted* and *not meditating*. Undistracted nonmeditation. These two words together actually form one essential expression. Undistracted nonmeditation. To hear this phrase and to understand the vital point communicated through these two words, we need to connect with the meaning of "meditation free of concepts," the nonconceptual state.

Without understanding this correctly, one may think, "Well then, it would be good enough not to practice if it's about nonmeditation," equating nonmeditation with *not practicing*. Then one just drinks alcohol, goes to the disco, or watches a movie; one does whatever one feels like, because these are all states of not meditating. Is that good enough? No, because the first word is missing: undistracted. These ways of distracting oneself are in themselves not good enough to progress in samadhi. How about the methods to remain undistracted? Usually they are called meditation. Meditative methods are applied to make sure that the attention doesn't constantly wander from one thing to another. But any deliberate technique to be undistracted is by definition conceptual.

Undistracted nonmeditation, the combination of the two words, means to be both undistracted and nonconceptual at the same time. That is the kind of hammer needed to smash conceptual mind. Shamatha is a way of being undistracted, but because it involves doing in terms of meditating, it is also conceptual. Shamatha means to conceptually try to be in or to cultivate an undistracted state. It is the activity of *trying* to be alert, *trying* to keep mindful of something, in this way cultivating a state of being undistracted. While shamatha is the act of meditating, vipashyana training, in this particular context, refers more to what happens after having recognized. It is to allow what naturally is to be as it is, without trying to modify or correct it in any way; to allow the continuity of this recognition to endure without hope, without fear, without trying to do anything. In the beginning, this doesn't necessarily last very long.

The Dzogchen teachings tell us: *don't meditate, but also don't be distracted.* When we are able to be that way, there's no choice other than to be the continuity of the innate nature. You can also call this unconditioned mindfulness. It's like the conceptual manager has retired, but the office is still functioning. The conceptual manager has been kicked out, fired. Who kicks out the conceptual manager? It couldn't be another conceptual attitude. If it was, concept number two would kick out concept number one and become boss. Concept number two is then kicked out as number three enters. The third is kicked out by the fourth, the fourth is kicked out by the fifth, sixth, seventh, and so on, a hundred times, endlessly. This is why it is absolutely essential to recognize the view.

Honestly, meditation is simply to sustain the view. It is nothing other than that. The continuity of whatever is recognized doesn't have to be improved or contrived or made up or extended. In the beginning, let it be whatever it is, however it is; just let whatever is known be that, without hope and fear. We call this continuity, however brief it might be, Baby Rigpa.

Keep this Baby Rigpa for a while, simply as he is. Don't try to squeeze him, and don't try to throw him away, or he may die. Just keep him nicely, but without too much expectation. If you're not such a good father, you might hold him so tightly that he vomits. You don't squeeze a baby. You just allow him to be, very nicely. Lift the head a little bit higher than the legs. In the same way, whatever is seen initially as being the view is exactly what you allow to continue. As Milarepa said, "The royal view is to be undistracted while not meditating."

Artificially trying to extend the recognition spoils it. You need to know how to allow it to continue. This is why the Dzogchen instructions are incredibly special. They deal with something so subtle, something that is the most special, the most secret.

It is not enough to see the view again and again. It needs to endure as a continuity. That is the whole point of Dzogchen: Dzogchen meditation is to sustain the continuity. It is to give Baby Rigpa breathing space. Up till now, he has been suffocating. Once your Dzogchen meditation is sufficiently accommodating, then rigpa, the view, can breathe freely. Through breathing more, your lungs start to function, your heart gets stronger, and gradually the baby starts to grow. It develops its strength. The baby should grow and develop its strength, and for that you need Dzogchen meditation. This meditation is not a conceptual act. It is the meditation we defined as undistracted while not meditating. Is that clear?

Isn't it true that you want your baby to grow? You let him be with his mother to drink milk, and when he is able to eat, you give him nice food. Then he starts growing. In the same way, for rigpa to last longer, the genuine Dzogchen way of meditation is required. It does not help to push. It does not help to sincerely hope to see it last longer, to keep hold of it as if hanging on for dear life. "I pray I won't lose it!"—that doesn't help. All that is conceptual. We need to let be: undistracted while not meditating. Through this kind of practice, does rigpa then last for a long time? At the beginning, it is not much more than an instant. If it were a meditative state in the general sense, it could be kept for quite a while, not as an unbroken continuity but as a "continuity of recurring resemblance" during which one conceptual moment of being at ease in a meditative state is replaced by the next conceptual moment, and a third one, and a fourth. Because they look alike, this series of reoccurring moments fools you into thinking that it is a continuous state. That's stability in the sense of the ordinary meditation state. The first moment of bliss is gone after a split second—bye-bye! But something that looks like it has already replaced it. People usually call this continuity.

The training in this case is in short moments repeated again and again and again. In order to progress, we supplicate our lineage masters. We supplicate the Buddha, we supplicate the Dharma, we supplicate the Sangha: "Grant your blessings that I may progress in this practice." By this supplication we keep reminding ourselves to recognize and allow this short moment, again and again. As with collecting raindrops from the eaves of a roof, the vessel is slowly filled. In the beginning, it seems quite difficult, but we should not lose heart just because it is not easy.

In the beginning, the awakened state of rigpa is like an infant. Slowly, as we train more and more, this state of rigpa will start to distinguish itself. It becomes more clear what is what. It becomes more evident to us what is a conceptual state of mind and what is rigpa. This happens to such an extent that sometimes a moment of conceptual mind in its launch turns into a state of rigpa. It doesn't really get a foothold; it doesn't really get the chance to cause harm. The two aspects called *strength and display* begin to happen. That is when the good times start—really. Anxiety, dread, and timidity become things of the past. You feel very spacious. You feel you can accommodate whatever happens, anything, without being caught up, because you know so clearly what it is not to be caught up and not to cling, as opposed to clinging. That is how confidence slowly takes its seat. At this point, qualities have begun to manifest. We start to feel good about ourselves—genuinely. "I'm great, I feel good, I'm Number One." That feeling begins to happen, but in a relaxed and authentic way, not a distorted and negative way.

At this stage you feel detached, you feel compassionate, you feel insightful. All sort of feelings accompany this. They are feelings without glue, nonstick feelings. We need feelings. We shouldn't be unfeeling people. But feelings are usually very sticky. And the thorough cut of the *Trekchö* view chops that stickiness again and again. I think this may be a new concept, honestly, at least new to the West. Or perhaps not just to the West, but rather a new concept to unspiritual people. It is unfamiliar ground whether you are a Tibetan or a Westerner, wherever you are from. For 99 percent of people, at any given moment, when something occurs one is immediately stuck in it. One is either stuck to it, or one becomes indifferent, or one switches to a state of vacancy, hostility, closed-mindedness, or attachment. Most of these reactions are unnoticed, unconscious. Most thoughts are unnoticed, but reacting either for or against something is biased either way. That's why Tilopa said to Naropa, "Son, perceptions don't bind, clinging does; so cut your clinging, Naropa." Whenever something happens, it is not the event itself that adheres but the clinging that binds us—the sticky stuff. That's what needs to be cut through. Some meditators misunderstand what clinging means. They hear it as "try to not perceive," as in try not to know, try not to see or hear anything. It becomes an ongoing battle.

All wholesome qualities manifest out of rigpa. To connect to rigpa authentically is "knowing one that frees all." If we miss it, on the other hand, it is called "knowing one hundred but missing one." Rechungpa was one of Milarepa's main disciples, and at one point he wanted desperately to go to India to learn poetry, grammar, astrology, black magic—all sorts of different topics. Before he was to go, Milarepa said to him, "I had great hopes for you. I thought you could be someone who by knowing one could liberate everything. But instead I fear you will know one hundred different topics but still miss one." Then Milarepa performed several miracles and Rechungpa changed his mind. He thought, "My guru is right. What was I thinking? It's a huge mistake to chase superficial knowledge." He stayed and practiced, and slowly he became like Milarepa himself.

Progress requires perseverance, a certain willingness to follow through. If we are already able to train in the view free of concepts, then we should do that. Additionally, we can train in the view with concepts from time to time. When we don't know how to train in the nonconceptual view, it's perfectly fine to train in the conceptual view of shamatha, or the general type of vipashyana. Whatever the case, the point is that we need to train. To train in the conceptual view is one type of training, and to train in the nonconceptual view is also training. Whatever the case is, we should train.

Any questions about this?

STUDENT: Two or three weeks ago I experienced the essence of mind, but since I didn't know what it was, as I had never read about it before, a great fear arose about what it could be. If this experience is very intense, can it be dangerous if I haven't received the proper introduction from a master?

RINPOCHE: It may be dangerous or not dangerous; it depends. Simply experiencing and recognizing mind essence is in itself never dangerous. But getting caught up in all the thoughts about it afterward could be dangerous: "What I recognized, is that really it? Or maybe I didn't recognize, maybe it wasn't it?" You could have all sorts of thoughts about it. But let's say that what you experienced a couple of weeks ago is exactly the same as what I am presenting here. Then there is no problem in that whatsoever. When, together with that experience, you also understand the method of training in mind essence, there is definitely no harm at all, no danger. It is the web of thoughts about the experience that can cause problems, not the experience itself. You may think, "Wow, it really happened! It was mind-blowing! I'm really special now. I've got something and it has totally transformed me. I don't know where it came from, maybe it came from above, but I'm a changed person now. This is it!" Those thoughts can cause significant trouble. But that's not what I am teaching here. I teach a simple method of how to repeat that experience in a very practical way. If you just understand the key points and proceed with the training, it is very good. There is no problem with that at all. If we keep a view that is as high as the sky, and at the same time we are conscientious about how we behave, applying a scrutiny as fine as barley flour, as *tsampa*, then there is no problem at all.

STUDENT: What is the difference between the real state of rigpa and the imitation?

RINPOCHE: Check whether or not there is any clinging, any sense of keeping hold of something. With conceptual rigpa you notice a sense of *trying to keep a state*, trying to maintain a state, trying to nurture a state. There is a sense of hope or fear and also a sense of being occupied. Understand? This *keeping* means there's a sense of protecting, of not wanting to lose it, in the back of the mind. This is not bad, it's good, and for some people there's no way around training like that in the beginning. Through training in this way, that conceptual aspect becomes increasingly refined and clarified.

So you practice more, more, more. Now you have more of a sense of openness, but still you're *holding* this openness. All right, then, let the openness go. Let's say that after two months you let it go. But still you're *staying* within the openness—so then you practice letting go of the staying. And somehow there is still a remnant of wanting to achieve it again. So you let that go as well, and slowly again let it go, let it go, until you become very much "just there," and finally very free and easy.

Also, if you notice that your meditative state shuts out other things to some extent, that you don't really want to receive any message about anything else, that you're closing off; if when something happens it feels like a disturbance, an irritation, that is a sign of conceptual meditation, of being occupied. Also, if you notice there's a huge difference between the state of composure and postmeditation, that's no good either.

You're meditating like this. *[Rinpoche demonstrates someone absorbed in his meditative state]* Somebody comes up, and you exclaim "Hey! What!" That's a sign that you were conceptually meditating, not really present. You are totally absorbed in your meditation and something happens that feels alarming, so that you really jump up out of your seat. Or it could be: "Oh, my! How very difficult to come out of this meditation state!" *[Rinpoche again demonstrates looking very preoccupied]* "Yeah? What did you say? Say again?"

That was also a sign that you were meditating. It means that cognizant nature was absorbed. It is no good to *maintain* an artificial meditative state. One description of rigpa is phrased like this: "Not dwelling in any way whatsoever, and yet totally present throughout everything." Please listen once more: Not dwelling in any way whatsoever, and yet totally present throughout everything.

Let's try this one more time: Not dwelling in any way whatsoever, and yet totally present throughout everything.

Just before Tulku Urgyen Rinpoche passed away, I had the great fortune to spend a couple of months at his hermitage, Nagi Gompa. At the same time, work was going on at Nagi Gompa; statues were being built downstairs in the temple hall. Often I had the task of carrying various messages between Tulku Urgyen Rinpoche and the workmen. One day, the workers were asking me how to go about a particular task. I couldn't settle the matter myself, so I took a note and went upstairs. Tulku Urgyen Rinpoche lived in a tiny room about nine by nine feet, just a tiny little room with one big window. There was a bed on the side with a high railing, and enough floor space for maybe seven or eight people to fit. At the door was a cloth door hanging, and before going in, I lifted the hanging aside a little and took a peek. Tulku Urgyen Rinpoche was sitting with his prayer beads, gently repeating his mantra, not in a rigid, upright posture, just leaning to one side, with his legs extended, half reclining, with his eyes very juicy and with his voice repeating the *mani [the mantra of Avalokiteshvara]*. I thought I better not go in; it might disturb him. So I waited outside for five or six minutes. Then I looked again. He was still like that. Again I waited. Three or four times, this sequence happened. The workmen downstairs were waiting for their job, so I finally thought, "Well, you gotta do what you gotta do." So I looked very carefully, then went inside. Whatever state Tulku Urgyen was in, he just turned from within that state and looked. And without losing that state at all, he started to have a conversation: "Hello, how are you," discussing the task at hand, then making a decision about it and settling it. And then as I went outside and looked back, I saw Tulku Urgyen Rinpoche just reclining right back into the posture he was in before. That really stuck in my mind. I had been totally wrong to think that I could disturb his meditation.

I'd been projecting my own understanding onto Tulku Urgyen Rinpoche. When somebody comes into my room while I'm practicing, I get annoyed. I have a certain time I need to sleep. In the afternoon, I have to nap. I have my private time, and if someone comes, I get irritable. Tulku Urgyen was not like that. His room was just open. Without breaking the continuity of his way of being, he started to communicate and deal with what had to be dealt with. While he was talking, his rigpa was not interrupted at all. Then when I left, he continued to be that way. I reflected a lot on this later, and I felt certain that he was really an embodiment of the meditation of nonmeditation.

Every now and then, when walking into someone's room I sense a frozen state. It's almost as if I cannot go in, cannot inhale, because the whole space seems blocked. Walking into Tulku Urgyen's room was not like that at all. His private room was so tiny, but it felt huge. It had a lot of air, a lot of room, because of his openness. Because of his capacity, it felt extremely spacious. That is how we should be in our practice. With that quality we can deal with our mundane tasks very beautifully. This is described as "being in the world but untainted by the world." This is the difference between meditation and nonmeditation. If we are rigidly meditating *on emptiness*, the whole house feels like iron. It makes the whole affair very constricted.

STUDENT: The preliminaries seem so conceptual. What is the reason to do them?

RINPOCHE: There are many purposes for ngöndro, the preliminary practices, otherwise known as the four foundations—one of them being to give conceptual mind a whack. In a way you're using one concept to beat another concept. The lazy mind receives a whole series of whacks from the persevering mind, until it gives up and surrenders. After you do 100,000 prostrations, "Well, sitting ten hours, no problem! So lucky! Just one or two hours, that's nothing. To sit four hours, that's easy!" All the aches and pains and the preoccupation with these have been chopped into pieces. It's like the laziness gets minced, chopped up into little tiny bits. That's one purpose of the ngöndro.

Another purpose is that doing ngöndro gives us little opportunities to let be in the state of rigpa, over and over again. In addition, the ngöndro training creates tremendous merit, which makes recognizing rigpa almost unavoidable. That is what merit does. You have almost no other choice than to recognize rigpa, because you repeatedly provide the circumstances for that. Ngöndro removes all chances for distraction. It's like you wanted to leave your meditation seat to drive to the disco in town to dance, only to find that merit has emptied your gas tank. You try to turn on the engine and it doesn't start, so you think: "Well, well, I might as well sit down and practice." *Ngöndro* makes distractions simply not happen, and good circumstances for practicing Dharma happen much more easily, without your having to try too hard. They just fall into place. You meet teachers more easily, you find yourself in places where the spiritual path is readily available, and this happens wherever you are, again and again. Merit simply makes everything fit. Meritorious karma arranges all these circumstances for you very neatly. Without merit, we have to try so hard to make good things happen.

For example, when Tulku Urgyen Rinpoche was alive, some people would call ahead long distance and get hold of Marcia, Erik, or Andreas to ask, "Is it all right to come? Is Tulku Urgyen Rinpoche available?" Then they would buy their plane ticket and fly all the way around the world to Kathmandu. But then Tulku Urgyen might be busy with something else, and for their whole stay they would get no teachings. Meanwhile, another person walks in out of nowhere, not even knowing that it's possible, and receives plenty of the vital instructions. Merit does make a difference. Merit makes favorable circumstances. That is why the accumulation of merit goes before, as an aspect of the preliminary practices. That is a reason for the ngöndro.

Westerners sometimes think ngöndro is *so difficult*: "Unless I do a three-year retreat, I can't do a ngöndro." It may seem like that sometimes, if one doesn't see its purpose. One hasn't understood its value, so one's heart is not in it. It seems so hard and challenging. If your heart is in it, it is not difficult at all. Of course, if one is old or frail, you can rightfully say prostrations are difficult, but you can still do the Vajrasattva recitation, the mandala offering, and guru yoga. There is also a way of doing half-prostrations that is fine, although ngöndro generally involves full prostrations, the extended ones. Some people may need to get their knees in shape from the prostrations of the previous day by soaking their knees in warm water. Other people just carry through doing these until the skin on their kneecaps wears off. Lymph and pus may flow from the wounds, and still they continue.

As I mentioned earlier, a genuine spiritual practitioner needs fortitude. This comes from understanding that Dharma practice overcomes negative emotions, and it's not to make one have a good time or feel good. The feel-good part is for the ego. Ego gets a little weak and you think, "I need a spiritual vitamin for my ego to feel good. Maybe I'll try some kind of special practice." The main focus here is to make *me* happy. "This will make me function better in my normal daily life. I can be a better lawyer, I can be a better writer, I can be a better businessman, I can be a better nurse or manager."

This motivation for spiritual practice is not particularly profound. It's all right—you can't say it's evil—but one who practices with this motivation does not deserve to be called a Dharma practitioner or a spiritual person. That is why motivation is so important. Most people forget its importance. But as we understand the Dharma more deeply, we also understand the value of right motivation more and more.

STUDENT: I have a question about distraction. When I notice that I am distracted, I have trouble letting go of the thought that I am distracted. I get lost in the object of thought. What do I do about that?

RINPOCHE: That's a good question. You need to let go of both the thought as the object and the watcher as the subject. Release both of these, together. When a thought is about to be formed, together with it is a noticing that the thought is about to be formed, which acts as the subject to the object. Both of these must be released together. The thought comes, and almost at the same time, release the thought *and* the noticing of the thought. At the same time, release them both.

STUDENT: Could you talk more about the two aspects of ignorance?

RINPOCHE: Coemergent ignorance is a conceptual attitude, but it's very subtle. You could almost call it instinctive, although it's not really unconscious, but more like one doesn't notice it afterward. It's like you consciously put your glasses up on top of your head, but then you immediately forget about them, so that later you walk around looking for your glasses. Coemergent ignorance is something that recurs through habit. It is a habit of not knowing. Because of it we do not remember what we did in any given situation. We simply weren't paying attention. This is probably more habitual for us than an action done while fully conscious. Of the two types of ignorance, you can say the coemergent ignorance is like a thief, in that you do not notice that your things disappear. Conceptualizing ignorance is more like a bandit that takes over by force.

Sometimes we find that there is just nothing to do: no matter how much we try to be lucid, sharp, and bright, it does not work. The twofold ignorance takes over repeatedly. That is when we need a practice other than simple mindfulness. This can be sincere supplication to our guru, imagining the lights in receiving the four empowerments, mingling our minds into one with the master's, or making Vajrasattva recitations, doing ngöndro, lighting butter lamps. In fact, the main reason for lighting butter lamps is to dispel the darkness of the twofold ignorance. While lighting the lamps, you make the sincere wish, "May this lamp completely dispel the darkness of ignorance!" The whole accumulation of merit through various practices removes that which causes twofold ignorance to recur. This is in fact the whole point of the ngöndro practice.

'Ngöndro' means prelude, the preliminary before the main part, and in the Tibetan tradition you do this first. After doing ngöndro, it's much, much easier to train in the main part. By going through the ngöndro you approach the main part having already accumulated a lot of merit, having already reduced the intensity of the emotions. You've already visualized Vajrasattva above your head, and by means of the four remedial powers you've dissolved, flushed, washed away, and cleansed all the pieces of ignorance, imagining that they all disappear. Afterward, when you try to let be in the state of the Great Perfection, you find that it automatically lasts for a long time. Sustaining rigpa becomes much easier. The preliminary practice is a very effective and pragmatic way of going about training in rigpa. It was not intentionally designed to give you a hard time. Slowly, slowly we discover its value, right?

The whole point is that attachment, anger, and closed-mindedness are *formed* attitudes. They're not natural—they get created, and therefore they can be undone. We simply need a strong enough remedy against them. In other words, emotions are not like automatic cameras that shoot off many frames at once; they're like manual cameras that have to be repositioned and reprogrammed repeatedly. The important point here is that something that is made can always be undone. Take this glass on my table—all you need is a hammer to smash it. It is not indestructible. With something less than a hammer, for example, a napkin, you can whack the glass again and again and you'll only wear down the napkin. Nothing happens to the glass. In other words, you need a spiritual practice that is effective, one that is appropriate to the situation at hand. An effective remedy against the emotional attitudes *does* dissolve them. If you were trying to destroy something that was unmade, unformed, it would be the same as trying to hammer away the sky. Even if you called 100,000 friends to help and each brought a hammer, then whacked away at space, nothing would happen, right? In the evening, your arms would be sore. You'd only accomplish the need for a massage: "I need some oil, ooooh. Please massage my arms!"

Emotional states are something formed, and therefore they can be destroyed by the proper remedies. That is the whole point of ngöndro: to reduce the intensity of emotional states, before the main part of practice.

LIBERATION

Freedom is the main objective. Freedom is the opposite of being powerless. Right now, when an emotion wells up, it seems to take you over so that you are no longer in charge. You are involuntarily carried away, caught up in that emotion, without any freedom. When we are moody, bored, angry, attached, and so forth, we can't just *be*. That is not freedom. We need to be free and in charge. We should become independent, so that the emotions can become the wisdoms that are the ministers of King Rigpa.

Now we have come to the fourth point: being free. This is among the most important points because, as it's been said, "Knowing how to meditate but not how to be free—isn't that like the meditation gods?" Being free is incredibly important. Isn't the awakened state of buddhahood called emancipation or liberation? This utterly depends upon knowing how to be free.

We must understand the difference between these two: being distracted and being undistracted. In this particular context, the undistracted state is composure, *nyamshak*, while postmeditation, *jetob*, includes all distracted states of mind. This is the Dzogchen definition, and it is different from the general definition. Generally speaking, composure is when your buttocks are placed on the cushion and your attention is one-pointed. Anything other than that—the four daily activities, walking around, eating, talking, and so on—falls into the category of postmeditation. From the Dzogchen perspective, however, remaining in the state of rigpa is considered composure, while straying from rigpa is postmeditation.

From the pure Dzogchen perspective, any state other than the nonconceptual is distracted. That doesn't mean that these states are superfluous—some of them are still necessary. I call these virtuous distractions, indicating that they are both good and valuable. These states of beneficial distraction are necessary, but this doesn't mean that we must keep hold of them with the thought "This is it, forevermore!" If we do, we will never be liberated. For instance, keeping hold of this beneficial distraction prevents shamatha from changing into vipashyana.

Clinging, grasping, and the 84,000 types of negative emotions are all generated by the alaya, the Alaya Bank. Distraction is whenever one gets caught up in one of these negative emotions. Don't believe that you will be able to avoid thoughts or emotions. As I mentioned earlier, we have a lot of karmic capital invested in Alaya Bank that keeps yielding interest, so we cannot prevent this abundant return right now. Nor do we have to reject or deny it. The realistic response at this point is simply this: do not reinvest the yield as it arises. Whether or not the yield is being reinvested depends on whether or not we cling. If we cling, we automatically reinvest in Alaya Bank; an automatic money transfer is made into the bank. Alaya Bank is very well informed indeed: it has your address, and every month you get your statement—maybe every day or even every second, if your balance is very high. If you don't cling, it's like you are spending or using up the money, but if you do cling, you are sending the money back. "I don't need this money right now; could you reinvest it for me?" Mr. Ego, the manager of Alaya Bank, replies, "Yes, I'm happy to reinvest your conceptual pattern! I will send it back to you frequently so that you can regularly get caught up in samsara. In fact, we will send you a credit card with an unlimited credit line to use in samsara! You can use it whenever you want!" If you refuse this credit card—if you do not cling, do not cling, do not cling—then one day you will go bankrupt. And that is what we really want: we want to ruin our account in this karmic bank. Slowly, slowly, we will destroy the bank building too—the alaya itself.

What I mean to say here is, don't expect your training in rigpa to utterly prevent the occurrence of thoughts or emotions. They will still appear due to karmic investment, but everything stands or falls with whether or not we cling to them. That issue is not so karmically fixed; it is a completely individual matter. We have the option to cling or not to cling. One cannot say that just because there is a thought occurrence it means that there is clinging and distraction. Actually, all sorts of options are available.

To reiterate, according to the extraordinary, unique instructions of Dzogchen, distraction is anything other than the state of self-knowing wakefulness. When we realize this, we are at the point of *being free*, or liberation. This is where Garab Dorje's *Three Words That Strike the Vital Point* comes in: recognize your own nature, decide on one point, gain confidence in liberation. For a spiritual practitioner, this confidence is of the utmost importance.

Among the three—view, meditation, and conduct—liberation has to do with the conduct aspect. Of course, if after being introduced to the Dzogchen view we could be in a state of composure all the time and never be distracted, that would be the best situation. But let's say that just by chance we happen to get distracted from the state of rigpa. Wouldn't it be nice to know how to liberate that distraction and arrive right back in the state of rigpa?

Gain confidence in liberation. Confidence, the state of being totally self-assured, does not come from being rich, nor from being proud of oneself. It also doesn't come from using personal power to drum it up. That's not real confidence. According to Dzogchen, true confidence comes from knowing how to be free in any thought and in any emotion. When that is the reality of our own experience, we are no longer afraid of ourselves.

We generally tend to attribute our fear to an external object, saying, "If such and such happens, I get scared." But this is not being really honest. We're just pointing the finger of blame somewhere else. What we really mean when we say that is, "I'm afraid that I won't be able to stand it, that I can't bear being in that situation. I don't know how to take it." It basically means "I'm afraid of myself." That's what fear actually is. We are afraid because we are unclear about our real state, our nature, what it really is. There's a vagueness involved here; it's like we're playing a game with ourselves. We are unclear about what we are. That's the reason to be afraid. All fear springs from that.

It is necessary to know how to be free. In other words, we must know how to liberate whatever occurs as the expression of our mind, how to allow it to be naturally liberated. The real meaning of recognizing the view, recognizing rigpa, recognizing mind essence, is to recognize exactly what we really are in terms of what our nature is, in actuality. We may have recognized rigpa, but this doesn't help much unless we can also recognize that our natural expression is devoid of a concrete identity. *The expression needs to be freed.*

There are three ways to be free. The first one is called *freed upon arising*. In this state, arising and being freed are simultaneous, like a drawing made on the surface of water. Second is *naturally freed*, a snake tied in a knot unties itself And the third is *freed beyond benefit and harm*. This is like a thief entering an empty house: there is nothing to find, nothing to steal.

Freed upon arising has two modes. Let's say we are in the state of composure, the continuity of rigpa. As we remain, it appears that the recognition of rigpa grows a little dim. That seeming dimming can take the form of coemergent ignorance or conceptual ignorance or a certain habit beginning to be activated; a thought is vaguely about to happen.

What triggers this distraction? There is rigpa's cognizant quality and somehow there is a diffusing of this cognizance. The noticing of the empty quality grows fainter, and together with that the cognizant quality to some extent freezes. Why does it freeze? It is due to neglecting or ignoring the empty essence. Cognizance is no longer really clear about its emptiness, so the cognizance becomes slightly stiff, although not totally so. Let's say about 20 percent of the cognizant quality dims, and that gives an opportunity for clinging to begin. This has nothing to do with whether or not sense perceptions occur. There could be perceptions or not; it makes no difference. The difference is in whether clinging occurs.

At this slight lapse of cognizance we need a certain mindful presence, one that is not conceptual or contrived but effortless and true. We need a mindful presence that is indivisible from the cognizant nature. We are not deliberately *trying* to be mindful, not at all, but are simply aware of what is happening during this state. When the cognizant quality is about to slip a little bit and we are just about to get distracted, we simply need to acknowledge its empty quality. There needs to be 100 percent emptiness.

When I was with Adeu Rinpoche in China, I questioned him about this very point. To not fall under the sway of distraction, he said, necessitates remaining undistracted through unfabricated mindfulness. Since the identity of mind and the identity of mindfulness are of the same nature, rigpa is sustained by sharpening up during this seeming dimming. At this point, you are not yet out of rigpa, but you are about to be, and by reasserting a mindful presence, you reconnect back to the full measure of 100 percent. The distraction is about to be formed, about to become a thought. Just as it is about to happen, rigpa is aware that the slip is taking place, and it becomes sharper because of that. The forming of the thought immediately dissolves, is freed. You are almost about to move away from rigpa but cannot. It is like a design drawn on the surface of water: it vanishes as you draw it.

Another way of formulating freed upon arising is to say that the thought occurrence and its dissolving are simultaneous. You are nearly distracted, but not really. When in mind essence, you stay with the nonmeditation without distraction. But a movement comes, a distraction is about to take over, and as soon as it presents itself you have the opportunity to release the movement before getting carried away. In the moment of almost straying, there is a refreshing of your own state that immediately dissolves the thought. In other words, the first onset of the thought does not mean that you are really distracted yet.

The traditional analogy likens this to drawing upon water: as soon as you draw the next line, the first has already dissolved. You are drawing "A B C" or "I love you" or whatever on the surface of the water, but nothing is there afterward. In the same way, when you are genuinely in mind essence, the thought dissolves at the very moment it begins to occur. Just as the drawing is gone the moment you lift your finger, the emotion or the thought that is about to occur dissolves, simultaneous with the knowing that it is about to be formed. To understand this point is wonderful, because you are then able to let rigpa remain for a long time. The duration of undistracted nonmeditation can be ongoing because of that. Please understand this principle: the arising and the dissolving of the thought can be simultaneous.

The moment a thought occurs, it can be simultaneously liberated in the recognition of mind essence. I mentioned two modes. One is during composure. We are in mind essence and are just about to lose it by becoming involved in a thought when the thought dissolves through nonclinging. The other is during postmeditation, having already become distracted. A strong thought comes suddenly, and that abrupt occurrence of a thought can push you back into rigpa. With a certain degree of training, the eruption of a thought or emotion can make you remember to recognize and thereby to arrive in rigpa. The very intensity of the thought causes us to recognize mind essence, and the thought dissolves right away.

Freed upon arising should mean that the arising of a thought and its dissolving occur simultaneously. The clinging to the arising of thought must dissolve. Once it does, the thought has no foothold, no life of its own, and so it vanishes. There is a subtle point in this context that we may not have noticed until now, but that is okay; there is no blaming going on here. There is a subtle distinction between the thought or emotion taking place and the clinging to it. We should let go of the clinging. That does not mean that the atmosphere of the thought vanishes instantaneously together with the clinging. The atmosphere of the thought may linger for a little while; it does not have to leave right away. The same with an emotion: the atmosphere of the emotion may slowly recede even though there is no clinging to maintain it. One might have expected that the thought *has to* vanish immediately together with letting go of the clinging, and if it doesn't, then one has the suspicion "This couldn't be rigpa!" because an echo of the thought or emotion lingers on. The remnant, in the form of its atmosphere or echo, may still reverberate for a while. The clinging, which is held or maintained by the sixth consciousness, is interrupted and is no more. So, one should not have the belief that this atmosphere would mean that the clinging still remains. But watch out for the other extreme, which is to believe that one can be free of clinging no matter what while engrossed in ordinary thoughts and emotions. This subject is very subtle and sensitive, and that is why one needs to verify one's understanding with a true master.

Freed upon arising means that the thought is liberated at the same time as the recognizing, without depending upon a remedy. This happens only through training and not without it. In mind essence, everything is free, unrestrained. Emotions are free to come, so you are not really blocking any situation: anything can come and go. You sit there and allow all the emotions, all the stuff, everything, to be very open, very clear. One thought and boom! you are clinging, about to reach out for it, then—"Hey!"—you realize, you let it go, and you do not depart from rigpa. You are about to cling and then you realize, so that the arising of the thought is freed or dissolves in itself. This actually happens very fast, so fast that the arising and the dissolving of the thought are simultaneous. Everything happening is within the expanse or stretch of rigpa itself.

The second type of freeing, *naturally freed*, is not something that comes afterward in a sequence. It is a different way of explaining how a thought dissolves. Please understand that whenever the word "thought," namtok, is used, it means *a thought while clinging*. But there is also a thought movement without clinging, which is called display of rigpa. This second mode of freeing comes about by recognizing the very fact that the *identity* of any type of thought is and always was rigpa. Recognizing that fact makes it so that no matter how much the thought jumps up and dances around, whatever it tries to do, the boss is still in charge. Rigpa is still in charge and can put it straight immediately, all by itself. It is never said that a separate remedy is necessary to do away with each type of thought.

In applying the Dzogchen instructions, we do not have to go through any sort of long intellectual procedure to solve the basic problem. No matter what mental state, thought, or emotion occurs, its nature is always the nature of mind, always the unconditioned nature of *dharmata*. To recognize that nature in actuality is the most powerful; the conditioned state is less powerful. When we don't recognize mind essence, however, the conditioned state is more powerful, while the unconditioned has no real power. Of course the unconditioned nature, dharmata, is always the most powerful, but from our perspective of not recognizing it, it is the conditioned state of mind that seems more overwhelming, more dominant. Our training leads to a certain point at which there is no need to depend upon any other remedy—rigpa is said to be like a sovereign king.

The metaphor for naturally freed is that of a snake untying its own knot. Some snakes are quite long and coil up in loops, but as they move, they just slide out of the twists all by themselves. Let's say there's a snake couple, Mommy and Daddy Snake, and that Daddy Snake is coiled up in a knot. Mommy Snake doesn't have to worry about it and go help him, because Daddy Snake is capable of untying himself. In the same way, rigpa is capable of being self-freed, capable of being untied by itself. This metaphor explains the fact that in recognizing the very nature of a thought or emotion as rigpa, you don't need many other techniques to undo that mental state.

We say that "rigpa is singularly sufficient," that it is "the single sufficient king." Wherever you are, whatever the thought or emotion, at that very place and moment recognize the self-knowing wakefulness, and immediately the emotion is liberated. Rigpa is described like this: "Since rigpa in itself has never been confused, all that is necessary is to acknowledge that liberated state. It does not need to be changed into anything else." Whatever takes place can be in harmony with rigpa. There's lots of space in that knowledge.

The pivotal point here concerning being free is *confidence*, and the basis for confidence is a sense of being in harmony. The basis for being in harmony is knowing how to be free. As we train in the meditation state, we therefore train in releasing the grip of clinging. Thoughts are formed, but as the clinging is released, they dissolve.

The third way of freeing, *freed beyond benefit and harm*, doesn't happen for beginners; it doesn't happen unless one is pretty experienced in Dzogchen meditation. The topic of discussion here is the natural expression of rigpa. As a matter of fact, whether we know it or not, everything already *is* the natural expression of rigpa. Delusion, recognition of mind essence, thoughts, emotions, wisdom, and so forth—everything is rigpa's natural expression. The heart of the matter is this; know this point well and for such a long time that you never move away from the continuity of rigpa. Whatever unfolds no longer harms or disturbs that continuity of rigpa: there's neither benefit nor harm.

The metaphor here is this: let's say there is a huge empty house. The owner is there, he's home, but there's nothing in the house. It's completely empty. A thief slowly opens the door. He sneaks inside and looks around, but there is nothing to see inside, so he relaxes. Then he sees the old guy sitting there, and there's nothing else to say but "Hi!" So the old guy says "Hi!" back. The old guy realizes the man is a thief, but since he has nothing to lose, he is very relaxed. The thief sees he has nothing to gain, so he too is quite relaxed and just says hello. The old guy says, "Come in! Come in!" So the thief comes inside and sits down. They talk and drink Chinese tea together. They become friends. One has nothing to gain and the other has nothing to lose.

The point here is that whatever thought may occur during the continuity of rigpa, the subject that otherwise could get involved in the thought, that could be triggered into clinging, has now vanished. There is no longer any ego left. Also, there is no getting into expecting a nice thought or a happy thought, nothing investing in wanting to improve the situation in any way, nor in fearing an unpleasant thought that might worsen it. There is no hope or fear. No matter what thought or emotion occurs, there's nothing for it to achieve. It can't cause any damage either, because immediately its essence is recognized as being just mind essence itself. So it is liberated, it dissolves. It is beyond any benefit or harm. The thief has not been shut out. He can come right in. There's nothing to lose.

In other words, any thought is welcome. Sense perceptions or memories, whatever occurs is fine; whatever occurs is naturally freed. Why? There is no hope or fear, because the whole setup of an object to get involved in, a subject who gets involved, and the involvement in clinging—the totality of what clings, the clinging, and what could be clung to—has all dissolved. It is liberated. When that happens, then enlightenment is just around the corner; it will happen quite fast. At that point, even if you regret becoming enlightened and want to stop the process, it's too late—enlightenment is inevitable. Even if you try to cling to thoughts again, you cannot put your whole heart into it. It's just like when you've boarded an airplane and it has taken off—it's too late to regret getting on and want to get off. It is simply too late.

This is the point at which emotions are no longer ordinary emotions but are now called wisdoms. Samsara is not rejected but is naturally purified in itself. Without samsara being rejected, it is naturally pure in itself.

Those were the three ways of liberation. There's sometimes a fourth one called *primordial liberation*, but we've already covered that under empty essence, which is originally free, already free, and doesn't have to be liberated. Another aspect, called *directly freed*, is also important to understand. It has to do with how liberation takes place. You're practicing, and let's say you become a little dull, a little sluggish, a little absentminded. Then you look more directly, becoming slightly more awake. You strengthen mind essence so that the five senses get a little brighter. It's like a straightening-up of your state. We could also say that you're sharpening it, brightening up your awareness through the vigor of self-recognition. Along with that, the five senses get sharper and more awake. This is just an occasional method or intervention, not an ongoing state to be maintained.

No matter how much we say about this, we're still trying to describe something about which one really can't say anything. Really. From the beginning till now, we have tried to think of what it is, again and again, but honestly it is not a *thing* about which one can think; it is not something to be thought of. The *Prajnaparamita*, also known as the Great Mother scriptures, says:

> Transcendent knowledge, beyond thought, word, and
> description,

Does not arise and does not cease, like the essence of space
    itself.
I salute this domain of individual, self-knowing wakefulness,
The mother of all conquerors.

As Tilopa said to Naropa:

Kyeho! This self-knowing wakefulness
Is not an object to be spoken of, nor is it an object of thought.
It is not something that I, Tilopa, can show you.
Understand that it is revealed to oneself by oneself.

This is how the nature of mind is described. If I keep on talking your
ears are going to start to ache. You can ask a few questions now.

STUDENT: Earlier you spoke about a seeming dimming of rigpa as
thoughts or emotions arise. If rigpa is naturally empty and cognizant,
how does this dimming take place at all?

RINPOCHE: Some dimming *does* takes place, as you may notice. Our basic
state is empty in essence and cognizant by nature, but even though there
is a knowing of rigpa, somehow it loses its footing. This slip begins by a
dimming of the cognizant quality, a losing track of its being empty.
Now you ask why this happens. There are several reasons: past karma,
habitual tendencies, and ignorance. The last of these has two aspects.
Coemergent ignorance is the intrinsic tendency to *not know* that reasserts
itself. This intrinsic unknowing simply means losing track of itself. The
second aspect is conceptualizing ignorance, which means that one gets
involved in clinging to and labeling a thought pattern or perception as it
is about to take place.

Ignorance means *not knowing*. Its antidote is to know. I mentioned
earlier a sharpening up, a readjusting, that dissolves the dimness. But
without knowing how to readjust in the right way, the attempt to readjust could prevent the state of rigpa. One time out, no problem. One
hundred times out, also no problem because you can always come back
in. We don't need to feel guilty about getting distracted from rigpa.
"But I am still happy, because I am going back in. While out, I do not
lose interest in going back in." The interest in returning to rigpa should
not be lost, nor should one feel guilty about slipping.

STUDENT: Rinpoche, you mentioned several ways to return from distraction, saying that a strong thought or a strong emotion can actually help. Because they are strong, they are easy to see. But how about when you are just drifting, distracted, and nothing strong comes along? What is it that brings you back then?

RINPOCHE: It's difficult, but it's not that difficult. Be present, really and strongly present. The strength of that keeps you from drifting into this undercurrent of absentminded thoughts. Let's say you are someone without much special training and that you are not in the state of rigpa during your daily activities. How do you deal with that in order not to be continually distracted? You must begin somewhere, and that is where shamatha comes in. The quality of shamatha means to be present, mindful, and alert. Also, nurture the attitude toward everything that it is all impermanent, like a magical illusion, a dream. These are tools to take hold of your mind, to guard or watch your mind. As we get more and more used to these, we progress. We need to deal with thoughts, whether they are forceful or gentle. The more obvious thoughts or emotional eruptions are more noticeable, but the vague meandering of thoughts must be dealt with as well. This is more a problem for older yogis who become too carefree. The instruction is this: be more strongly present; have the bright and mindful presence of awareness. What will counter absentminded thoughts besides this mindful presence?

Maintenance

Earlier I mentioned a famous phrase: "Knowing how to meditate but not how to be free—isn't that like the meditation gods?" Certainly we must possess the vital point of practice, but that doesn't mean we grasp on to or try to own that experience too seriously. Allow it to be opened up completely. After recognizing, we can emphasize looseness rather than trying to keep a tight grip on rigpa. It is taught that after recognizing rigpa we can from time to time give importance to three qualities: one is *looseness*, another is *brightness*, and the third is *lucidity*. Brightness has to do with having vivid senses—when, for instance, sitting outside in the practice of mingling the threefold sky. The five senses are wide open, not closed in on themselves, simply present. Lucidity is more a quality of being clear that is not dependent upon sensory clarity. Rather it has to do with the clarity of rigpa itself, independent of whether the senses are bright or dull.

It is taught that as soon as rigpa is introduced and recognized, the most important thing to do for a couple of days is just to emphasize a sense of looseness. Do not keep hold of it at all. Be very open, very free, very relaxed about the whole matter. Cultivate an attitude of abandon. One does not really care too much about keeping that which has been recognized; one simply allows it. Focus simply on this for a couple of days. Then, within that state, emphasize a bright presence of mind. After a while, you add the lucid quality. When you train like this, you arrive in a very genuine way at undivided and aware emptiness.

When a beginner recognizes the awakened state of rigpa for the first time, it is of course a big deal because it may be something that one has waited for and looked forward to for quite a while. It is so important, so precious. Therefore, of course, one tries one's best to maintain it and hold on to it: "This shouldn't slip away. This is so special, I must keep it!" The psychology of that self-conscious attitude, not wanting to let it slip away, makes us tense and the looseness disappears. Therefore, especially remember this: be loose and relaxed. When you have this loose-ness, then emphasize a bright or sharp quality. Please understand this point.

As I mentioned earlier, the Dzogchen definition of "meditation state" is *while the duration of rigpa lasts*. This state of composure is while you have not strayed from the continuity of rigpa. When straying, it is con-sidered postmeditation, as it's no longer the state of rigpa. Thus, the dividing line between composure and postmeditation consists in dis-traction or nondistraction. When distracted, it is postmeditation; when undistracted, it is composure. When distracted, it is dualistic mind; when undistracted, it is rigpa.

A lot of questions usually come up at this point: Is shamatha training a state of distraction? Is the act of visualizing during development stage a state of distraction? Is recitation of mantras a state of distraction? How about cultivating loving-kindness? When one is explaining the Dzogchen teachings on their own terms, the answer is yes, those are states of distraction. But one must add that these are first-class states of distraction, especially loving-kindness. For most people it is quite diffi-cult to be distracted in those noble ways even when they try. Isn't it true that most people find it quite difficult to be continuously loving and kind? To have very clear visualization in the development stage is also not easy. To have one-pointed concentration in shamatha is easier said than done, isn't it? So from time to time it is perfectly all right to make the wish "May I attain that type of distraction."

In terms of the teachings of the Great Perfection, we have to agree that those states are still dualistic mind, albeit a very fine type of dualis-tic mind, one that we sometimes need. Nevertheless, the states of dis-traction *are* distracted states. Occasionally people blunder at exactly this point and lose interest in cultivating any dualistic state such as loving-kindness, one-pointedness of shamatha, or development stage. That is surely a mistake. From time to time we should certainly cultivate those.

The real problem is if one frowns upon dualistic practices because of hearing that the nondual state of rigpa is the real thing. One might in-correctly feel that trying to be compassionate and cultivating noble qualities is an inferior type of practice, so why bother? Unfortunately, the loving-kindness and compassion that should be spontaneously pre-sent within the awakened state haven't manifested yet. One is in a vacant and dry blankness where nothing much happens. To fixate one's mind on the unconditioned while rejecting noble qualities is an obstacle. It is a self-created hindrance for practitioners of particularly this type of practice. This obstacle is called "the demonic view of black dissipation," a view that gives credence to neither good nor evil. You could say that it is "Mara's blessing" that causes one to go astray. One feels no interest in cultivating good qualities because such practice is "too conceptual," but one does not naturally have any good qualities either, so nothing happens. That is a big obstacle, and it is one of the reasons the Dzogchen teachings are kept secret. Not because there is anything wrong with the teachings—there is absolutely nothing wrong when they are practiced correctly—but it is possible for an individual to misconstrue the process, and this is where the danger lies. We don't want to do anyone a disservice, do we? The obstacle is definitely not the fault of the Dzogchen teachings, nor is it some kind of built-in flaw in the state of rigpa. It is the individual practitioner's fault for not understanding how to practice correctly.

One can also misunderstand at the outset of the practice how rigpa really is. Yes, it is spacious and open, but it's not simply an extroverted spacious ego. In this distortion, ego is not dissolved, it just makes itself outwardly spacious: "There is so much space there. I am so open. I am *so* open!" And then one stays like that, vacant and frozen. One trains again and again in keeping this open, vacant, frozen state that is definitely not rigpa. If it were truly rigpa, the compassionate qualities and devotion would naturally appear. True practitioners of rigpa sincerely appreciate their guru and the lineage of teachings. True practitioners understand the futility of samsaric aims, and renunciation genuinely arises within their mind. But since it isn't really rigpa, these qualities are not allowed to unfold.

A specific psychological problem accompanies this particular distortion of rigpa, arising as a sort of side effect. It reveals itself whenever one is confronted with doing something noble or meaningful. The misguided Dzogchen yogi tells himself or herself, "I shouldn't do this, because it's dualistic." If compelled to take part in dualistic practices, one feels guilty, as if one had betrayed this vacant, spacious ego. Ego is not self-liberated at this point, not at all, because the knowing of its empty essence is missing. There is a plastered-over, empty feeling, and cultivating this habit becomes a problem because one becomes stuck there. One simply does not want to create any type of meritorious attitude because one imagines this would be betraying the Dzogchen teachings. One would rather not develop any further.

This distortion is potentially a huge obstacle. If this arises, one especially needs to supplicate one's guru, receive more instruction, and then dive into the conceptual practices of loving-kindness, training in compassion, and so forth in order to perfect the accumulations. Give up altogether the "state of rigpa" that one was hanging on to so seriously and say, "I don't care for this; let me continue along the path. Obviously I took a wrong turn; let me go on now."

Being caught up in this distortion is actually one huge distraction. It is not the true path. You know the two aspects of means and knowledge? All the different practices that belong to means have very few sidetracks. There is really nothing that can be turned upside down, inverted and distorted. The practice I have taught here belongs more to the knowledge aspect, especially the view of the Great Perfection. The path of means has few sidetracks, so that one doesn't really go wrong while trying to accumulate merit. Some pitfalls are possible when doing completion stage with attributes such as *tummo* practice, *tsa-lung*, and the like, but otherwise not much can go wrong.

About this issue Nagarjuna said, "To regard things as concrete is to be as stupid as a cow, but to regard things as inconcrete is to be even more foolish." We may do good actions with the attitude "This is real; this is concrete, solid reality." This attitude is not really so bad, because some good still comes out of it, and the opportunity for realizing the illusory nature of everything remains open. On the other hand, the fixation on the nihilistic view that nothing is real is very hard to cure by means of the Dharma teachings, because one has already decided that nothing is real; one has denied everything. To switch to again acknowledging that there is a certain degree of reality is very difficult. It is much easier to change from believing that everything is real to believing that it is unreal than the opposite.

We may hold these notions in mind: "There is a buddha, and enlightenment is wonderful. There are these offerings, and there is me. I like to give them. I am giving them. I will get something out of it in my future life. It is all good!" This is not such a big mistake. Of course, we are being similar to a cow here, but at least we are no worse than a cow. The other attitude is: "This is all useless! Why should I do that? What is the use of lighting a candle? It's just a candle; it's merely oil in a lamp.

How can there be any merit in lighting the wick of a butter lamp? All right, molecules are heated up to a higher temperature so that they emit light, and that light extends into various directions, but where is the merit? I don't see it anywhere. I don't see how lighting something is going to help me. They say there is a buddha named Amitabha in a buddhafield, but I haven't seen one; he's never spoken to me. As far as I'm concerned, he doesn't exist!"

That kind of cynical attitude makes it easy to settle one's mind upon the idea that *there is nothing*—in other words, upon a nihilistic view. There is a certain nihilistic attitude that can be dressed up as spirituality. It goes like this: "I only want the main point. I don't need any of these cultural or religious trappings; they are not for me. When disturbed I want to be calm. Calm is necessary, I understand, and I need it. Whenever I am selfish I should be more kind, because it works, and I feel better, so I need that. But please keep all the other complicated stuff away from me!" Seen from the traditional Buddhist point of view, this is a poor attitude. One does oneself a grave disservice by thinking like this. One is depleting one's own merit and making oneself unfortunate for no reason. I feel it is necessary to be aware of this way of going astray.

Getting back to the heart of the matter: as you get distracted, you stray from rigpa. You are undistracted when simply allowing the continuity of rigpa to carry on, to endure. While you remain composed, undistracted from the continuity of rigpa, two types of distraction can happen. One is not even noticing when after only a few minutes you find yourself already out of rigpa. How you came out of it you don't know, but suddenly you realize it. The other is that during the continuity of composure, something begins to move about in the periphery. It catches your attention and carries you off, even though you are aware of it. That is mainly the way a beginner gets distracted. The first type happens more to practitioners who have the confidence of being "advanced meditators." The looseness is perhaps too loose, so that one does not care too much to apply a remedy against whatever happens. That is why it is possible to slide away.

What is necessary? When one is distracted, what is it that gets distracted? It is the cognizant quality that gets distracted. How does the cognizant quality wander off? Because of forgetting its empty essence. What is the job of this cognizant nature? To *re-recognize* its empty essence. Having recognized its empty essence, this cognizant or awake quality is already complete. Its job is done. The problem here could be that the cognizant quality tries to make empty essence into a concrete meditation object, and then, because of holding it strongly in mind, distraction occurs. In fact, empty essence means there is no object. Making it into a concrete meditation object would mean attempting to render it almost tangible, like when I try to touch this gong. Recognizing empty essence means *recognizing that there is no object*. If emptiness were an object, then it could be touched, but it is not an object. It is like touching nothing, then simply leaving that nothing open. But because of coemergent ignorance, because of our innate habit of not knowing, cognizant nature gets kind of fidgety. It is not happy with no "thing" to touch and begins to look around for something to grab. This is the root cause of getting distracted from the state of rigpa.

There is possibly an instance when cognizant nature begins to look for an object, a very particular object; it won't settle for anger, attachment, or belief. Rather, it turns space into an object. This is when spaced-out meditation happens. At this point rigpa is definitely lost—or maybe it was not correctly recognized to begin with. One begins to solidify the spaciousness as an object of meditation. Does this make sense to you?

STUDENT: That spaciousness becomes the object?

RINPOCHE: Yes, the cognizant quality begins to objectify space. It takes itself as subject and space as object. This obviously becomes a dualistic state of mind. It is possible that you all are very intelligent and that you get this point immediately, but somehow I'm not sure that you've gotten it, so I keep repeating myself. You are welcome to say, "That's enough! I've got it."

There are several ways of being distracted, a so-called similar type and a dissimilar type. It is much easier to notice when distracted by a dissimilar type, meaning entirely different from rigpa. If it is a similar type, something that feels like rigpa, then it's not so easy to notice. Making spaciousness into an object held in mind is a state of distraction that resembles rigpa. It is not entirely different, because rigpa *is* empty and spacious. The difference is that rigpa's spaciousness is not an object held in mind. The spaciousness of rigpa is very natural, open, and free, whereas making space into an object means we form the *notion of spaciousness* and then try to maintain this notion. It might feel as if it is rigpa, but it definitely is not; it is a state of distraction. Because it is similar, though, it's hard to notice.

As a general rule, the similar type is much more difficult to get out of than the dissimilar type. An example of the dissimilar type would be anger, which is completely different from the state of rigpa. Its very presence alerts you and makes you feel, "Of course, now I am distracted." It's the same with strong drowsiness, for example; you can easily feel that you got distracted there.

I just explained how distraction occurs. The next subject is how to deal with it. Distraction slowly begins when the cognizant quality seemingly dims. I mentioned before the dimming of the light and the beginning of darkness. This awake quality, the cognizant nature, seemingly begins to dim, and together with that is a freezing of the attention toward something. When this occurs to such an extent that the cognizance loses track of being empty, then distraction has begun. But if you are aware of this just as it is about to happen—if you are aware that your attention is about to move into a thought, about to become distracted, and at that moment you re-recognize the empty quality of this awake state—then there is no distraction. The quality of freedom is re-established.

Earlier I mentioned three styles of freedom: freed upon arising, naturally freed, and freed beyond benefit and harm. The situation I am currently discussing is freed upon arising, which has two manifestations. Re-recognizing is one type of freed upon arising. As the thought is about to be formed, it dissolves again. The analogy for that is like drawing on water. This whole process takes place during the state of composure. Another aspect of freed upon arising occurs during the postmeditation. Together with knowing you're being distracted, you remember and immediately arrive in rigpa. For example, you are just about to get angry. You notice, "I am getting angry," and you immediately recognize rigpa. Based on the anger, you recognize rigpa: "I am getting carried off here. I am not in rigpa." Simply because of noticing this, you are immediately back in nondual awareness: "Oh, now I am out. Wait. Look. See." You do not need to go through this whole process step by step. You arrive directly. Certainly it's not easy to notice every time you get carried away, and this does not come readily for most people. During a two-hour stretch it rarely occurs even once. Mostly it comes in the evening when one is really tired and says, "Hey, I am really distracted here. I really got carried off." Then one notices, but otherwise it is a rare thought.

The second type of freeing is naturally freed. Natural freeing means "not dependent upon a remedy." When recognizing the wakefulness of knowing, no matter what type of object distracts you, the distraction dissolves without the use of any other remedy. The adept meditator does not have to take the support of a specific remedy against each particular object of distraction. Whatever state of mind might arise, if you can recognize rigpa during it, it is freed. It's the same for thoughts and emotions: there is the ability for these knots to be untied by themselves, without any other remedy, if you simply recognize rigpa. Rigpa is truly the single sufficient king.

The third way of freeing is freed beyond benefit and harm, and it is compared to a thief entering an empty house. Here, at this rather advanced level, you have recognized in actuality that all phenomena, whether belonging to samsara or to nirvana, are nothing other than the play of rigpa. When you have become familiar with that, then even though thoughts still move as the flow of karmic patterns, they don't have anything to hook into. Not only are all phenomena seen as empty, but the thought flow itself, all the various patterns, are seen as empty as well. At this point, there is no real danger of losing anything to any thought or emotion that arises. The thoughts "know" by now there is no longer anything to get, since they lost so many times before, but they still have to come because it is their job. There is still some karma left that is not yet purified. The thoughts are still being spewed forth to a certain extent, but that is not such a big deal, because there is no real danger of getting anything or losing anything.

STUDENT: How is rigpa maintained?

RINPOCHE: In America and Europe, general maintenance is considered very important, right? In Nepal the idea of regular maintenance does not even come up; people speak of obtaining something or building a structure, but not of keeping it in good condition afterward. Look at how the houses are built in Nepal. After a month or two they don't look new any longer—they look like they were custom-tailored to look old. It's living proof that maintenance is very important.

Once we have recognized rigpa, how is it maintained afterward? This is the next key point I would like to cover. Is it by trying so hard to be one-pointedly mindful, trying not to be distracted? Or just looking into rigpa once and then going to sleep—is that the way? Other, more tangible kinds of teachings are easier to maintain. If the view is tangible, then the meditation training to maintain it will also be tangible. But here the view is beyond the tangible, so your maintaining must also be intangible.

Let's say that the view is comprehensible, that it is something graspable to keep in mind. Doing that, of course, would be called *maintaining*. But what if the view is no *thing* to hold in mind—an intangible view? How do we maintain that? That is why we have the sequence of first looking, then seeing, and then letting be. There is another term for letting be: not fabricating. How do we *do* "not fabricating" or "not contriving"? If we *do* it, it is by definition fabricated. If we don't maintain it, we lose rigpa. So, how to maintain the view? Do you understand this dilemma?

We have to use words to communicate, and here are some important words: First, see the view of the Great Perfection; next, maintain it. The Dzogchen teachings use a name for this maintenance: *training in the threefold motionlessness*. Remember this phrase. There is a relationship between not fabricating and motionlessness, because the moment we try to create something artificial there is immediately a moving away from the natural state. The finest way of motionlessness is to not fabricate anything artificial.

The first aspect of the threefold motionlessness is the *unmoving body like the king of mountains*, like Mount Everest. This is how to place your body at the beginning. *[Rinpoche demonstrates the sitting posture]* After mastering it, you can place your body however you want. Putting your butt up in the air and your head down is fine. Having closed eyes is okay; open eyes are fine too. You can sit on a chair or in your car, or you can lie face down on your bed; it does not matter. Squeezing your nose flat is also okay. For us Tibetans it is very easy to flatten the nose, but for Westerners with their long noses it is more problematic. *[Laughs]* Honestly, sometimes I actually do sleep face down, no problem. Some people say you shouldn't sleep like that because your nose will get crooked, but I don't mind.

Once we attain stability in the correct body position, it does not matter how we sit. In fact, we should try to seek out what is difficult. Go to a scary place or an uncomfortable place, a situation where we are not at home or comfy, maybe somewhere crowded with many people, a place with all sorts of turmoil, a place where we get flattered, criticized, have pleasant or unpleasant experiences—all different types of places. In doing this, we should take support of the *symbolic master of experiences* who is teaching us at that very moment, because in those situations we can recognize mind essence and still be free. The liberated quality of the experience at that time is "the true master of natural knowing."

There are four types of teachers, two of which I have mentioned here. One is our ability to learn and progress during difficulties. This is the symbolic master of experiences. Another is when we are able to recognize the natural knowing during an unpleasant experience and capable of overcoming the unpleasantness. The sense of freedom here is the *true master of natural knowing.* The quality of being free in the emptiness during difficulties is also a teacher. There are two additional kinds of teachers that we will return to later.

The point is, when we are able to recognize the liberated state within any difficult situation or any body posture, then it doesn't matter how we sit. But right now, while we are training, our mind is in some way dependent upon the channels, energies, and essences. Mind is supported by the essences, the *bindus.* The essences in turn are supported by the energies, while the energies are supported by the channels. The channels themselves are supported by or dependent upon the physical material body. Therefore, the 72,000 channels in the body are in their naturally aligned mode when this material body is placed in an upright, straight position. With the 72,000 channels in their natural mode, the energies that move within them—the upward-moving, the downward-clearing, and so on—all flow freely and can dissolve within the central channel. When the energy currents are in their natural mode, when they are purified in this way, then unnecessary thought movements diminish. Why? Because the pathways through which the thought currents move have been eliminated, cut off. When the energy currents move nicely, the pure form of the essences, which are interconnected with mind, are in their natural mode as well. We experience this as a state of mind that is at ease and feels more natural, relaxed. When mind is at peace, it has a greater opportunity to recognize its own nature. A kind of natural intelligence is revealed. On the other hand, if there is a lot of disturbance, turmoil, and constriction, then our sense of intelligence is preoccupied. Therefore, sit with a straight back for this practice.

There is also a posture called the sevenfold posture of Vairochana, which is quite difficult, especially for Westerners. Westerners have long arms, right? And their arms do not seem to fit easily in that particular posture. So either we need an amputation or we need special pillows under our butts. The arms should be like this, and the legs in the vajra posture. *[Rinpoche demonstrates]* I have short arms; if I had long arms it would be more difficult. This sevenfold posture of Vairochana is especially important if one is doing the *tsa-lung* type of tantric yoga, which is a way of forcing the energy currents into the central channel. For Dzogchen practice, though, it's not that important. Those of you with long arms, place your hands on your knees, like Longchen Rabjam. This is known as the posture of mental ease. There's another way of placing the hands, which is used in Zen and other practice traditions—you place your hands in your lap, one on top of the other. I personally prefer placing my palms on my knees. Shoulders are drawn slightly back and down. There could be a bubbling energy, a difficult-to-explain feeling of a rush—just let it settle. Let the belly area relax a bit. This is known as the soft breath. There is also the vase-shaped soft breath. If you practice that a lot you will develop a slight potbelly. For people who are very concerned with their looks it might not be such a good idea! But do a couple of push-ups, a couple of sit-ups, and it goes away Many people experience a constriction in the belly area. The shoulders go up a bit, the neck goes down, and there develops a traffic jam in the energy currents, a sort of congestion. The remedy for this is to let it settle, relaxing the shoulders down. Then you just sit there not moving, not fidgeting. You sit and just drop every concern about having or not having a body. Sit loose, happy, and relaxed, but still keeping your shape. This is all about the first motionlessness, the unmoving body that is like the king of mountains.

Next are the *unmoving senses like planets and stars reflected in a lake.* It's a serene lake here, not a turbulent one. All your senses are open. Your ears are not blocked, nor are your eyes closed; you have feeling in all the pores of your body, and the thoughts in your mind are not blocked either. Nothing is obstructed. You are not looking right and left, fidgeting about trying to listen to this and that. "While keeping my ears open like Tsoknyi Rinpoche told me, should I now listen carefully to every single sound that comes along?" No, that is not what's meant. You do not have to listen deliberately or intently, and yet all senses are simply wide open.

At this point, breathe through the mouth, between the teeth. The lips and teeth are just slightly parted so that the breathing flows naturally, unforced—not like this. *[Rinpoche opens his mouth and gasps]* You can keep the teeth just touching if you want; that is fine. The mouth is slightly open so that the breath can flow as it pleases. The mouth is neither gaping wide open nor closed so that you're breathing through the nose. Leave the mouth slightly open and let the breathing be totally unforced. It is better to grow accustomed to this slowly so that the inhalations and exhalations become long and relaxed, so that we are not so nervous, palpitating and panting. Long, easy breaths. The eyes look straight ahead. The gaze is simply left there to itself.

Wide-open senses may be a bit uncomfortable for someone who has been used to meditating with closed eyes, but you can adjust slowly. In fact, it is best to train with open eyes, because when we get up and walk around, we need to do that with open eyes. If you were to continue training with closed eyes when you walk around, wouldn't you bump into things and hurt your head? People would have to call the ambulance. "What happened to you?" "Well, uh, I was meditating!" The ambulance driver asks, "*This* is what happens when one meditates?" What are you going to say, other than "Uhhhh, yes!" At the next retreat we may need an ambulance on call for mindless meditators!

In other words, leave all the senses very open and alive, not necessarily reaching out toward objects, but simply aware. Our lineage masters all agreed that you do not have to be *deliberately aware* of things. Rather, just allow them to be reflected, to appear by themselves. When you look at the placid surface of a clear, quiet lake at night, the planets and stars just appear there. They present themselves, and when the surface is very serene and quiet, you can see them very clearly. It's the same way with our senses when they are left wide open.

This second motionlessness, the unmoving senses like planets and stars reflected in a lake, is a very important point. Placing your sense faculties in the correct way facilitates a particular type of intelligence—the intelligence that discerns all phenomena thoroughly and fully—unfolding as you progress. You now see very clearly what is correct and incorrect. One could say that the circumstance of the senses being left wide open facilitates that intelligence or allows for it to happen.

The third motionlessness is *unmoving mind essence like a cloudless sky*. The mind itself resembles a clear sky, totally lucid and bright, not forming any clouds at all. When we leave ourselves in this threefold way of motionlessness, that is called maintaining rigpa. But it is possible to maintain rigpa only after having recognized it. If we are unaware of what rigpa is, then there is no maintaining it either.

Another point is that there are two aspects of getting rid of what needs to be eliminated: through understanding and through training. Through the process of training, getting more and more accustomed to this way of being, certain factors are discarded. The way of training here, the key point of maintenance according to the specific terminology of Dzogchen, is to be *undistracted while not meditating*.

What happens if one is meditating? You can say whatever you want, but do say something.

STUDENT: There is some fixing or clinging.

STUDENT 2: Conceptualizing.

RINPOCHE: That is why the key point is *while not meditating*, right? But undistracted. What happens if one is distracted?

STUDENT: One is taken away by the thoughts.

RINPOCHE: Right! Therefore, undistracted. So why combine these two terms, "undistracted" and "not meditating"? How about "undistracted" but not training in that? Will one get good at that without training? Unless we train, isn't it true that we will just remain distracted? To be undistracted, don't we need to train and grow accustomed to it? Yet the instruction says "while *not* meditating." Doesn't that sound like "don't train"? No? What does it sound like then?

STUDENT: Train, but don't get distracted and don't meditate.

[Laughter]

STUDENT 2: "Undistracted" means maintaining clarity or lucidity. "While not meditating" means maintaining the emptiness. There is no subject or object; you are not *doing* anything.

RINPOCHE: Yes, it is like that. The cognizant nature needs to be allowed to be cognizant naturally, by itself, not by our trying to make it so by meditating.

So how do we *do* rigpa? Is it by meditating? The question arises, "Then what is there for me to do? Rigpa is just automatic and natural. There is nothing I have to do about it. I'm told that anything I try to do is just conceptual—so what do I need to do? Won't I go crazy?" No, you won't go crazy.

Our task here is first to recognize the essence, rigpa itself. We don't need to *do* anything about rigpa after that. Rigpa does not require our assistance. All we need to do is simply refrain from accepting the invitations that come along to be distracted, to disturb rigpa. The distractions come and say, "Let's disturb rigpa now! Let's cover it up!" But we simply refrain from accepting that request, again and again. That is our task. We do not need to improve rigpa. Let's say there is a glimpse of recognizing the awakened state that is rigpa. There is no way we can expand it, even if we try to. Trying to do anything to it just covers it up more. Some people misunderstand this point. They think, "I should *get* rigpa, *hold* rigpa." If they try to do that, though, the nondual state will never last. That is how it is.

The phrase is *undistracted while not meditating* because if our meditation is conceptual, we are by definition distracted, in the sense of ordinary people who are always distracted. Usually, in order to not be distracted, we try to keep mindful, right? What is it that maintains shamatha, the state of mental stability? The best way is mindfulness, right? To keep undistracted in shamatha, we remain mindful. The main purpose of mindfulness is to be undistracted. The Dzogchen perspective is different, and in fact this is one of the main distinctions between shamatha and rigpa. Rigpa of course needs to be undistracted as well, but the rigpa that needs to be *kept* undistracted by means of mindfulness will only turn into a conceptual state. Here there seem to be two possibilities: being undistracted by keeping mindful, and being undistracted *without* trying to keep mindful. Rigpa's type of undistractedness is the latter; it is not kept by being deliberately mindful.

The Dzogchen teachings actually mention four types of mindfulness: deliberate mindfulness, effortless mindfulness, true mindfulness, and supreme mindfulness. Briefly, however, we can just operate with two types: deliberate and effortless, one for shamatha, the other for Dzogchen. Deliberate mindfulness is used in shamatha training, while effortless mindfulness is during vipashyana, in the Dzogchen sense. From a Mahamudra perspective, the true mindfulness is during One Taste, while king like supreme mindfulness is during Nonmeditation.

One might sit and think, "I should *not* be distracted. I should remain quiet and still ... quiet, still ... just knowing this ... quiet ... undistracted. Of course this is very nice and is necessary—I am not criticizing it. Please don't misunderstand this point. Explaining the distinctive features of Dzogchen may sometimes sound like criticizing shamatha. Some of Milarepa's poetry even sounds like a critique of the Buddha, but it surely wasn't. It is just that in one specific context special qualities need to be brought forth in order to be seen more clearly. The issue is this: the view is supposed to be nonconceptual, but what happens if the training in the nonconceptual view turns conceptual? When view and training are in conflict, we hamper progress.

STUDENT: How do we train in the threefold sky practice?

RINPOCHE: From time to time in our practice, we may feel obscured, dull, or sluggish. As a remedy for those states, train in *mingling the threefold sky*. Mingling the threefold sky could be spoken of as a specific practice, as an enhancement of the Trekchö view. But don't obsess with mingling the threefold sky; it is not just another practice to *do*. It is simply about the Trekchö view, the *thorough cut*.

The outer sky is the circumstance here, so find a good location, a wide-open vista that is cloudless, without mist or haze. If you're staying in a village, go find a hilltop. If you're staying downtown in a big city, go up to the top of a tall building. The optimal condition is to "wear the hillside as your collar," meaning the hillside continues up behind you as a support, but in front of you the sky opens up so that you don't have to sit and look upward at too sharp an angle. Simply look straight ahead into the vast, open sky. In Tibet, Dzogchen practitioners would search out a practice place like this. Regarding your eyes, there are two ways to look. One is to look into space as if you're holding a spear, so that your gaze and space itself mingle into one. But remember that your mind, your attention, should not be directed outwardly in the same way as the eyes. The other way is more like throwing your gaze into the sky and just leaving it like that. You should practice this in combination with your teacher's oral instructions.

Next is the inner sky, which is your empty mind. This means that the attention should not be grasping at space, as in: "I should see it. I should hold it. I should aim at it." Avoid that form of strong intent. Let it fall away and give way to an awake quality that simply acknowledges *how it is*. You are not aiming at space outside but simply acknowledging its own intrinsic, spacious quality. In other words, the cognizant nature recognizes its empty essence. In this way, outside there is the empty quality of the spaciousness; inside there is the empty quality of mind not clinging; and there is the empty quality of rigpa itself being acknowledged. The practice of mingling simply consists in recognizing the empty quality of these three aspects—outer, inner, and innermost—then allowing that state to be as it naturally is. Remaining naturally composed in that way is called the *innermost sky of the luminous vajra essence*. Here, "luminous" means cognizant or awake, "vajra" means unchanging, and "essence" means acknowledging these as one identity.

If you focus too much on this practice of mingling the threefold sky, there is a danger of getting too spaced-out. It is more beneficial to train in it once in a while as an enhancement to the view. If you feel too closed in, too dull, too hazy, then mingling the threefold sky clears up your dullness and mental haze; they dissolve simply through a sharpening or strengthening of awareness. After that, just return to being very ordinary and normal. During the practice, have your eyes wide open and face the sky. Don't wear too much clothing.

Earlier I mentioned two ways of gazing: looking piercingly into the sky with your eyes aimed like a spear, and a way that is more like throwing your gaze into the sky and just leaving it like that. Most of the time we just let go when looking at the sky, but once in a while we should try to look very piercingly, very directly. Why? When we aim at the sky, because there is no "thing" there to aim at, the support or target vanishes. There is a reason for practicing in both these ways. Looking directly into the sky sharpens or brightens the awake presence. The thinking mind is suspended in rigpa; together with that, you just aim into the sky as if holding a spear. The other way is more relaxed—just leave the gaze open in space.

If you are really in the state of the luminous vajra essence, the positioning of the eyes doesn't matter, but otherwise there is a certain connection. This is an individual matter that varies from person to person. Sometimes, however, if you maintain this loose quality for too long, the whole affair becomes hazy or vague, blurred, as if there were several levels in space. Or, if you are too absorbed in the external spaciousness, and at the same time there are thoughts and concepts going on inside, you can become disconnected. There is an external spaciousness, sure, but the thought flow inside is not liberated. You just sit there, vague, eyes out of focus like an unfocused camera lens. If you train like that for too long, one day this outward attention doesn't know what to do and you become blurred on the inside also. Instead of training in being out of focus, you need to sharpen up. All three skies should be brought together and mingled: the outer empty sky, the inner empty mind nature, and the innermost empty rigpa.

STUDENT: Would you say that devotion and receptivity are states of distraction? What is the relationship between awareness and these states of mind, with regard to being in a conceptual state?

RINPOCHE: It's possible to be in a state of devotion while undistracted. You could also be distracted in devotion if you get addicted to the feeling and absorbed in it. But if the devotion is allowed to dawn as an adornment, an embellishment to the state of rigpa, just like a reflection in a mirror, without losing the quality of empty essence, then it's not distraction.

There are two ways of being undistracted. Remember, we can be un-distracted while meditating, or undistracted while *not* meditating. I talk about the second type. You can check for yourself whether that is your situation. If your state of being undistracted is because of remaining focused, it's not meditation in the Dzogchen sense of the word. It is meditation, definitely, and it's still good—but it's not Dzogchen medi-tation. Being mindful and undistracted is still a conceptual state of meditation, and this type of mindfulness is not unconditioned mindful-ness, but rather a mindfulness *by a subject, on an object*. As I mentioned in detail before, the word "meditation" in the Dzogchen context means to be undistracted while not meditating.

Concerning receptivity, having the five senses wide open, left totally free, is one specific quality mentioned within the Dzogchen instructions. We must be very clear about what it means so that it doesn't become another way of being spaced out. It's not that one merely submits to the five senses, totally letting the attention be caught up in or absorbed into the fields of the five sense impressions. That would be a particular meditative discipline: a training in being spaced-out, which is *not* Dzog-chen meditation. Dzogchen meditation is to give freedom to the five senses by allowing whatever is presented as the five sense impressions to just occur, without blocking out anything. At the same time, you are not particularly encouraging anything, nor are you keeping hold of or pur-suing anything. It's more like just being a mirror in which everything is allowed to be reflected. Within the accommodating and spacious empty essence, the wide-awake cognizant quality allows everything to be reflected without a problem.

DEALING WITH
EMOTIONS

The Buddha taught three principal ways to deal with negative emotions. The first is to keep a certain distance from emotions, trying your best to avoid them. You go to a peaceful place where you don't get emotionally involved, a place without many temptations. Doing this is called *abandoning emotions*. You haven't cut emotions at their very root, but there is not much "reinvestment" taking place. The second method is *transforming emotions*, and the third is called *acknowledging the nature of emotions*.

The first technique, abandonment, is prevalent in the Hinayana teachings. You may have noticed skeletons hanging on the walls of some Buddhist temples, or images of skeletons painted there, especially in Burma and Thailand. In Tibet too there are a lot of paintings of skeletons in the temples and some hanging there as well. This is for the benefit of monks and nuns, an antidote for desire arising in their minds. When desire arises, they're told: "Consider the body's interior. Peel the skin off, and what's inside? Are you attracted to that? We are all carrying a portable toilet in our gut. Do you have desire for that? When a dead body is opened up and you see the rotting organs, how do you feel? What if you found yourself lying in bed next to that person?" The Hinayana tradition has a lot of instructions of this type. However, this kind of attitude creates another hindrance—the emotion of disgust, as in "How filthy!" or "People who don't brush their teeth, how disgusting!"

Along this line, Shantideva asks in *The Way of the Bodhisattva*, "Honestly, what is it that you are so attracted to?" He makes you consider a whole series of attractive objects, one after the other, and then ruins your attachment to each. But each time it is ruined, you have a new problem. You are no longer attached to that particular object, but your attachment, your desire, is still alive, and it reaches for something else.

You ruin a particular desire, but then a substitute replaces it. To remove the substitute, another remedy is necessary. This is how we end up with 84,000 types of Dharma teachings.

The Dzogchen system teaches that if you continue like that, grasping at one thing after another, the process could be endless. The Dzogchen principle here, however, is that it is not necessary to rely on another remedy. When anger or desire arises it can be allowed to dissolve into itself. Only when you are unable to let it be naturally liberated must you resort to an external remedy. If an emotion doesn't get freed immediately, then you simply give it a little more room. Allow two or three minutes, then let it go. For example, if the anger is really intense, you don't try to let it go right away. You give it a little love, a little sympathy, a little room, and it starts to soften. You recognize its essence within that softening.

In a certain context, an intense emotion could actually help rigpa become more fresh and vivid. The strong emotion can bring a certain further strength. As a matter of fact, as you progress you discover that each emotion can be accompanied by a sense of basic wakefulness. You have heard that the five poisons are the five wisdoms, right? This teaching is very interesting and very important but also quite risky. There is a danger in a sentence like "The more emotions, the more wisdom." Yet, honestly, it could be for real.

Often you see that important, powerful people have most vigorous minds. They can be very bright, very intelligent, but full of ego at the same time. They can have strong passions as well as being very compassionate. They can become incredibly furious, have strong drive, be very clever, and also be totally stupid in another area, with huge blind spots. If a person in an important position wasn't competitive, he or she wouldn't have the drive to keep going. Because of ego's drive, the dominant part of the person's energy goes into the patterns of the five poisons and not the five wisdoms. That is why office bosses can be so aggressive even though they are quite bright. They become boss because they are intelligent, but you may not like to work with them because they can also be infuriating.

These kinds of people exemplify the certain potential inherent in strong passions. Along with the passions, existing simultaneously with them, there is the potential for their transformation—for allowing the five wisdoms. These wisdoms are connected with the five buddha families, which are naturally related to certain types of people, certain types of mind-sets, and particular Vajrayana deities.

It is taught that Vajrayana practice is especially suited to people whose emotional states are more forceful. I am not quite sure I can explain this difficult point satisfactorily. There is something on my mind about this topic, and I often try to express it, but I'm not sure I have been able to really articulate it yet. While I teach, I always look at people's faces to see whether they are getting the point, to see if I'm getting through or not. That hesitation actually clouds me over. If people don't get this point correctly, it could be very dangerous. One might think, "All right! I get aggressive and pushy, but that is okay because the teacher said that's how one should be to express basic wisdom." How about that? Not good, right?

There is another type of person who prefers to be like a vegetable—a good, pure, organic vegetable. This person likes to remain uninvolved, doesn't have much emotional drive, doesn't get too angry, too passionate, or too jealous. However, he is also not overly compassionate either; he doesn't try to reach out to other people. Still, he is good and decent, quiet and relaxed. I am not saying that's bad, but a certain gutsy strength seems to be missing.

Sometimes you find practitioners of Dzogchen who have fierce negative emotions, ablaze like fire, but at the same time, when these emotions are not that active, these people can be very intelligent, very sharp. Sometimes they are very loving, very kind, very compassionate; sometimes they are full of devotion. When they get angry, they rage, but they can also be very sharp. When such a person who has both intense passions and a very sharp mind connects with a qualified master, he or she may truly understand the Dzogchen teachings; that's how it's taught. For someone whose emotions are in 100 percent full bloom, it is also possible that intelligence or sharp-mindedness can be 100 percent activated, that devotion or compassion can be 100 percent fully manifested. There are a lot of people like that in this present age.

A Vajrayana practitioner is not supposed to criticize the emotions as something awful. Rather, one should let go of the grasping within an emotion and recognize its pure quality, using the strength of the emotion to recognize rigpa. That's a very important point. But the emotion *must* be liberated through this process. What does it mean for an emotion to become liberated? It doesn't mean we prevent an emotion from arising, like closing the door. Nor does it mean we should take hold of whatever arises, whatever unfolds, with a clinging to "I" and "other." Rather, just allow it to dissolve, dissolve, and again dissolve; then the energy in the emotion becomes full-fledged, fully blossomed. This most vital point—that the emotions are the five wisdoms—is an extraordinary, unique feature within the Vajra Vehicle of Secret Mantra. Failing to understand this point correctly can become a grave mistake. But when you really understand it, there's major progress in understanding. Truthfully! There wouldn't be much success from trying to suppress the emotions, trying not to feel. I have given this issue a lot of thought, and I feel this point is really precious, honestly! The main quality of Vajrayana is how to deal effectively with emotions.

Now, while you don't suppress an emotion, there is no benefit from just getting carried away by the emotion and doing whatever it says. It would be very easy just to kick back and surrender to the emotions, but that is not the Dzogchen way. Say you leave the door to your house wide open, and fifty emotions march in. The emotions tell you, "Get up now. Let's go rob that bank! You have to come along." If you reply "Okay, no problem, I'll join you," you're finished. The Dzogchen approach is not to fight with the emotions, true, but you don't obey them either. This is entirely different from closing your doors and windows and pretending not to be home when the emotions come knocking. So what do you do? Just let the emotions come right in. You're sitting down, and they each point a rifle at you, saying, "If you don't come with us, we'll shoot!" What to do? At that moment, you surely need the key instruction of Vajrayana. If you let yourself get overwhelmed and join forces with the emotions, you are no different from an ordinary person. And if you try to prevent them from entering, by closing all the doors and windows, then there's no adornment, you're just sitting there all alone, like in shamatha. We need to allow rigpa's natural strength to be fully present. Faced with rigpa's natural strength, fully manifest, all the emotions lose their power and become part of rigpa.

To truly liberate emotions through the practice of rigpa, you have to make sure that you have recognized rigpa to begin with. Recognizing your own nature basically means that dualistic mind is introduced to itself, to its own basic nature—which, as you have heard by now, is empty in essence and cognizant by nature. You must also have heard that these two cannot be separated in any way whatsoever; they are an indivisible unity. Cognizant nature means a natural intelligence, an alertness that is simply present, completely aware of what happens. Rigpa is not a dim-witted, vacant state of mind. It is not absentminded, unaware of what is going on. Nor is it a conceptual manner of being aware. There is a certain presence in rigpa, but that mindful presence is not made deliberately. It is intrinsically present together with this empty essence. It is simply a matter of this state knowing itself.

Let me illustrate this point with a candle and its flame. Let's say there is no electricity in the room, only a lit candle. Do you need to turn on a flashlight to see the flame? No, the flame is self-illuminating. You could say it has two aspects: it illuminates darkness, and it illuminates its own flame. But take this chant book in my hand, for example: do you need a flashlight to see it? Yes, because it is not self-illuminating. To see the chant book you need two things: the flashlight and the book; just like you need a subject and object to conceptually know something. But rigpa is entirely different. Rigpa is a *self-knowing natural cognizance.* It's *as if* a flame could know itself.

The pointing-out instruction for recognizing mind essence involves dualistic mind being introduced to itself. Mind is led to know its nature. We are told how to recognize our empty cognizance. To put it in a nutshell: your basic state of mind is not *another* state to arrive at later. This present way of experiencing simply acknowledges that it is actually empty in essence and, while not losing track of being empty, is still able to perceive and to function.

This mind is supposed to recognize its emptiness, but not as an object. The moment this mind recognizes emptiness, rigpa is an immediate actuality. If this cognizance sees its own emptiness as a separate object, then there is duality in that the knowing becomes the subject, with emptiness as its object. That is the opposite of recognizing rigpa. The moment of rigpa is alert, casual, spontaneous, not meditating, not keeping hold, not rejecting. All five senses are open. It is not a thing but a beautiful, fresh moment. We also call this moment *ordinary mind.*

First, acknowledging it is called *recognizing one's nature.* Next, we must be decisive about what is recognized. This is more complicated, because who really decides? Is it conceptual mind that settles it? Or is it rigpa itself that decides? Or is it your teacher who makes up your mind—"The guru said so, so it must be true"? Or will modern technology validate it for you? Could you go to the Rigpa Lab and check your heart and brain with instruments to decide if your rigpa is fine and fit, if your nonduality is in good shape?

How do you resolve this point? It may be tough to have to immediately endorse our own experience, but we can decide upon it if we feel even 60 percent confident that it's actually rigpa. As the basis for verifying, we use our teacher's words, the words of an authentic scripture, and our own experience. When our state of experiencing rigpa really *is* rigpa, there is within that an automatic feeling of certainty. To arrive at that certainty you need to give some time to the process, and you also need to have passion. There is a point at which the certainty is built-in, automatic certainty. Once we get to this natural, unshakable certainty, we feel so sure that even if the Buddha himself came before us and said, "Hey, you're wrong, it's not rigpa!" we would thank him for coming, but it would not change our certainty at all. At a certain point the qualities of empty essence, cognizant nature, and unconfined capacity become so utterly obvious that we *really* know. At this point, we have gained the certainty that whatever occurs in our minds can be freed by itself.

This process of resolving and settling the authenticity of rigpa seems to have two aspects. One aspect is that we don't doubt "today's rigpa." The other is confidence regarding how we deal with phenomena and emotions—how we deal with whatever occurs in our minds, within our field of perception. We must decide on recognizing the *self-knowing wakefulness*, rigpa, in whatever the moment may be. In a moment of anger, recognize rigpa. In a moment of desire, recognize rigpa. If you already know how to recognize rigpa, do not resort to another remedy to pacify or destroy that particular emotional state. In other words, no matter which of the 84,000 different types of negative emotions may well up, once we have recognized rigpa, the solution to any state is simply to recognize rigpa again and again. There is really no other way. Unless we make up our minds in this way, we might be scrambling endlessly for ways to cope with various situations. Without certainty in rigpa as the universal remedy, there would always be a need to *do* and *apply* in the present moment, to run for cover or prepare for battle, instead of simply recognizing the very essence of rigpa right here as the single remedy for whatever emotional state may take place.

We can place an object in midair, but does it stay there? No, it doesn't. In the same way, emotions have no foothold in the moment of recognizing rigpa. Emotions cannot remain in the face of rigpa. I am not saying that emotions can never happen in a Dzogchen practitioner. Paltrul Rinpoche phrased the vital point this way: "The way they arise is the same as before, but the way they are freed is a major distinction."

Let's say there is a fairly advanced yogi in a crowd of people. The way he or she gets angry or experiences a thought is exactly the same way all the other people do—there is no difference. But how that emotion or thought is subsequently allowed to dissolve is entirely different. I am not talking about a completely realized yogi, which would be a different situation, but just a fairly advanced practitioner. The point here is that thoughts, emotions, and perceptions do occur during the state of rigpa. As a matter of fact, they should. They occur while we are training, and we use them as training opportunities. Trying to block off perception in order to train throws us into one of the two extremes of eternalism or nihilism, and we never have the middle way that is so tremendously valuable. Just as our basic ground is neither permanent nor nothing, rigpa, which is part of the ground, is also neither permanent nor nothing.

In my teachings, I first emphasize the way to be sure you have the right rigpa. After that point, the arising of phenomena is the basis for training. Phenomena, appearance, experience, feeling, or perception—all are called *nangwa* in Tibetan. There are many kinds of nangwa, both subtle and coarse. Something appears in the mind, whether it is a vision, a memory, an emotion, an experience, or a perception. Since perceptions occur, they can be liberated within the vast expanse of emptiness. Based on these perceptions, these nangwa, we can have liberation or confusion. It is also on the basis of nangwa that we can become an accomplished being, a siddha. In short, nangwa is whatever comes from and through the natural cognizance of mind. It is said, "While empty, phenomena appear, and while appearing, they are still empty." That is the way we work with phenomena, with our perceptions. In this tradition, we do not seek to merge perceptions as the object with the perceiver as the subject. Instead, we allow perceptions to be freed upon arising.

I have mentioned nonfabrication as a key point of meditation training. We are supposed to simply let be in the continuity of rigpa, without fabrication. You could also say that meditation training means *not losing the continuity* of rigpa. The first meditation moment is that of seeing the nature of mind. Let's say that this first moment is allowed to endure for three minutes. The meditation is still fresh; we say that the continuity of the view has endured. The first moment of recognizing is allowed to continue, so that after three minutes it is still the first moment. But during those three minutes, at the various points where we are just about to get distracted from the continuity of rigpa's awakened state, the onsets of distraction must be freed upon arising. How? The awake quality of cognizant nature re-recognizes its own emptiness and— "freed upon arising" happens.

The key point of the meditation training is nonfabrication—not plotting or constructing the natural state, just allowing the continuity of the view to carry on. Whenever this is the case, there is no distraction. If distraction does occur, simply remind yourself to recognize again and start afresh. That is how to continue the training.

Let's say that rigpa continues for a three-minute period and that during this time perceptions do occur. We do not need to expect that the duration of rigpa will be without anything happening. It *is* possible that nothing will happen; that could either be the completely naked state of rigpa, or it could be the blind alley of having blocked off all perceptions. Therefore, the presence or absence of sensory input does not define the true state of rigpa. There can be rigpa with perceptions, and there can be rigpa without sensory impressions. The yardstick is whether emptiness is recognized either during perceptions or in their absence. Please understand here that "emptiness" does not mean going blank. But, while perceiving, if the perceived is kept hold of, this is also wrong. The teachings say: "Neither stuck in being empty nor fixated on perceiving."

Within emptiness, we can welcome perceptions. Here, emptiness is not a theoretical construct; emptiness means *the recognition of not clinging.* I am not discussing the philosophical articulation of emptiness as that within which perceptions occur, because, as a matter of fact, all experience already occurs within emptiness and always has. There is nothing new about that. I am talking about *actually* acknowledging this spacious quality and allowing perceptions to occur within this recognition.

Take the example of a strong warrior. He might not look like much if he's just sitting down. He needs a circumstance, a setting, to display his power. Some opponent must appear and challenge him with a weapon. Then he stands up and shows his full strength. You see this in the movies—the hero needs a villain so that he can demonstrate his full might. In the same way, rigpa needs the occasion of an emotion to rouse its natural strength. Once this strength is roused, the emotion has no chance. It has to give up. Like a nicely burning fire—the more wood you throw at it, the more it blazes up. Sometimes you can even toss water on a really hot fire and it simply vaporizes; the blaze seems even more intense than before. We need that type of strength in dealing with emotions. If we try merely to evade them, acting as if we have nothing to do with them, then that innate strength is unable to manifest.

Here is another example. On the narrow roads in Nepal you find cows, chickens, people, everything, all sharing the space. Nepali cows are very peculiar in that they can sleep in the middle of the road. Exactly where it is busiest, they just peacefully lie down and sleep!. Imagine you are driving in Kathmandu. You are not a great driver, just acceptable, but still you're not too sure about which pedal is the brake and which is the accelerator. All of a sudden, a chicken darts out in front of you. First you remember, "Well, I have two legs, and there are two pedals. Now, which one is the brake and which one is the accelerator?" If you have to think about it like that, by the time you've figured it out, there is no more chicken—it has become chicken curry. Likewise, if in the presence of a strong emotion you first have to think, "All right. Shamatha… breathing… aaahh … let me see, where is my mind?" First, you try to find your mind, then that there is no mind. As a matter of fact, you don't have time to do that, do you? And second, the emotion will have already gotten hold of you if you need to think it out laboriously like that, so is too late. You might then think, "Okay, I'll let it go," but it has already caught you. It is very difficult to liberate thoughts or emotions with that level of skill.

Conversely, the moment a good driver sees a chicken, he immediately slams on the brakes. The sight of the chicken makes him put his foot on the brake. He doesn't have to think; the braking reflex is automatic. Without a chicken, there's no need to brake; because of the chicken, he steps on the brakes. Applying this analogy to the emotions, we could say that the thought or emotion throws you back into rigpa. In other words, when you are able to practice this way, the odds of you getting really sucked into emotional states will be less and less. The very moment an emotion arises, you acknowledge the wakeful knowing, and the emotion is like a drawing upon water. We need to be like that. The past masters said that freed upon arising is the most important of the three ways of liberation.

I consider this principle of not suppressing emotions very important when you have children. You look at your children and train them accordingly. Some children are very smart, very aggressive, very feisty—they may seem like they're about to break the whole table, right now; it's that sort of energy. But then the next moment they can be so loving and kind, so beautiful, so relaxed, so clear, so juicy. They can be very naughty, full of energy, and at the same time so pure, so full of life. I have noticed that in many Western countries children are constantly told, "Don't do this! Don't do that! You shouldn't, you can't!" To always restrict children hampers their natural ability as they grow up and curbs their strength. They might be given very reasonable, psychologically correct explanations as to why they shouldn't do this or that. In Tibet children get told not to do things and are sometimes given a whack, while in the West it is said sweetly, with a kiss on the cheek. Whether it is done roughly or sweetly, the children are still being suppressed. This will cause them to be timid as adults, to hold themselves back. Sometimes I see children around eleven or twelve years old who already have adult worries in their minds. I can see their minds almost ready to start thinking because you give them too much reason to do this or not to do that. They do something a little bit wrong and are made to feel in the wrong. They are psychologically trapped. I don't feel that this is such a healthy way to bring children up. It teaches children to have no self-confidence.

I am suggesting here that we could treat our mind as if it were an energetic kid. We need to teach our mind, as well as our child, to be in charge of itself—to teach it how to steer itself. This is really necessary, rather than imposing all sorts of external restrictions. The other way may be very reasonable, of course, but it's like Mom and Dad are constantly arranging a ring of thorns around the child. No matter what direction she moves, they warn, "You will bump into a thorn and it will hurt you." Eventually the child becomes trapped, unable to move, because there are thorns in all directions. She hasn't even had the chance to touch them yet, to learn from her own experience, but Mom and Dad have told her not to—it'll hurt! The child thus becomes completely surrounded by psychological thorns. I don't think that is very healthy.

I have children myself. I have one daughter who is about nine. I have been observing her very carefully, and I've observed that the healthiest situation is when her mind is educated, so that she can think for herself. This is something like what you find in Daniel Goleman's book *Emotional Intelligence*—allowing people to take charge of themselves. I am now teaching her a bit of meditation practice. I am not teaching her any psychological meditation, no teachings on the theory of impermanence. There seem to be too many psychological theories being bandied about, upsetting people and causing worry. I honestly feel that the problem is too much psychology, not too little. I am not teaching my daughter any psychology right now, but just allowing her to be at ease with herself, peacefully, and then telling her to be aware of her thoughts as they occur. I tell her, "It's not such a big deal—thoughts happen, just let them go." Children often take their thoughts very seriously. So if I succeed in undoing her tendency to take her own thoughts too seriously, she can adjust: "Oh! I can change my state of mind!" She can let it go. Then she will feel more confident because she is in charge of whether or not she changes her state of mind. Therefore, as she grows up, she won't take life too seriously and have all the problems that come with taking it too seriously. I feel that children who are brought up this way improve as they grow.

Let me restate my point. Children have a certain energy that is part of their basic character, and I don't think that it is our job to make them be psychologically different, to somehow shape them into *not* being that way. Rather, we should teach children to be in charge of themselves and steer themselves. Some children can be so wild one minute, and the next so loving and compassionate. To disturb those qualities is not healthy. Those energies *are* the children. If you do meddle with this, it's like their spark, their radiance, is reduced. On the other hand, if they're not taught how to be in charge of themselves and you just allow their energy to manifest in an uncontrolled form, it can grow into excessive patterns, and that is no good either.

Let's apply this to ourselves. If every time a thought occurs we tell ourselves, wagging a finger, "You are bad, you have a thought!" and we do this again and again—"You are bad, you have a thought, you are bad!" we'll start to feel guilty every time a thought occurs. The thoughts get very timid; they don't dare arise. The thoughts start to shrink back in fear, and more and more fear is created. From the Dzogchen perspective, so what if a thought arises? It is no big deal. Emotions arise, fine, no matter. Emotions have a right to arise, and you have the right not to cling to them. We should neither disturb the emotion's freedom nor our right not to get influenced and carried away.

If we educate ourselves in this way, we become much more capable of moving in any direction we choose. We become flexible people who are unafraid of ourselves. Most people suffer from being afraid of themselves, afraid of not being able to liberate the thought or emotion that is about to arise. At the moment the thought arises, they single it out as no good. You often hear that negative emotions are bad, but you don't know how to let them go. All these negative traits have been in you. But you can't *not* be how you are, so what do you do? For the unrealized person, there is only one solution: be depressed about it. All spiritual systems say negative thoughts are bad. You cannot find any that say negative thoughts are good. Really, are there any? Maybe some of them say that you should express them, let them out, but that is still because they know that negative thoughts are no good, that if you did not let them out you would just keep them festering inside. It is merely a different way of phrasing the same depressing information.

The main point is to be free of negative thought and emotion. The methods of getting rid of these differ, of course. There are oceans of books written about how to do so, from both spiritual and psychological points of view. We all understand that attachment, aggression, closed-mindedness, and all the other selfish emotions make problems for people. There is a broad agreement that negative emotional states are difficult, painful, and bad because they cause problems for ourselves and for others. Everybody is in agreement about that. But how to be free, for real? That is not a settled matter. There is a lack of clarity about how to be truly free. No matter how much it is explained or discussed or thought about, the problem remains largely unsolved. Honestly, there is only one solution: set your buttocks down on the meditation cushion and train in how to be free. As far as I am concerned, that is the only way.

There are two ways of being free. One is the general way: when an emotion is present, you use a remedy against it to make it subside and to ensure that it does not arise again. The second is the particular Dzogchen style, in which you don't apply a separate remedy but simply recognize the self-knowing wakefulness within the emotion so that it dissolves. In fact, one recognizes that the emotion does not exist to begin with.

I would like to tell a story about Angtrin, a remarkable *yogi* who lives in Tashi Jong, northern India. His spiritual tradition is the Drukpa Kagyu but his practice is Nyingma, Dzogchen, like me. When he lived in Tibet, he practiced meditation a lot and became very peaceful. He stayed in solitary retreat for six years, and the retreat situation was very comfortable, very nice. In those days, people would bring food to yogis on retreat, or if the yogi had his own ingredients, he could cook up a nice little meal for himself. There was lots of firewood around; when the sun was shining it could be quite warm; and one might even see a wide-open vista of sky. There were trees all around and various animals could be seen in the forest. The yogi might have some pride: "I am practicing the Dharma. I am very happy; it is very comfortable for me here. There are no negative emotions, no difficulties, no obstacles. I'm still young." After six years Angtrin felt that his practice was going very well indeed. But then he thought, "Well, who knows, maybe this practice has just turned me into a tranquil vegetable." So he asked his master, Khamtrul Rinpoche, "Wouldn't it perhaps be better if I went to a scary place, a rough, rugged, unpleasant place?" Khamtrul Rinpoche said, "Yes, definitely, you should go to such a place," and he gave directions to a particular location.

Arriving there, Angtrin found a huge cave where the sun never shone, with water trickling down the entrance. In the evening, a large flock of pigeons flew around inside, making a lot of noise while shitting down on him. The first day he didn't know what was going on. He put out various containers to collect the water trickling down, but when he drank from it, he said, "What is this? It has a strange taste." Later he realized it was urine from the pigeons. The cave was cold and damp, noisy, and scary at night. As he practiced there he found that his former peace of mind was tracelessly gone. He thought, "My practice has gone to pieces. Now what should I do?" And he felt that whatever he had done in the past didn't amount to much, so now he really had to practice. It was very difficult in the beginning, with the restless pigeons flying around in the dark. It was like being in the bardo, with all the turmoil and noise. Angtrin tried to cultivate this inner strength of rigpa by not surrendering himself to the distraction, by not getting carried away with the noise. He trained like that over and over again. He stayed in that place for maybe another six years. And now, whatever happens, whether it is pleasant or unpleasant, *really* doesn't affect him. He doesn't care anymore. But that doesn't mean that he ignores everything.

I believe that when Angtrin dies, he probably won't have that much trouble in the bardo. For him, all emotions are, as they say, subsumed within the expanse of rigpa. In other words, he's free. Until we reach that level, we need to practice. We must grow used to this freedom. Use as a yardstick your ability to cope with whatever emotion arises. We shouldn't aim at just feeling good when practicing. We must transcend being hijacked by the current emotion, being on the defensive against it, or trying to get rid of it. We reach this gradually, as we become more and more stable and confident in empty essence, cognizant nature, and unconfined capacity. Then we discover that the emotion does not necessarily run us over, and we don't need to get caught up in it either. We don't have to prevent or suppress the emotion. Rather, we simply allow it, spontaneously and naturally, to become an embellishment of rigpa.

STUDENT: I was going to ask about anger. I noticed I was feeling angry last night and this morning, and also feeling bad about myself for feeling angry. In practice I tried to recognize who was angry, but the thoughts kept coming and coming. Next, I switched to supported shamatha and then unsupported and then back to rigpa, which I'm not good at anyway. I wondered if you could help me—I'm not sure what to do.

RINPOCHE: Continue practicing, that's good.

STUDENT: Which practice?

RINPOCHE: All the practices—do the ngöndro, do yidam practice, practice shamatha, practice vipashyana, recognize mind essence, supplicate the guru, contemplate the four mind-changings, everything. Do prostrations and train in exchanging yourself with others, sending and taking. When you get angry, then think, "Fine, I am so lucky that this anger comes here! May this anger deplete the anger in all other beings; may this bring an end to anger in everyone else!"

STUDENT: But perhaps it perpetuates anger. If you have anger, there's the possibility of creating more anger.

RINPOCHE: It's impossible to be only angry, as if anger were an absolute. There's always a combination of different factors. As a matter of fact, nothing exists completely on its own—there's no entity like that.

There's always a support, some kind of prop to support the anger. Either it is attachment, or the feeling of "me" or of something that "should have happened but didn't." There are all sorts of thoughts that team up to justify to oneself the reason to be angry. And if some of these are taken away, the anger cannot really hold itself up as easily as before. Sometimes the issue is that "I didn't get what I wanted" or "It didn't go my way," and because of that attachment, as well as the deluded notion of "I," there is a platform for the anger. Or it could be: "I came all the way up to Nagi Gompa. I didn't come up here to be angry, but now I'm angry! This is really bad; what should I do? I must not be angry. Now I'm angry with myself for being angry." And it gets worse and worse. This is also possible.

At the moment anger arises, as with any other emotion, take a carefree attitude: "Well, I may not understand the Dharma completely, but that's how I am at present. Now I'm angry. Sometimes I'm not angry, so what? It doesn't matter that much; just let it come, let it go." If you take that kind of unworried attitude, the anger doesn't have that much of a hold, so it can't get entrenched. As I mentioned, the ego belief is anger's basis. If the ego is allowed to just dissolve, anger cannot lie around by itself, completely disconnected. It too must dissolve. If you're really smart, then cheat the ego. To cheat the ego, what must you do? You befriend ego, not as in being its real friend, but just acting like you're a friend of ego. Then ego thinks, "Great! He's very honest with me, no problem." [Laughs]

STUDENT: Is it possible to love your anger?

RINPOCHE: Sure, definitely. This is an important point. It is difficult, but possible. Giving love to the anger means giving space to the anger, telling the anger, "You seem to be so crowded here. Why don't I give you a little more room?" Giving it room could be called love, love as *giving space to*. Love here does not necessarily mean obeying anger blindly; it is another type of love, which is just to give room. It's like when your brain, your head, is really tired: giving love to the brain is to give it a break, a rest. When you're angry, you feel very confused. It's like there's a traffic jam in your emotions—you don't know what to do or how to deal with it. So just give it space, open up, don't cling, but love and accept what's going on. Don't immediately judge the anger or any other emotion as being awful; just give it some room, give it space.

STUDENT: When anger comes up, I have tried some "looking and seeing." I find the anger is still there, but it doesn't possess me. I have a little bit of distance.

RINPOCHE: That's very good, because now you are not giving all your energy to the anger, and when you are not infusing it with energy, slowly it deflates. That is entirely different from thinking, "I must get rid of it, rid of it, rid of it."

Take this example: There's a balloon in front of you, representing the anger, and the pump to inflate it is located right under your bum. You're meditating. You're saying, "Meditation, rigpa, letting go of the anger. I don't want anger. I don't want anger. Rigpa come back. I don't want anger." [*Rinpoche rocks from side to side*] Doing this, you are pumping, pumping, pumping, and the balloon inflates more and more. "I must let anger go. Rigpa must let it go." You're still pumping, pumping, pumping, and the balloon keeps filling up. Automatically, you're linked to the anger, although this is not an event that unfolds in physical space but in your mental field. Different rules apply here—if it were happening out in physical space, then you could throw something at the balloon, pop it, and the whole thing would be over. But in the mental field the energy of a situation comes from your mind, your attention, so giving credence to the anger actually pumps it up.

Shantideva mentioned that if you want to walk on a smooth, soft surface everywhere you go, it won't help to cover the entire earth with soft leather. As a matter of fact, it is impossible, so it's much more practical to just put leather under the soles of your feet, so that wherever you walk you are touching that soft leather. Similarly, we cannot control all the objects we experience, to have them be just right, although we surely try. Ordinary people fool themselves with their dualistic clinging to subject and object. meditators can fool themselves by trying to orchestrate their meditation experience. One could cling to the feeling of bliss or of being clear. But it is much better to sort out the perceiver, to handle the mind—then everything is automatically right. This is an enormously important point.

Experiences
and the Real

At a certain point we come to know how rigpa actually is, not just intellectually but in an experiential way. This is not really a complicated matter at all. At this stage it is no longer necessary to scrutinize or try to figure out rigpa. We don't need to rationally discern while experiencing rigpa—that was before recognizing, when we tried to understand the idea of it, tried to wrap our minds around it. The actual experience of rigpa is very simple, completely normal, very natural, totally straightforward. Before we have this experience, we might misunderstand it; we might have too much expectation about it. Because rigpa is explained as being so entirely different from the ordinary way of thinking, we may expect our mind to be totally blown away when the experience of rigpa finally happens, as if everything should be completely different. Or we might even try to cultivate rigpa as a paranormal experience, but honestly, rigpa is not like that, not by any means. Of course, the experience of rigpa does have the qualities of being beyond permanence and nothingness. It does not arise, dwell, or cease; it is something very subtle. Those qualities are certainly present, but not in an overwhelming sort of way that wipes out everything else. Rigpa is very normal, very gentle, very simple. We acknowledge rigpa as purely an accommodating, open state.

Look at this mala. To get rid of just one bead, it is not so easy to simply pull the bead off, is it? The bead hangs on a cord tying the whole mala together. There is a sort of holding together here. The recognition of rigpa dissolves the cord that usually holds thoughts together. The clinging doesn't announce its departure: "I am about to leave now. Now I am going. Bye!" *In the mere recognizing it is already dissolved.* Just as when the string in the rosary is gone, the whole affair naturally falls apart. You don't have to pull each bead off one by one. There is simply nothing that the beads are hanging on to any longer. In the same way, without our having to force our emotions and thoughts away, the moment the clinging is released they fall apart naturally.

Now some people are not satisfied when that happens. They don't want their beads to slowly trickle away; they desire a spectacular drama, an action scene with thoughts and emotions being blown into pieces. Formidable rigpa dramatically enters to blow the thoughts and emotions away—that would be satisfying. It's quite likely that every so often we naturally arrive in the state of rigpa, a state in which the thoughts and emotions have already dissolved, but we are still not really satisfied. We have the preconceived idea or expectation that rigpa should be *powerful*, something much more extravagant, incredibly blissful, with clarity in all directions, totally free of thought, some sort of fantastic experience. While the awakened state of rigpa is plain and simple, lucid, present, and undisturbed, we refuse to acknowledge that it is actually rigpa, because it is not fascinating enough.

About this stumbling block, all the enlightened qualities may not be fully manifest, but it is still rigpa at the beginning stage. As we train further in the true state of rigpa, these qualities gradually begin to manifest more and more, as an atmosphere of compassion and devotion. Moreover, a deeper sense of intelligence starts to become more obvious. This happens as a natural progression. To be discontent and reject the beginning stage of rigpa prevents us from training in it, and that prevents the qualities from manifesting. I would like you to be content and decisive. Baby Rigpa is very simple, very easy, very neat and smooth. Slowly allow yourself to settle evenly in that. Then, grow more and more used to it.

Right now our situation is one of nurturing Baby Rigpa, allowing its growth in the sense of *sustaining the continuity* of rigpa. As we train in this way, all types of experiences unfold—sense impressions, physical impressions, mental impressions. When awareness gets caught up in the impressions as they are presented and starts to zoom in on them, selecting certain ones and rejecting others, and is carried away by that event, this is called distraction. The continuity is interrupted by this kind of fixation. But when sense impressions and all the other input are just allowed to be experienced without loss of the continuity of rigpa's aware quality, then they are freed. Experience is liberated by our remaining undistracted.

Now here is a problem for a beginning yogi: the tendency to want so badly to establish the nature of emptiness and rest in it that he sees nangwa—experiences and perceptions—as an intruder, an opponent. The enemy has arrived: "The object appears, and *that is why* I become distracted." That warpath mentality is the actual problem. A meditator might habitually oppose objects as they arise because "they disturb my meditation; they ruin my emptiness." The basic attitude here is that the object should be wiped out, and this attitude is an obstacle to progress. Nyoshul Khen Rinpoche told me many times that in order to progress, one should have a more welcoming and inviting attitude toward sense impressions and whatever else unfolds. This sort of attitude says, "Welcome! All right, please come here, it is fine. Feel free to disturb my meditation; I don't mind." Cultivate that kind of attitude instead. Remember, nangwa includes memories and sense impressions—sights, sounds, smells, tastes, textures, and so forth—anything that could be regarded as an object. Unless you learn to relinquish the importance you assign to nangwa and don't regard it as such a big deal, you are holding yourself back from becoming an advanced meditator. The bottom line is, you can be *aware emptiness* even though perceived objects do not vanish.

There are stories of retreatants who get into a fight over a single piece of firewood and end up killing each other. Why? Because of not being able to liberate their own nangwa, their present experience. Confidence in liberation has to do with the way we experience nangwa. Everything springs from this nangwa. All the buddhafields with their amazing scenery and adornments of enlightenment are nangwa, as are all the various experiences of the six classes of beings. They are merely different ways of experiencing. We must make nangwa—our way of experiencing—very pliant, very flexible, rather than rigid like an old, hardened cowhide. The way is to know the key point of liberation. This is what it's all about for spiritual practitioners: the extent to which we are able to soften up the way we experience. Staying at a high-altitude retreat, wearing white garments, and growing our hair long are not enough for us to be called advanced meditators.

The great Kagyu masters told us, "Recognize emptiness and strengthen while experiencing." First you should recognize the open, spacious quality; then, no matter what phenomena you are experiencing, you have to acknowledge that the basic nature of that experience—the identity of that experience, the real home of whatever is being experienced—also has that empty, spacious quality. And you need to do this each and every time. The cognizant nature is never really apart, even for a second, from the empty, spacious quality. Once we acknowledge this fact, we can truly say that experience and emptiness are an indivisible unity. That is the point when pure experience can unfold. The Vajrayana principle of pure perception is possible when we allow the open, spacious quality to be acknowledged within the way we experience. Every moment of experience becomes very open and free. That is truly pure perception.

What we need here is confidence. The Tibetan word for confidence also has a connotation of being naturally capable. How does this capability come about? It comes through *knowing how to be free*. At the beginning of our training in being undistracted while not meditating, certain experiences can take place, called bliss, clarity, and nonthought. The Tibetan word for these is *nyam*, which is usually mentioned as the second of three aspects. First is theory or technical understanding, next is nyam, or the meditative experience, and the third is realization. We should take extra care not to mistake these three. In a country where the Dharma is new, there is always a mixing-up of what is seeming and what is real, the superficial and the ultimately true. There is always a tendency to confuse temporary meditation experiences, nyam, for realization. There is a famous statement: "Theory is like patchwork; it wears out and falls off. Meditation experience is like mist; it fades and vanishes. But realization is unchanging like space." Theory is just getting the idea of something: "Ah-ha! This is how it is." But it's never guaranteed how long we can maintain such an insight. It's like a patch. In Tibet when you got a tear in your clothes you'd put on a patch. It might not be stitched on with much skill, just stuck on haphazardly, so that after a while it would fall off. That is the metaphor for intellectual insight.

A meditative experience may at times arrive most compellingly, but like mist, it eventually vanishes and then the sun shines again. Then another cloud comes and the thunder cracks. The weather changes all the time. Are these nyam experiences good or not? They are good, not bad. They happen because of meditation practice. What is the problem then? The problem comes when one believes they are the state of realization. A disciple of the sixteenth Karmapa came for an interview after a spectacular nyam and said, "My body feels like it's made out of rainbows. I don't feel obstructed in any direction. I am almost sure I am enlightened. I can't find any flaw anywhere." The Karmapa replied, "It is very easy to settle whether you are enlightened or not. Go up to the top of that building over there and jump. If you are not dead after you hit the ground, you must be a buddha. If you die, of course, it is a shame, but we will do some meritorious rituals for your benefit." That test is a bit tough, isn't it? Please don't try it!

I'll give you a less drastic test to check whether a particular state is nyam or realization. Sometimes a nyam can be "I am totally enlightened. My entire body is bliss, clarity, transparent. Wow! This is enlightenment. Nothing can harm me. I am also full of compassion. I am nothing. I am so blissful, so full of care! I am going to save the entire world! Oh, come to me, everyone! Come here, I will teach you! Bewildered masses, I will help you." You can certainly have this type of nyam. In one way it is good because it shows that you are *approaching* the true state of practice. Meditation can produce this sort of temporary experience. To test it, light a big candle and put your finger into the flame. If you can still say, "I am enlightened. I love everyone. I am so full of goodness" without getting burned, then, wow, I bow to you! But if it is terribly painful, then keep practicing, taking refuge, accumulating merit, and developing compassion. You still need to progress in rigpa.

Realization and enlightenment have different meaning in Buddhist terminology. You can be realized to a certain extent but not yet enlightened. In the West the word "enlightenment" is used in various ways, but in my tradition enlightenment takes a little longer to reach: it is the completely awakened state of buddhahood. There are two aspects to liberation, one being mental liberation free of emotions and so on, and the other a physical liberation free of all karmic bonds. Until that second phase happens, please carefully observe the law of cause and effect. You are still under its rule! When you forget, you can always put your finger in the flame and see if it still affects you.

Among the three kinds of nyam—bliss, clarity, and nonthought—the experience of nonthought comes from empty essence. This experience of having no conceptual thought whatsoever can sometimes last an hour or two without any thought at all, just very serene and peaceful. It can even last for several days, which is very good. The problem lies in mistaking this for something else; it could be mistaken for realization. It is not a problem to experience this state; the problem is clinging to it. "Wow! No thoughts! Now karma has ceased. Nothing obscures me. No pollution, nothing covers my state." Even if you have that sort of experience, don't be fascinated. Don't cling. It is just the *experience* of nonthought.

Second is the nyam of clarity, which you can say is a reflection of, or an expression of, having grown more accustomed to the cognizant nature.[2] Whenever you grow used to something there is an effect—an indirect effect and an authentic effect. The indirect effect is the nyam of clarity: "Wow! I know everybody's mind! What he is thinking is so clear. I know what is happening far away. I can see what is happening in other people's rooms. My friend is going to come." Sometimes that clarity experience could be slightly affected by realization, but mostly it's not. The real clarity is clairvoyance and, even further, realization of the three times. One can ask a buddha any question about past, present, or future, and instantaneously there is an answer.

Let me tell you a story about enlightened clairvoyance. At the time of the Buddha there was a man who had attained accomplishment in his particular path. From the Buddhist point of view it was a mundane path, meaning a refinement of dualistic mind. This man had a certain degree of clairvoyance, but he did not have complete omniscience like the Buddha. One day, he thought, "The Buddha cannot be for real. He must be brought down a notch or two!" So he called his followers to help him with an elaborate test. They gathered around an enormous tree that had recently been cut down and spent a long time counting all the leaves, twigs, and branches very exactly. It took several months to make an accurate count, and they wrote it all down very carefully. Since the Buddha would pass by every morning on his way to receive alms, they invited him to their village, asked him to take a seat, and gathered around him. The teacher then asked the Buddha, "How many leaves were on that tree?" The Buddha immediately told the exact number of leaves. They were dumbfounded. What had taken them so long to laboriously calculate the Buddha knew in a fraction of a second. The story goes that the teacher was so shocked that he dropped dead on the spot, because the Buddha knew immediately what he had taken so much trouble to find.

The Buddha's way of knowing is not a process of inference, not a "this because of that," but rather a way of perceiving directly, an *immedi-*

---

[2] Cognizance and clarity are the same Tibetan word.

ate perception. For example, you see smoke on a mountainside and then reason that there must be a fire burning there. You do not see the flames directly, but rather you infer that they are there. A buddha's way of knowing is not through deduction but through direct perception. That ability stems from the cognizant nature. The basic sense of knowing has, in the case of a buddha, become unimpeded. Haven't I told you many times that rigpa has a natural knowing that does not cling? Its perfection is a buddha's knowing. Before it is perfected we encounter various experiences, different nyam. When faced with these nyam, some people feel, "Wow! I am enlightened now." But they get into trouble if they start to behave as if they are enlightened. Some people know deep down they are not enlightened, but they still pretend. I have no doubt some other people sincerely *believe* they are enlightened. It makes me feel very sorry for them because they blindly trust it and don't know my simple finger-in-a-flame test to check it. I will happily sponsor the candle. *[Laughs]*

Empty essence and cognizant nature are an indivisible unity. As we become more accustomed to this unity, we experience a deep sense of ease, and that is the bliss experience, the bliss nyam. As you train more and more, it can suffuse the entire body. It feels as if even the nails and hair are blissful. The whole body is blissful from top to bottom, as well as everything we perceive, even people. You think, "I used to hate New York, but now I like it so much. Times Square is wonderful! There is no problem here, no stress. New York is so pleasant. It is not difficult to survive here. Everyone in New York is so nice." If that is happening on your cushion, while you're not in New York, then it is nyam. If it is happening while you are in New York, it could be realization. *[Laughs]* Sitting in your room, you may feel that there is not a problem in the world, but really, there is one problem: you are clinging to that feeling of ease and well-being.

We do not have to sidestep these experiences, these meditation moods. They are part of the practice package, so to speak. Attempting to avoid them by suppressing their arising only hampers realization. They should be allowed to happen and seen for what they are: indicators of meditation training. Just don't cling to them.

Here is another example of the difference between these meditation moods and actual realization. It happened to me, but maybe not to you. When I was young and living in India, I went with a couple of monks to see a Bruce Lee movie. We walked out of the cinema hall feeling like Bruce Lee. Seeing a couple of young Indian boys, we felt, "They are no match for us, we can easily knock them out!" This was the Bruce Lee nyam. In reality, if one of us had walked over to the Indians to mouth off, he would probably have been punched in the face and had his nose slit and his ear chopped off. He was not Bruce Lee, but only had a *feeling* of being Bruce Lee from having seen him in the movie. Likewise, you can say rigpa has a similar effect, so that any state that comes close to it gets affected by its atmosphere of realization.

A real kung fu expert is entirely different. Even surrounded by twenty people he can still outdo them. But I don't think the true kung fu expert gets into the nyam of a kung fu expert. He has something better: confidence. The best situation is someone who is confident and compassionate—not just the mood but the real thing. For example, imagine this movie scene of a kung fu expert: an old man who is shorter than me, big in the belly, comes in carrying a bottle of wine. He is smiling, not frozen, but peaceful, kind, and confident. He gives the impression of someone who can handle anything. He laughs and fights at the same time; the camera circles him panoramically. Sometimes he throws the wine bottle up in the air, fights a bit, then catches the bottle and has a drink. You can see he is relaxed. This is the example of a good meditator. You have a very open, relaxed, unoccupied attitude; you are not absorbed in your own stuff, so your mind is clear and ready. The best meditator is always simple—more simple than simple. Emptiness is more simple than simple, in the sense that you cannot find any *thing*. It is always open, relaxed, fresh. Any enemy that comes—anger, attachment, anything—you don't reject it, you just let it be self-liberated. That is quite different from kung fu.

In short, do not mistake nyam meditation moods for realization. You do not need to reject them either. They are fine to have—just don't cling to them. If you do not cling, you can continue to progress. Progress is made through devotion to the buddhas and your own root and lineage masters, compassion for sentient beings, and also renunciation—the will to be free. In short, you progress through loving-kindness, compassion, the view, and perseverance in meditation training.

Follow a basic rhythm for progress. You only have two legs to walk on. You can ask, "How do I walk by a beautiful person? How do I walk by an ugly person? How do I walk if there is a flower garden?" Each of these questions has the same answer, and that answer is very simple: keep the basic rhythm of walking. Because you walk, you see the flower; because you walk, you see the garden; you walk, you see. It's a natural rhythm. You don't need to *do* much to anything you see, just keep walking. Regardless of whether it feels blissful or clear or free of thought, no matter what, continue in the continuity of rigpa.

STUDENT: Is there an ultimate lesson to learn in any of the nyam, even if we do not cling?

RINPOCHE: Let's distinguish here between relative and ultimate truth. You are moving along in daily life and something requires your attention. You relate to the matter at hand because there is a need. You could call that a lesson, as there is an obvious reason to deal with it. Sitting on a meditation cushion, however, you do not have to *do* anything about what happens. As a matter of fact, since nyam is merely a temporary experience, there is nothing to it. You don't always have to decipher the message, not at all. If you get a strong feeling that a tiger is coming from behind, and it is a *really* strong feeling, maybe you should just turn your head and see if in fact there is a tiger, and if there is, then run away. Other than this, you do not have to label it "meditative inspiration." Suppose you live in an iron house: even if a hundred tigers come, they can't get in. If you find you are still scared that a tiger may come inside, then you should realize it is a pointless meditation mood, and so you don't follow it—you let it go. You know whether something requires attention; the cognizant nature knows. This cognizant nature is intelligent enough to know whether something needs to be taken seriously. If it is a matter of life and death, a matter of survival, then you take it seriously. Respect it because you are not yet enlightened. You are still affected by such things.

We shouldn't mix up the relative and ultimate truth, even though it seems quite popular to do so. There is a huge difference between believing what is seemingly real and seeing what is actually real. The first situation occurs when we do not look closely; the second when we look carefully and see how it actually is. The difference is due only to not looking. Once we look closely, there is no longer any real dividing line. We are not fooled by what is seeming but simply see what is real.

STUDENT: What about drowsiness clouding the cognizant nature?

RINPOCHE: There are two ways of being drowsy. One type of drowsiness is simple fatigue, physical tiredness due to many things—imbalances in the flow of energies and essences, a certain low energy, or having concentrated too hard, having worked a lot so that naturally the body feels drowsy and tired. That doesn't necessarily mean that rigpa is obscured—not at all. The other type of drowsiness is usually called cognitive obscuration or basic unknowing. This happens on a mental level and of course obscures because it is the opposite of rigpa. With physical tiredness, it is possible to not be obscured. Within the physically caused drowsiness, it is possible not to lose rigpa's continuity and instead feel more open and lucid even though the body is tired and seemingly nodding off. One could use that situation to expand rigpa even further. This depends entirely upon what you understand by cognitive nature, how you identified it initially. If it's the clarity of the senses, then when the senses go dim you think cognitive nature has grown dim. This is where *distinguishing* is essential—distinguishing between dualistic mind and rigpa, between sensory brightness and rigpa's lucidity.

These ways of distinguishing are very important; otherwise, we can be mistaken. You are awake in the daytime and your senses have a bright quality—how you see, hear, and so forth—which is related to the physical situation. It is interconnected with the essences in the body being recharged, so that you feel invigorated, alive, and present. Suppose you now identify that as being cognizant nature, rigpa's awake quality. Then when you get tired it feels as if rigpa is somehow diminished or only half there. In other words, to identify rigpa as the physical clarity of the senses makes you feel as if the cognizant quality has dimmed when you are tired or drowsy. This is because of having initially misidentified rigpa. We may then believe that we need to expand the spaciousness in the physical clarity of the senses, and that the state of rigpa is to rest in sensory brightness. This being so, "rigpa" is lost every time we get tired and drowsy. The person who trains in this way will of course find it impossible to be liberated into dharmakaya at the moment of death.

The empty essence has a spaciousness together with a lucid cognizance that is independent of what is happening on the screen of perception. Rigpa is *not* defined by sensory clarity, which comes and goes. You can notice this difference when you catch the flu, for example. Your sinuses are congested, all your senses are blocked, and you feel very heavy. That is a good time to notice the cognizant quality. Or maybe you are really exhausted and your physical energy has gone way down— but that does not mean that the openness, the atmosphere that hosts the whole event, has disappeared. This lucid emptiness can host the drowsiness as well. It is still there; it never goes anywhere. This is true whether the guest is anger, drowsiness, or anything else. That is why we must distinguish between sensory brightness and the lucid quality of rigpa. Otherwise we may think, "Now I can't practice. There is no clarity, so I can't recognize." We may have misidentified the cognizant quality.

Of course it feels better to be well. There is no question about that; our meditative state feels more smooth. We are healthy and energetic, and there is more brightness, an uplifted quality to the whole affair. Let me say this one more time: we should *not* confuse this with cognizance, because then it can seem that rigpa's quality depends upon the sharpness of the senses, and this is not true. We should aim higher than that, not at a "cognizant quality" that is anchored in the material body. There is certainly a connection between the two right now, but we should identify the true cognizant quality, rigpa's lucidity, as *not* based in physical matter.

This is why I sometimes ask students to suddenly close their eyes in the state of rigpa. This is to prevent them from being too dependent upon the clarity of the eyesight, on the brightness of visual input, which is *not* the cognizant nature. We need to put our awareness to the test in different situations—sometimes sitting in a brightly lit, open area, sometimes in pitch-black darkness, sometimes with open eyes, sometimes with closed eyes, and in all sorts of physical positions. We should test rigpa in this way so that we become more independent of sensory clarity.

The physical body with the senses has a certain structure of channels, energies, and essences. The unfolding of sensory experience is connected with bindu essences. It is connected with the brain and with the white and red essences that were initially received from one's father and mother. As long as all of that circulates and is kept alive in a body, there is a certain vibrancy or vivid quality to each moment of sensory experience. But that is entirely different from rigpa's lucid quality. Whatever is connected with the body is interrupted at the moment of death, but the cognizant quality is much more fundamental. It is intrinsic to mind, and mind is not physical matter. That is why sensory experience ceases at death but cognizance doesn't. The cognizant quality is uninterrupted at death. It carries on through the bardo, the next life and the next life, on and on continuously until buddhahood. After complete enlightenment, the cognizant quality is named the omniscience that sees the nature as it is and perceives whatever possibly exists.

This cognizant quality does not vanish when you are unconscious either. It is rather that there is a lack of recognizing it. If somebody knocks you out with a big stick, it is not that mind vanishes, just that you become unconscious; your sense consciousnesses withdraw like when you fall asleep at night. You wake up again in the morning, right?

While encased in a physical body, dualistic mind is cognizant, but this cognizance is constantly involved in conditioned ways of perceiving, labeling, and thinking. "Conditioned" means there is a certain dependence upon sensory input. In the case of an ordinary person, not an advanced practitioner, this dependency is a very strong habit. At the moment of death, such a person's conditioned mode of perceiving falls apart, since the physical support for sensory cognition disintegrates. The mind that is dependent upon that input no longer feels the presence of anything solid, so it panics and faints.

Just because mind is cognizant does not mean that it knows itself. The empty essence of this cognizant quality is not necessarily obvious to the conditioned mind, not even at the moment of death. Don't think that every sentient being has an automatic recognition of mind essence; it simply doesn't happen. Rather than knowing itself at the moment of death, the normal person's mind faints. But this state of unconsciousness is only temporary, not permanent. Something starts to happen again, and the mind looks around, notices what is going on, and is soon in the bardo of becoming.

I would like to introduce three aspects here. One is that all experience unfolds due to a combination of channels, energies, essences and mind. Pure and impure experience is all based on a certain way that energy moves in the channels. When cognitive scientists try to figure out how experience unfolds while one is alive in a human body, they may be looking at one level of channels and energies—the neural network and its currents—but there are two more levels. There is the conditioned perceiver, meaning the functioning of conditioned mind, which is the second factor. And there is the third factor, which is the basic nature of this mind, explained in this book as essence, nature, and capacity. While we are in a body, all visual experience is dependent upon this structure of energies in the channels and how they move. The other sensory input also depends upon the channels and energies. When we communicate and talk, when you hear words being said, all of that takes place within the system of channels, energy currents, and so forth. Now please understand that there is also the *perceiving of all that input,* which is the conditioned mind. At present, this perceiving mind seems to take its support from the sensory input.

Death interrupts the body-based channels and energy currents, but this does not mean that the perceiving mind and its basic nature is interrupted. Nor does this mean that it becomes enlightened. It is still conditioned, but because it is receiving no input, its conditioned way of perceiving is temporarily suspended. In other words, it doesn't *feel* as it did before. The perceiving mind hears no words being spoken; there is no feeling of physical touch, no light taken in through the eyes—all of that is halted. This disembodied mind—which we call the bardo being or spirit—clearly does not experience the world as we do right now. There is no solidity anywhere. Experience feels totally different, but the conditioned mind is still perceiving. It has a new situation, and this setup is called a mental body. Again, being disembodied does *not* guarantee that mind recognizes its own nature and awakens to enlightenment. It just continues being conditioned. The opportunity is certainly there. Suppose this mind was a practitioner with prior training who knew how to recognize his or her own nature; then it would be possible for this mind to attain true and complete enlightenment by recognizing dharmakaya and attaining stability in that. The option is still open.

The conditioned mind is so used to being in a physical body. It is habituated to always getting input presented through the nerve channels and energy currents. When all of a sudden the stream of input is cut off, it is so surprised, shocked, ultra-traumatized, that it faints. It shuts off for a short while, usually mentioned as a couple of days. Then something starts to happen again, a sort of waking up. What unfolds then is the bardo experience, which is entirely different from how we normally experience things.

STUDENT: If our experience of rigpa changes back and forth, how can we ever gain confidence in what true rigpa is?

RINPOCHE: It has a lot to do with your personal aspirations and how you resolve to persevere. Determination makes all the difference, because our rigpa does fluctuate, experientially, until we reach the first bodhisattva level. From that point onward there is no more falling back or straying into confusion. The path is now a steady, smooth journey. Before that, we forget, then we remember, we forget, then we remember—flickering back and forth. Don't expect that because yesterday we were introduced to rigpa, we recognized it as a glimpse, now we are set. A glimpse of experience isn't going to transform everything or carry us all the way to enlightenment. It doesn't happen like that. Only at the first bodhisattva level do you have true confidence, a confidence that does not waver any longer.

So how can we be confident right now? How can we really trust in the awakened state? A lot of factors need to come together. One component is trust in your guru and his instructions. Another is your understanding, your own sense of intelligence, and in this regard it may make sense to study more teachings and philosophy so you can settle the matter intellectually. A third component is the creation of merit that lifts you and pushes you forward. Many other factors as well combine to make you move in the right direction and feel more confident. But at this early point, right now, if you rely only on your own confidence, the whole affair is quite shaky, flickering back and forth. Sometimes your experience is clear, sometimes not. So it is not enough to rely only on ourselves at this point: we need something more.

There comes a point when we are almost self-reliant, known as the path of joining, which is after the path of accumulation. When you arrive at the path of seeing, which corresponds to the first bodhisattva level, you are completely independent. Your own experience is then the actuality of rigpa, with no confusion any longer. From then on you are independent, absolutely self-reliant in proceeding onward to a buddha's true and complete enlightenment.

I'll give you a very simple example. Say you want to go to Hawaii: that is called *your mind turning to the Dharma.* You look for a travel agent, and you either walk there in person or you call up on the telephone. You give your credit card number and your address, and you say, "Send me a ticket." That is *Dharma becoming the path.* The journey has become real: you now have the ticket in hand, but it is still not certain that you will be traveling. Circumstances could change matters—your finances, health, family, lover can all influence you. Your initial wish in itself is not enough, as you can still be influenced. Even though you are booked to go on the first of January, it is still not guaranteed. Therefore you need to make some prayers, and you must create merit. You need the blessings from your girlfriend, from your bank account, from your good health. When the time comes and you are in your car on the way to the airport, you still need to pray, because you haven't reached the airport yet. Then you get to the check-in counter and they check you in, but it is still not guaranteed; the situation could still change. Now you are walking up the stairs to the airplane, but as you have seen in the movies so many times, it is still possible to turn back. People exit the airplane at the last moment. Now they close the doors and start the engines, but even here it is still not sure. Takeoff is really the decisive moment. Once you are in the air, there is no saying, "I won't go," unless you somehow hijack the plane and force it to turn around. After takeoff, you are no longer dependent upon your girlfriend's permission or on a bank statement or anything. You are moving in the desired direction automatically, and if there are no major obstacles in the air, you will land in Hawaii. Likewise, once you reach the first bodhisattva level, you may want to say, "Actually, I changed my mind, I don't want enlightenment. I want to return to samsaric confusion!" But it is too late. You cannot go back.

Right now, we need to depend upon the instructions of a qualified master, the accumulation of merit, our own determination and will, and many other factors to move in the right direction. As we chant in the morning, "Until I attain enlightenment, I ask you for help. I take refuge." Implicitly this means, "Once I get there I don't need you any longer." We don't have to read this in a negative way, but once you have fully arrived, you no longer need any external support because you yourself are there.

The main point I would like to get across is this: it is quite likely that we have recognized the view of the Great Perfection, and it is quite likely that we experience the view of the Great Perfection on a daily basis, but for some reason we are just not happy with it; we want something else. It is not satisfying enough. We want to keep something in mind instead, a conditioned state; we want to *do* something. At the same time, we would like to pretend that the habit of mental doing is Dzogchen. That's a problem! The dilemma here is that you mistake the fabrication for rigpa. The reality is that a mistaken pretension is nothing but another conditioned state. So watch out for that. Our habit is to bite and chew on *something*. While in rigpa there is nothing to chew on, so the thought arises: "I wish there were something to chew. Maybe I should cultivate the calm state of shamatha, or maybe do some tsa-lung, some yoga, to conjure up a special state or recite a mantra to accomplish something. Then the job would be done. There would be something to chew on there." If that is the intention—to find something to chew on—a year could pass like that, another year, and so on, then we look back and say, "I have practiced Dzogchen for five years now, and what have I gotten out of it? Nothing!"

Dzogchen is not to fall for the habitual tendency of getting something to chew on. Hoping that the result of chewing is Dzogchen only leads to a big disappointment. Each type of training has its own outcome, its own result. So it would be a bit confused to hope for a different outcome from what a practice leads to.

To conclude, please understand that it is possible to be extremely simple and ordinary in the state of rigpa. The message is: be happy with it, be content. Don't expect it to be something amazing—it isn't. You may want something fabulous, but the hankering after something amazing is nothing other than desire.

The awakened state of mind is entirely the opposite of complicated. It is not a bomb to explode dualistic mind. If rigpa were a material entity, you could have a situation of one thing that blows away another. Well, it isn't. Rigpa is not an explosive that blows away all your concepts. It is much more gentle than that. You could say that it is the atmosphere that allows clinging to dissolve. Rigpa is not the antidote to thoughts and emotions, because then it would be one conditioned article getting rid of another. Do not develop the battlefield mentality that rigpa must wipe out its opponent. Neither is rigpa a powerful storm that moves in to scatter whatever needs to be gotten rid of and then, with lightning and tornadoes whirling about, somehow zaps your mind clean. It is not as though a specific announcement is necessary, with horns blowing and trumpets blaring, and then rigpa walks in like a king or a high lama arriving in a grand procession. Rather, rigpa seeps in beneath you, sneaks up from behind. Without any prior notice, rigpa is already present in the moment of being recognized. Within that atmosphere, your everyday clinging is not being driven out by an enforcer. Rigpa is not your policeman, but more like the atmosphere within which clinging naturally dissolves.

FEARLESSNESS

Over time, whether or not we feel that our practice is flourishing, we must occasionally examine ourselves. We can detect our progress from certain external signs, just as we can infer fire from seeing smoke. We definitely must progress, otherwise there's not much use in practicing. Change by itself is not enough—one could also change for the worse. We need to change in a good way.

The kind of change I bring up we don't necessarily notice from one day to the next; it's seen more over the course of several years. Three or four years from now, we should look back to when we received the Dzogchen teachings and ask ourselves: "During this time, what has happened? Have I improved or not?" This is the point at which we should be able to notice a difference between how we used to be and how we are now. The first line of the Four Dharmas of Gampopa is this wish: "Grant your blessings that my mind may turn to the Dharma." That wish has already been fulfilled, otherwise we wouldn't be studying the Buddhist teachings. It's the second of the Four Dharmas we should look out for: whether or not our spiritual practice has become the path, the real path.

There are three signs that show whether we are progressing: devotion, compassion, and intelligence. The presence of these three is proof that our Dharma practice is going well. Intelligence in this context refers to our recognition of original wakefulness, which is empty in essence, cognizant by nature, and unconfined in its capacity. It is through recognizing and training in this wakefulness that devotion and compassion can unfold as its natural expression. The main theme I teach is the third—intelligence or insight, which in Tibetan is *sherab*—but I hope and expect that when we thoroughly develop intelligence, devotion and compassion will naturally follow. Without true intelligence it's very hard to have real devotion and compassion. But whether it actually happens is an individual matter.

How does true devotion come about? Let's say that you not only recognized the empty essence of your mind but also have gained a certain confidence in being freed from the bondage of selfish emotions. You feel genuinely assured that no matter the emotion, you're able to be free. This is something you did not know before, so you find yourself delighted at such a discovery: "This is the way to solve the problem of negative emotions!" For the first time you become a friend to yourself and to your emotions. You are not rejecting them, and they don't rob or steal from you. "No problem. Fine. Anything may happen in my mind. I know how to liberate it." And because of that liberation, you achieve a very strong confidence inside yourself. That self-confidence brings you a profound peace and also a sense of joy.

At this point, you gently reflect on how you were before and realize: "Oh, well, I made a fair number of mistakes, but I'm not going to hate myself for it." So you reflect first on your mistakes, and at the same time you're happy because you now know the key point. You have released a nagging worry, and you continue to practice more. And somehow you find you enjoy the emotions, but not in the same old self-righteous way. You have a lot of openness, so that anything may come along, absolutely anything. If an emotion is useful, you walk along with it, you talk with it, you use that emotion. If an emotion is not so useful, you know how to let it go. You take charge of the emotion rather than being its slave. To any emotion that comes you say, "Welcome!" It becomes very easy for you to be with it, and because of this you are unworried, at ease, and joyful. In addition, you have a strong confidence that is grounded in liberation.

Because of this training in being free, you can gradually begin to like yourself. You can truly appreciate yourself. "This practice is really good. I'm so lucky. I'm born in America. I'm happy to be in samsara." At this point, somehow you enjoy staying in samsara. You don't see samsara as especially negative. You see that it is simply a mental projection, which you know how to liberate. Staying in samsara doesn't scare you anymore. This confidence arises from your recognition of mind essence. On top of that you now have very strong trust in the Dharma, especially in Mahayana and the Dzogchen teachings: "These teachings are really alive; they've changed me and they've changed my attitude. The teachings are so great!"

Such growing appreciation of this way of being—so free and easy—comes about through having practiced the teaching of recognizing mind essence. So, automatically, you really treasure the instructions on how to be free. These teachings are transmitted through a lineage of masters. You understand that it is this way of liberation that all the masters have realized and have passed on. You cannot help really appreciating not only the realization you have now tasted, not only the teachings that bring forth this realization, but also all the masters through whom the teachings have passed. And this appreciation, this rejoicing in the value of the teachings and trusting them, and your trust in the lineage masters all fuse together into something that can be called devotion.

Devotion is not just one entity, one single feeling. It's a combination of all these factors. Mainly it is to appreciate and rejoice in something that is for real, based on your personal experience. You have already experienced what it's really about, and therefore you can appreciate, you can trust, you can rejoice in its value. This is devotion: taking sincere delight in the teachings. This devotion is something that you cannot help feeling. It arises involuntarily as a sense of sincere appreciation. This type of devotion is deeply linked with blessings.

We need to receive the blessings, and devotion is necessary in order for this to happen. Without devotion, the blessings never manifest. First there is this open, carefree state, where you feel good about yourself. You rejoice in this way of being. It's a feeling that this is really your natural state. Because of this, no matter what is experienced, it's really no trouble. It doesn't bother you. It feels like arriving home—it feels that good. It's the true feeling of home, of being safe, secure, and embraced by comfort from all directions. It's that type of well-being. So you really appreciate the value of the Dzogchen teachings that brought about such confidence: "Without this confidence, I would always have been caught up in *the perceived*, like frozen ice. Now I feel as fluid as water. I really respect the value of these teachings!" There is a sense of deep appreciation: "Being like this is thanks to the Dharma, thanks to the Great Perfection. My true home is thanks to the blessings of the lineage masters—Dharmakaya Buddha Samantabhadra, buddhas of the five families, Vajrasattva, Garab Dorje, Manjushrimitra, Shri Singha, Vimalamitra, Padmasambhava, twenty-five disciples, and 108 major tertöns, Chokgyur Lingpa, Tsewang Norbu, Samten Gyatso, Dilgo Khyentse Rinpoche,

Tulku Urgyen Rinpoche, Nyoshul Khen Rinpoche—I really appreciate all of you, thanks a lot!"

Devotion lets the blessings mature in your stream of being. When devotion is really strong it blows your heart open. Devotion is a feeling, and when this strong feeling arises, dualistic mind cannot keep hold of everything. It gets overwhelmed, is at a complete loss about what to grasp at any longer, and just falls to pieces. Now you are genuinely open.

Devotion is the first of the three signs of progress. The second, true compassion, comes about in the same way as devotion: through recognizing your own essence and taking delight in knowing how to liberate every confused state of mind. You understand that confusion occurs, you understand how to free that confusion, and you feel extremely at ease with that freedom. It's a very deep feeling of rejoicing, delight, harmony, and well-being.

You're not afraid of yourself; you have a sense of harmony, well-being, and freedom. With devotion, the main feeling was that of appreciation. In compassion, the main feeling is a sense of taking responsibility: "Thanks to the Dzogchen teachings, I'm able to liberate all these emotions. This is so precious! And the same possibility exists for every other sentient being. It's not acceptable to relax alone and feel good all by myself. I must do something, but what should I do? All sentient beings get helplessly carried away by their emotions, which are so strong. They're unfree. I cannot really be angry at other people who act selfishly only because they get swept away by their emotions. They're not in charge of themselves; they're out of control." As you consider this, you *are* compassionate. As a matter of fact, compassion comes spontaneously just from thinking in this way. And inevitably, the next feeling you have is, "It's not good enough just to be at ease for my own benefit. What can I do?"

Your compassion is not yet capable of liberating all beings, but it is basically present. You feel somewhat sad and at the same time joyful. You want to take responsibility for others' well-being, but you don't know how. It's a very peculiar feeling. You feel at ease, and yet you're troubled. You feel happy yet sad at the same time. It's a bittersweet feeling. This compassion creates a deeper sense of perseverance in practice. You notice that your capability is not fully developed, but still you really want to help others, you *must* help them, so you feel the need to practice much more than in the past. Such compassion should and does happen spontaneously as the result of Dzogchen training.

This compassionate atmosphere is not necessarily directed at a particular person for a specific reason, as in "He's sick, poor guy!" It's more like *being* the compassion itself. You have now arrived at the authentic Dzogchen way of developing compassion: being the very atmosphere of compassion. Because you as a person and the compassion are identical, of the same identity, you are automatically a compassionate person, and whatever you do is an expression of this compassion. Benevolent deeds come naturally. Rather than mentally fabricating compassion or mentally fabricating devotion, they well up or manifest out of the natural state.

This is how to have strong confidence, deep confidence. You are confident because the selfish emotions really do vanish. When the selfish emotions dissolve, there's no enemy anywhere; and as you have no adversary, you can be completely at ease. You can now truly rejoice in yourself! Not only do you rejoice in yourself; you start to like other people as well. Earlier there was a certain resistance to appreciating your mother-in-law, perhaps, but now it feels easier. You discover you actually like her! You take pleasure in dealing with people who previously seemed challenging with whom you had a hard time. You're happy to be with them.

Together with this delight and this self-assurance comes a growing sense of being responsible, of wanting to take responsibility. You start to care more and more about others and are concerned for their welfare: "This potential for being free that I have discovered and am confident in is also present in everyone else. What is wrong with them? I wish they were also free. Why aren't they? They have the potential, but they don't seem to recognize it. They don't seem to acknowledge that this way of being is possible." You feel somewhat saddened, but at the same time, because you're seeing the possibility, you're also delighted that they can be free. It's a sweet-and-sour feeling, a mixture of sadness and joy. As it starts to grow in you, you become willing to take on even greater responsibility for the well-being of others. This compassion is the root from which the bodhisattva's benevolent attitude grows.

This basic compassionate attitude is a mixture of being confident in oneself, of taking delight in oneself, and of liking others. It's a caring for others, not wanting to turn one's back on them any longer, not forsaking a single sentient being, but really wanting others to be happy. And also there's a sense of being a little frustrated: "Why aren't other beings free? Why don't they just see? What can I do about this? I must *do* something! But if I just tell them, they don't seem to understand." You care; you're frustrated and a little bit sad also. But in the sadness, there is some sense of well-being. It's like a good chili pepper. You like it, but it burns you, but still you like it. A very, very good chili is hard for your tongue, and not only hard for your tongue, but at the other end there is a problem as well. You know all this, but still you like to eat the chili pepper. So it's a mixed feeling. On the one hand, you want to give up on sentient beings because they don't understand. But on the other hand, you can't give up on them because they *can* understand; the possibility is still there. They have the capacity to understand, just as you did. You care and you want to take responsibility; you want to help. This caring attitude of compassion needs to have open eyes. It needs the eyes of wisdom or intelligence in order to be true compassion, in order to be capable of showing the method to be free.

Problems can arise when compassion and intelligence are out of balance. Too much understanding of emptiness without compassion can be a problem, and so can compassion without intelligence. We need all three: devotion, compassion, and intelligence. As you practice genuinely with all three qualities, as your compassion and trust develop further, conflicts among people diminish and personal problems tend to dissolve.

Let me give an example. A lot of people have asked me over the years: "My mother and father don't like the Dharma. What should I do to make them become Buddhists? What should I tell them?" There is nothing to say to them, really, because your mother and father love you no matter how you are. As a sign of practice you may become a more responsible person and not so wild and rebellious as in the past. You become more kind and more in charge of yourself. Your parents, of course, look at you all the time, and they notice the difference. So they say to themselves: "I used to think he went to India and Nepal just to take drugs, but it seems he actually has improved. I wonder what happened?" Then your parents will ask you: "What happened, what are you doing?" That's the opportunity to speak, not before. Now you can explain, with respect for them, and the evidence is with you, because you *have* changed. That is the only way to effectively convince your parents—or anyone else, for that matter. If instead you have grown worse—more antagonistic, more emotional, more dogmatic, and more closed-minded—and then you begin to talk about the Buddha—"He said this, compassion is like this, emptiness is like that"—people will close their eyes and ears and seal them with glue. They will never listen but just say, "Total nonsense!" and walk away. To sum up, we need to change ourselves, become more compassionate, more confident, and have more insight. When that really happens, then you have true signs that your Buddhist practice is going well.

Along with devotion and compassion, the third quality is intelligence, which is what I mainly try to teach. Intelligence in this context means to be unobscured and lucid, an atmosphere of being present in a way that is willing to accommodate any situation. Whenever that is the case, there is a clarity that liberates any moment of negative emotion. That is *real* intelligence, and that is how our training should be.

Suppose you notice after three, five, or six years of practice that, rather than experiencing more devotion, you have only become more prejudiced and more closed-minded, that you have less appreciation for the Dharma, and that rather than being more insightful you feel dull and obscured. Rather than being more compassionate, you are more aggressive, irritable, and selfish. If this is the case, you should really watch out.

Of course we may get angry from time to time. Of course we occasionally feel dull or attached, but that is not the point here—that is just a fleeting upheaval, a temporary obstacle on the path, and not a major concern. It can be dealt with. What I mention here is something else: if we have trained ourselves to become more irritable, more unreasonable, to such an extent that we are almost irritation itself or animosity itself, attachment or closed-mindedness itself, we have surely trained in a wrong view. If that is the case, we should *really* watch out.

The momentary occurrence of negative emotion is not such a big deal, because our mind can think any possible thought. There is no limit to the thoughts and emotions that can arise. Sometimes one may even think that the Dharma is totally worthless, while at other times one may think it is so wonderful. Any thought is possible—but still, behind it all, we are very confident that spiritual practice is truly valuable. Momentary thoughts are not really a problem.

If after five or six years you find that you are really moving in the wrong direction, then you definitely need a consultation with your root guru, whoever that may be. Go see your main teacher, or one of the many great masters alive, and ask for advice. Tell him honestly, "This and this are happening to me. What should I do? How can I improve?" Many of you present-day practitioners are very fortunate. You have connected with authentic guides, real masters who have received advice, teachings, and instructions from their own masters. Communicate with your guru directly, so you can clear up any misunderstanding. If you follow your teacher in the right way, you won't go in the wrong direction. There are also many centers in all different parts of the world, Dharma study and practice groups. To connect with and use the support of fellow practitioners is also a great help in avoiding a wrong path.

If none of this helps and you still feel you're taking a wrong track, then it's time for a vacation from the Dharma. Just take a break from spiritual practice. Go and sit in a cafe instead, and talk to people there. Have a little chat, drink a little wine, whatever. Otherwise you are merely doing yourself a disservice. To practice a "spiritual path" while at the same time getting worse and worse—wouldn't that be useless?

As we practice the teachings—correctly—our confusion and negative emotions steadily diminish and disappear, until there is no confused experience whatsoever and we reach enlightenment. That which at the path stage we saw as empty essence, cognizant nature, and the unconfined capacity we have now realized as being dharmakaya, sambhogakaya, and nirmanakaya. In this way, we awaken to true and complete enlightenment as the three kayas. Attaining enlightenment means that the ground has been totally realized, completely actualized. The confusion at the path stage covered the ground, but now it is totally removed. Confusion has dawned as wisdom. The ground is revealed. That is the fruition. Once you awaken to true and complete enlightenment, you don't just hang out there—you manifest again for the benefit of beings. Out of dharmakaya please manifest sambhogakaya; out of sambhogakaya please manifest nirmanakaya, in countless numbers, to benefit and guide sentient beings in all directions, endlessly.

STUDENT: How do I definitively overcome the undercurrent of fear that colors all my experience?

RINPOCHE: I believe you *can* be fearless. Right now, you are not sure what will happen in your mind. In fact, anything can happen within our minds, and you're not ready for that. You don't know what might come up, and you don't know how you will react to any experience, any nangwa that comes. So deep down, you are scared of your own experience. Nangwa doesn't always arise in positive form; nangwa can come in any possible form. Now please understand that the basis of all nangwa is freedom, since all nangwa unfold from emptiness. Emptiness never says, "He is a little bit weak, so don't disturb him." Emptiness says, "My job is to accommodate. Your job is to be free in whatever happens. Whether you let it be a buddhafield or a hell realm is your responsibility." Fear creates the obstacle of not being confident in yourself, so you don't want to listen and you refuse to see. Because of this, your mind becomes increasingly closed, and the experience feels more constricted. This reaction to nangwa closes off more and more of your openness, until eventually all your nangwa become frozen and you lose the juice, you lose the openness, you lose the compassion. You're completely uptight and then you go crazy. How can you be compassionate toward other people when your mind is totally preoccupied with yourself and your own neuroses? The key here is in softening your approach to the nangwa.

In the context of relating to your nangwa, I would like to bring up *the symbolic master of experiences*, meaning difficulties turning into friends and becoming helpers. As I mentioned earlier, we encounter various types of teachers in our lives: the teacher consisting of the statements of the enlightened ones, the teacher that is the living lineage master, the symbolic teacher of experiences, and the ultimate teacher of your innate nature. Here's the bottom line: circumstances have become your friend when you can arrive in rigpa no matter what happens. At that moment you are liberated, and all phenomena—all the events of samsara and nirvana, everything that appears and exists—arises and manifests like a dance, like a feast. Both accumulations—the accumulation of merit with reference point and the accumulation of wisdom beyond concepts—are included within that. The accumulation of wisdom is not to part from the empty essence of awareness. The accumulation of merit is to allow the display of phenomena to unfold unimpededly, in all possible ways, like a big feast, a party, a huge drama. Do you know how to enjoy this feast?

You may now understand at least to some extent the relationship between nangwa and emptiness, and also what it means to be free and not free. When you gain actual experience of this relationship, I'm sure you will have a greater sense of well-being that stems from not being afraid of yourself any longer. Remember, any nangwa can happen, because the very nature of nangwa is openness; experience can unfold since its nature is emptiness. Through practice, you know how to relate to your unimpeded nangwa without clinging. You deal with it in the three ways of freeing, and through that you experience a certain well-being. Your mind is now in harmony with phenomena; you're not fighting with nangwa any more, and that is the best well-being. Your open, spacious mind invites any nangwa to come out and play. You are neither caught up in nor rejecting the nangwa. Everything happens very simply.

Whenever you allow such openness—which is essentially emptiness—everything is harmonious. This way of being unafraid of oneself gives room for a certain delight, an easy feeling, which is basic well-being. As we train in being composed like that, free of hope and free of fear, we encounter two natural expressions of rigpa, which I like to call the two kinds of juice.

At this stage, your emptiness and nangwa enjoy a good relationship, a good partnership. When images of deities in union are explained, we often hear that the male is nangwa, the female is emptiness, and their offspring is great bliss. This harmonious relationship between phenomena and emptiness, a perfect union, a perfect match, bears a lot of first-rate offspring. These children are compassion, devotion, deep insight into the nature of all things, and more. They are all the magical display of unified experience and emptiness. To practice in a harmonious, open, spacious way allows devotion, compassion, and intelligence to naturally manifest.

The openness of the empty quality is likened to a grandfather who has a very strong presence but is also very kind. His sons and daughters and grandchildren all get along so wonderfully whenever they're together, because of his benevolent inspiration. He has the ability to put everybody at ease and make them get along. When he's absent, they all fight among one another. The moment he comes back, everybody calms down. The openness is like that—strong yet accommodating.

Whenever we just *let be* in rigpa, which is empty in essence and cognizant by nature, whatever occurs as the natural expression of rigpa—

devotion, desire, whatever—is in harmony. That is when real peace can occur. The basis for peace—isn't that harmony? So within rigpa, all phenomena are influenced in a harmonious way. The Tibetan word for bodhichitta, awakened mind, is *jangchub*. *Jang* here means refined or purified in a subtle way rather than coarse, solid phenomena, while *chub* is the accommodating quality, a very open atmosphere, a sense of having opened up. Every conceivable entity is accommodated within this spaciousness; there's plenty of room for everything to arise and exist. That is the basic atmosphere of bodhichitta—a sort of *total roominess*. There's a basic harmony, because empty essence is present throughout all phenomena. In this way, all phenomena are in harmony within the expanse of empty essence. When one is really experiencing this spacious harmony, it's very enjoyable.

There's an abundance of practitioners' songs expressing this joyfulness. You're enjoying it, and while enjoying you don't have to step out of mind essence. When you completely let be in empty essence and cognizant nature, it's like all of a sudden there's so much room. Everything is available in this spaciousness. There's plenty of housing, plenty of food, plenty of cars, plenty of everything. It's completely accommodating, and everything is present in a very easygoing way. All types of nangwa are in total harmony

Even though the identity of everything is the same in being empty essence, within the vastness of rigpa, at the same time, everything is still distinct, revealing its own qualities, keeping its own attributes. Desire is still expressed as desire, devotion is still devotion, detachment is still detachment, and being at ease is still being at ease. Nothing gets blurred or mixed together just because it's identical in essence. It's like the way Granddaddy keeps everyone in harmony, yet at the same time the children are allowed to be individuals and express themselves. Another way to define the grandfatherly quality that keeps everything in the harmony of one essence is as *dharmadhatu wisdom*. Granddaddy's expansiveness, his generosity in being able to accommodate the entire family, is the dharmadhatu wisdom. And the very fact that whatever is accommodated is in complete harmony with Granddaddy is the *wisdom of equality*.

Nevertheless, the children are not dominated by Granddaddy. They are allowed to express themselves freely in their individual ways. One grandchild is a lawyer, and that's perfectly fine; he expresses his lawyer quality completely. One is a tailor, and that's also all right. He expresses his tailor qualities. Granddaddy doesn't suppress any of those distinct qualities. That's the *discriminating wisdom*. *All-accomplishing wisdom* is that Granddaddy's capacity is not restricted in any way, as if the entire family is carrying out his intentions about whatever needs to be accomplished. Whether it's in a mode that pacifies, enriches, magnetizes, or subjugates, everything is spontaneously accomplished. That's the all-accomplishing wisdom.

Last there's the *mirrorlike wisdom*, which means that at any moment, in any instance, the basic intent of Granddaddy is never lost. None of the grandchildren are in any way obscured, nor do they forget about what Granddaddy's main intent is. You can say that his atmosphere permeates every single activity the grandchildren are carrying out. No matter what occurs, whether it is desire, anger, devotion, or compassion, at that same moment, the empty cognizance that is their very nature is never lost or forgotten, not for a single instant. That is the mirrorlike wisdom quality of being basically unobscured. When that's the case, there's no problem whatsoever. Whatever occurs is like a thief entering an empty house— there's no sense of loss or risk at all.

Granddaddy himself is in no way worried about whatever unfolds at any moment. He knows that there is harmony in this big, happy family as long as he's present. He doesn't have to do anything to enforce it. There's natural harmony, there's plenty to eat, and everybody gets along. The grandchildren are not fighting with one another; there's plenty of room. This is the supreme way of being at ease. It's also known as great bliss, which is complete ease in whatever happens. This is the root from which all the great qualities grow, the source of their unfolding. It's very enjoyable, very delightful. And while being delighted at this way of being, one still doesn't forget Granddaddy's kindness. Why? Because there's no leaving behind empty essence. And yet, whatever one's ability is, it is allowed to be fully expressed, without the need to leave behind the expanse of empty essence. This is an extremely delightful way of being. This is what a true yogi enjoys. There are so many songs describing this state: "This great ease, this great bliss, ah la la." Great masters and true yogis express this great joy out of their direct experience, as an actuality.

The dilemma of life and death is one of the most serious issues for human beings living in this world. For a true yogi, however, the prospect of personal death is just a joke. Someone undaunted by death can be pretty much at ease, right? What else could bother you at that point? If you recognize that death is dharmakaya, there's really no dying. Death is merely another concept. Dying or not dying—it's just a thought making that up. That's how it probably is; I don't know from my own experience. To tell the truth, I'm still afraid of dying. But for a true practitioner, there's not even as much of a hair-tip of fear of death. That doesn't mean being pretentiously defiant, claiming, "I'm not afraid of death" and jumping into a situation of mortal danger—that would only be stupid. The moment of death reveals whether someone is truly a great practitioner: can you honestly be fearless at that point? It's certainly the toughest spot we can imagine, isn't it?

All the complaints we make about this and that during this lifetime pale in comparison to the moment of facing death. Practitioners in eastern Tibet were often told, "Now listen, don't be a disgrace. The moment you die reveals everything." Fearlessness in the face of death doesn't have to be pretentious. It can be for real when it springs from genuinely experiencing the fact that within the *ongoingness* of rigpa, life and death are simply the arising of one thought, which dissolves, the arising of another thought, which dissolves. That is what life and death really are. I've read many of the songs of the great yogis of the past. I've gotten a lot of teachings. And just thinking about it from the intellectual angle, I reflect that everything takes place within the continuity of the unformed essence. Something unfolds, then it vanishes; unfolds, vanishes. Being continuously caught up in this unfolding is what we usually call "my life"—one long string of concepts arising and ceasing. That is what one identifies as being one's life. But it's all something that vanishes, vanishes, vanishes, whereas the environment within which it vanishes, the unformed essence itself, cannot be subject to birth and death. It's not something that comes and goes. Therefore, birth and death have only to do with that which unfolds and vanishes, unfolds and vanishes. When I think of it from that angle, even though I don't have any personal experience, I feel this is probably what those great yogis meant.

I was present when Tulku Urgyen Rinpoche passed on. When Nyoshul Khen Rinpoche died, I was there a few days before. I've also witnessed many other practitioners, lamas, and normal people dying. I've been asked to come to their deathbeds or to visit them after they were dead, to do ceremonies like performing the *phowa* ejection of consciousness and the like. But one mark was evident with masters like Tulku Urgyen Rinpoche or Nyoshul Khen Rinpoche: they were totally without fear of death. There was no anxiety such as "I'm going to die, oh no, what to do?" Not at all.

I've seen so many worldly people die. They say, "Do something, please, save my life!" Some time back, I was the president of the Tashi Jong community for a term, and while I was there, my secretary was dying. I went to his deathbed, and he said, "Rinpoche, it's not my time to die. I don't want to die. I have a wife, I have children." He was the same age as me. He begged, "Do something, please. Do whatever you can. Call some other masters. Ask them to give me any necessary empowerment or blessing." He was so afraid, so worried. But there was nothing to do.

Great masters never say, "I'm about to die and I don't know what to do." Somehow they know that they're dying. They don't make so many preparations, writing their wills with all sorts of worry or attachment, instructing "do this, do that"—nothing like that. They simply sit. When they die, they die knowingly and with acceptance, as if they are going next door. Nyoshul Khen Rinpoche and Tulku Urgyen Rinpoche just left. They didn't make a big fuss about it. They didn't need to write any letters, spelling details out for others. If they hadn't known that they were going to die, it would have been a different matter, but they knew. For them, it was so easy. Isn't it true that when you move house, it's such a big deal! Just checking out of a hotel can be a complex task. When you go trekking, how much preparation do you need in order to trek for one week? How much hope and fear is involved? How many pieces of luggage? But masters like them don't need to prepare at all. They don't make any big deal about it whatsoever. They just leave, like going from one room to the next. I was pretty amazed at that. At first I was concerned with whether there would be any auspicious signs and watched out for them. But then later, when reflecting on it, I realized that actually the most auspicious sign is the ease with which someone can depart, like going to sleep at night, without the slightest anxiety or fear.

JUICE

True Dzogchen training in the awakened state of rigpa has a sequence of three points: recognizing, developing strength in it, and attaining stability. First of all we need to recognize rigpa, the awakened state itself, which is endowed with the three aspects of original wakefulness: empty in essence, cognizant by nature, and unconfined in its capacity. Having recognized this in actuality, we need to develop its strength through training in rigpa's natural expression. Rigpa is not some kind of incapable, vacant, impotent state—not at all. There's a tremendous capacity or capability in rigpa that starts to show itself. When this ability of the awakened state begins to radiate, to manifest and be expressed, we must recognize that it is our natural expression, meaning rigpa's natural expression. During this manifestation of rigpa's qualities, train in not parting from its empty essence. *That* is the training. As I mentioned before, all sorts of manifestations take place. We should relate to whatever is arising in complete harmony, so that the continuity of whatever occurs is the state of rigpa.

I also mentioned how the various expressions of rigpa are identical in nature, yet they individually express their own qualities. They're in harmony with rigpa, and they're able to fulfill a particular function. Now I'd like to go into more detail about the two juices, which are the natural expression of rigpa. These two juices are very important. The first brand is devotion, orange juice. The second brand, compassion, is apple juice. We can't do without these juices.

There's a certain connection between devotion and blessings. Blessing is a capacity that infuses our being when circumstances are right. Just as all things have their own innate capacity, there is a certain capacity in the state of realization, and it becomes present in anyone for whom the innate nature is an actuality. The converse is also true: there's a negative sort of capacity in someone who has trained thoroughly and continuously in being ignorant of his or her own nature, who is continuously involved in being either attached, hostile, or closed-minded. That type of "blessing" we already know.

Tulku Urgyen Rinpoche often gave the example of blessings being as natural as sunlight, the rays of the sun that simply shine. But if a cave entrance happens to face north or is closed off in some way, the sunlight doesn't reach inside. No matter how many centuries go by, the sun doesn't have the opportunity to dispel the darkness in the northern facing cave. Why doesn't it dispel the cave's darkness? It's not the sun's fault—it's the cave's location that is to blame. In the same way, all the buddhas and bodhisattvas, the enlightened masters of the lineage, have enormous blessings simply by virtue of their state of being—a fact tried and proven by Buddhist "scientists." Countless practitioners have put this matter to the test in their personal "experiments" and discovered that, yes, there are such blessings that can be received, that are realized through the pointing-out instruction. Hundreds of thousands of these Buddhist scientists have attained liberation by training in what they recognized through the pointing-out instruction.

Here's a metaphor for the relationship between blessings and devotion: someone with a cold or the flu will sneeze a lot, and the people sitting close by may well catch the sickness. It's as if buddhas and bodhisattvas are constantly sneezing on us, passing on the germs of enlightenment. But if the solid cocoon of our ego-clinging has its immune system operating at 100 percent, they can be sneezing for twenty-four hours and we still won't catch the cold. The shell of ego-clinging is so tight, so solid that there's no way for the blessings to enter. Devotion is what makes the immune system go down. It lowers ego's guard.

I'd like to add that devotion in this context is not a thing but rather a combination of many different factors. It's not just one feeling. Let's say that you're resting in composure, in the essence of nondual awareness. You are sitting in a very harmonious way. You are totally untroubled, totally at ease, in a delightful way that is completely unobscured, with self-knowing wakefulness that perceives everything. Whatever the situation is, it is clearly perceived. In this state, coming and going can take place freely. It's very spacious, and there is a good feeling about being this way that is very delightful but not absorbed or submerged into feeling good. There is an appreciation of your way of being so at ease. But this appreciation is not stupid, not imagining something unreal. It's more really recognizing what you actually are, what your true identity is. You appreciate yourself in that way. And the intelligence that is present, which sees what you really are, is also appreciated in a confident sort of way. Because you know how to let whatever emotion occurs naturally dissolve, you feel completely unafraid. Of course the physical body can still get into trouble, but mentally you are completely untroubled, unafraid of whatever may happen.

On the mental level, however complex a situation may be, however much trouble you may face, it's not a big deal, because you know how to relate to it. Such understanding is much greater, much more profound than anything you ever knew. There are many factors that combine in this feeling, but mainly there's a sense of real appreciation, because you understand the value of training in being this way. It's the application of the Dzogchen instructions that causes you to be this way, and therefore you consider the Dzogchen instructions to be incredibly precious: "Hey! Now I understand their value. But the Dzogchen instructions did not introduce a new state. They are simply the method to reveal and recognize in actuality what my basic nature is. Now I see it clearly. I truly respect the value of that. Thanks a lot, Dzogchen teachings!" It's that sort of appreciation. That is how we can trust the teachings. That is real devotion, real faith.

It becomes very clear to us: "This experience has been transmitted from Buddha Samantabhadra down until this very day through a lineage of masters. They have kept it alive and fresh, so that I as well, being at the receiving end of this long line of transmission, have been able to taste it in my own experience. And I have realized only a tiny bit; imagine how much more a realized master must experience! I really appreciate how they have kept this realization alive and passed it on. I'm very grateful for this! This transmission through the masters is something really special. I deeply appreciate it! I am able to be free of delusion about my basic being, about what is what, rather than chasing an illusory goal or driving in the wrong direction. I know how to proceed. I really appreciate that!"

That feeling is one of being delighted, spacious, appreciative, feeling good about yourself. It's one of trusting the instructions, with devotion and dedication. It is not stupid trust: it's based on your own experience, without delusion. It's not a sense of being intoxicated by devotion but rather a genuine, intelligent appreciation. Yet, no matter how appreciative one is, one does not lose track of the empty essence; and at the same time there is a feeling of being completely at ease about the whole affair. When all this comes together, we call it devotion. And when this feeling is very strong, there is simply no longer any room for ego-clinging: the manager, the ego who always claims ownership, completely falls apart. For a short while at least, ego-clinging has dispersed. That is the gap when the blessings of the buddhas and enlightened masters can enter your stream of being.

As a matter of fact, the blessings don't *belong* to certain masters. They exist naturally. Blessings just happen the very moment in which the innate nature is an actuality. It's not like we supplicate the lineage masters and they are somehow pleased by that, or that when we forget and don't do it, they get annoyed. It has nothing to do with that at all. The devotion in our hearts makes a difference in ourselves. Through devotion, we allow the blessings to happen. If you don't care about yourself at all, then this is not so important, but if you value your own well-being, if you want to be good to yourself, then develop some more devotion.

The buddhas and the lineage masters don't need your devotion—it makes absolutely no difference to them. If it did, if there were a buddha who felt happy because of your devotion and unhappy with your lack of it, that would not be a buddha, because a buddha is someone who is already free of ego-clinging. A buddha is freed through realization, and that means that any basis for the ignorant notion of self has totally dissolved. Someone who regards himself or herself as a focus of devotion and who is pleased at the presence of it or displeased at its absence is definitely not enlightened.

If you are annoyed at or hostile toward a particular buddha, he will have empathy and compassion. If you love him and supplicate him, he will have empathy and compassion. If you beat a buddha statue or put shit on it or chop off a leg or whatever, he will just feel empathy and compassion. It makes no difference. It's not like the buddha will think, "Ough, he hurt me." In Tibet so many monasteries were burned down to the ground; the Dharma scriptures were destroyed; the statues were ruined. But buddhas and bodhisattvas, from their point of view, only have empathy and compassion. They simply perceive that these people were not in charge of themselves, that they were carried away by their own negative thoughts and emotions. How sad for them!

During deep-felt, sincere devotion, the dualistic attitude falls to pieces. The maintenance of a subject and object falls apart. That doesn't mean that we should somehow sink into devotion, savoring its taste or blissing out. Rather, we should experience devotion while not losing the recognition of mind essence. About the time of devotion, it is said, "In the moment of love, the empty essence dawns nakedly." In other words, it's much easier to recognize mind essence during devotion. So when we're just about to lose mind essence, if we apply devotion it's easier to recognize again.

Combine this with the guru yoga or the guru *sadhana*, sincerely supplicate your teacher and allow your mind and his to mingle. Near the end of the practice, you imagine that the enlightened mind of the guru and your own state of mind intermingle, and then you simply let be in the state of this indivisible, awakened mind. Allow the dualistic attitude to dissolve and remain composed like that, while in devotion. If you put your mind into the guru's, what happens? You get blessings.

Of course it's fine if you're someone who can just be yourself in the sense of the awakened state, without depending upon anything, and through your own capacity be totally liberated. But if you find that it's not always so easy, then it might be a good idea to use the structure of guru yoga to imagine that all the buddhas and bodhisattvas dissolve into your primary teacher, your root guru, and that you then dissolve him into you. Let your mind and his mind intermingle. Then it is possible that some of the moisture of the awakened state may saturate you. Often I mention that a little miracle is necessary. That's the time when it happens.

If you only analyze and analyze intellectually, you're unable to train in Dzogchen meditation, because you're not letting go of the conceptual attitude. It is through the blessings that happen when letting go into the indivisible state of the guru's mind and your own that you're able to let go of the intellectualized meditation state. In this way, guru yoga is immensely helpful.

Devotion results from your own experience of the teachings, and through that you gain even deeper appreciation and trust. Through this trust you're able to receive more blessings; through the blessings you're able to deepen your experience, gain more appreciation and confidence, and so it goes on and on.

Westerners often think, "That's nice," when they first hear of blessings and devotion. Then after a few days they start to wonder, "Is this really necessary? I don't know." When I meet people I often believe they understand the need for devotion and blessings. But when I meet them again after a couple of months, I'm not sure they actually did get it. It's a hard point. Intelligence alone is not sufficient. It needs to be accompanied by other factors to be useful. The same goes for compassion, which has the same basis as I just explained for devotion. In addition, with compassion there's a feeling of taking responsibility, feeling responsible.

To gain stability in rigpa, we need to give rise to genuine bodhichitta in our stream of being. For this to be sincere and authentic, it needs assistance from the experience of emptiness, because emptiness reveals our natural state. Real compassion happens in the recognition of our natural state. We must *be* compassion. In order to be compassion, we need to recognize our natural state. There's also a way of being compassionate without knowing the natural state, but that is not compassion in the ultimate sense.

We always have some compassion, though it may not be the perfect type. It's the nature of any sentient being to be compassionate; no one is totally and completely hard-hearted. It is simply not possible. Even someone who kills a lot of other beings may have a wife and children or someone else he loves. It's impossible for any being to be totally without compassion and love. The *Uttaratantra Shastra* tells us that one of the proofs that all beings have buddha nature is their natural capacity to be compassionate. Every sentient being from time to time reveals this natural empathy, which proves that every single being has an enlightened essence.

Everyone can be compassionate from time to time, but there's a huge difference in how this empathy shows itself. Sometimes it can be partial compassion, sometimes only 5 percent or 2 percent or 1 percent, or even a tiny little fraction. Still, it cannot help showing itself now and then. That is not the same type of compassion that I am speaking about here. Here I am addressing 100 percent compassion, the *totality* of compassion. For us it's not yet fully manifest. What we currently possess is the basis for it, the root from which the 100 percent total compassion can grow. Among the three types of compassion that are traditionally explained— the compassion that holds sentient beings as its focus, the compassion that holds truth as its focus, and the compassion that holds no focus whatsoever—the type I teach here is like a mixture of the second and the third.

We need to *be* compassion, to be in such a way that our identity is compassion itself. When compassion saturates our being, like juice that is everywhere in us, then whatever we touch, however we express ourselves, becomes a way of being compassionate. If you turn into charcoal, whatever you rub against will bear a black mark. In the same way, when you *are* compassion, every way you express yourself becomes a way of showing compassion. Your very being has become compassion itself.

Take the example of a kilo of real, pure gold. It doesn't matter whom it belongs to; whether it is in the hands of a king or a beggar, it still has the value of pure gold. Regardless of where it is, the value remains unchanged. In the same way, to *be* compassion means that its value is present in any situation. It will always show itself as being compassionate.

Unlike conditioned compassion that is directed at particular circumstances or people, real compassion is directed at the deluded machinery of samsara. It's a feeling of compassion for delusion. To allow this compassion to arise and sincerely express itself makes us automatically feel totally at ease. We feel relaxed, brave, courageous, and unselfish. This is not just for *me*—rather, there's a deep concern for others, a feeling of being responsible. Nobody asked for it, but still you feel responsible for the welfare of others. This is something very precious.

To believe that one is a Dzogchen practitioner while paying no attention to devotion and compassion, thinking of these qualities as unimportant, is a surely wrong path. It is "dry Dzogchen," with no juice, no cream, no moisturizers. You are in a high-altitude place where everything is very dry. Or even worse, you don't care for anything. In fact, all the wrong traits develop out of this. There's no feeling for others, because everything is emptiness. "I must have peace, ahhhh, now peace is there. I must be relaxed, ahhhh, very good." Or "I have this emotional meditative problem; I must cure it." Or "I need a very good life in samsara. I do Dzogchen practice because there's a certain gap that I can escape into." If one is that type of practitioner, it's not Dzogchen. I can guarantee you that.

As we practice progressively, we discover that there's more and more juice, automatically. That is of course the best situation. But when it doesn't happen so naturally, then we should apply some methods. We can read inspiring books, receive further teachings, or use a practice that activates a feeling of devotion. It's the same with compassion: together with training in Dzogchen, we use other methods until it happens all by itself. Read, for example, Shantideva's *Way of the Bodhisattva*, think of other beings, and try to improve your motivation again and again, until compassion comes more naturally. When you feel a real sincerity of devotion and compassion, then recognize rigpa. When the rigpa's continuity is full of the juice of devotion and compassion, you have reached a very good level. At that point, your meditation is not mistaken. I'll explain more about this later on.

Blessings also help in clarifying rigpa. There are many benefits to the blessings, and I believe you can understand them. You're intelligent, well-educated people. People from each country have certain strengths and certain weaknesses. In the West, people are well educated and intelligent, and they are also willing to persevere, at least to some extent. They can be really interested, usually in the beginning, but this interest tends to wear off after a while, because dealing with emotional states is a difficult, though not an impossible task. As one trains further and further, the emotions become less intense, and one is able to progress more smoothly. But it's important not to give up and also not to be too unfeeling. That's quite important. We should make sure that we don't lose contact with *being compassion* and having a sense of devotion. As a matter of fact, this is not just a problem for Westerners, nor only for Dharma practitioners; it's a risk for all spiritual practitioners.

Another important point is this: don't regard the instructions as personal property, or any experience or realization as *mine*. Rather, treat them as something that can be used to help. We cultivate spiritual qualities so that we can be like a dispensary providing whatever is needed for other beings, rather than making a boundary around our feeling of peace and isolating ourselves. That's another risk. with some practitioners, the older they become, the more selfish they get, not necessarily about material things but about *my private space* and *my peace*. Be careful about this attitude! "I'm doing meditation, don't bother me." Trying to be in solitude, of course, is one way of beginning, but then you may become a little too uptight. You feel, "Anything that disturbs me is bad, because I'm doing good. It's very unfair that you are negative to me, because I'm doing good." That is very far from compassionate radiance. Everything bothers you, so where's the compassion? It decreased. Earlier on, you had some juice. When you began, there was some juice in your eyes, some water, some moisture. You've lost it.

I'm not saying that this happens to everyone; it's just something to watch out for. It's mentioned many times in the guidance manuals. There is a story of a meditator staying in a cave high up in the mountains who picked fights with meditators in other caves. Really, it does happen. They quarrel about small issues like "He rang his bell before me, or after me." The main preventive measure against this is the attitude of bodhichitta, which avoids all problems.

In the same way, it's not hard or tiring to practice when you are motivated by compassion in a deep way. "I am tired" is simply a thought, an attitude. First you believe you're tired, then you feel tired. You make yourself tired, then you become really tired. But it's the concept that makes you tired. You know this: it doesn't matter whether it's day or night—if you're deeply motivated, the task doesn't feel tiring no matter how big it is. Isn't that true?

Once you are compassion itself, this is different from the pursuit of compassion. "I need compassion, so I must look for compassion and get it." It's the same with wisdom and the Buddha. It's not that a buddha has wisdom, not at all. A buddha simply *is* wisdom, *is* original wakefulness. It's not that the sense of "I" is still there when you're being compassionate. The "I" is gone and there is just compassion. Compassion has become you. The wisdom has become you.

To proceed with devotion and compassion, keep rigpa as the core of your practice, and allow it to be expressed as devotion and compassion. You now discover that these natural expressions of rigpa develop its strength further and further. To practice like this allows us to progress incredibly fast and is also extraordinarily effective in destroying delusion's evil machinery. While you train like this in essence and expression—essence being rigpa and expression being bodhichitta—there is no source for confusion. There are no emotions or thoughts that could spring from anywhere other than from failing to recognize essence and being caught up in the expression. There's no other source of confusion than this: losing the recognition of essence and being overinvolved in the expression. While the essence is not forgotten but is recognized as rigpa, and you are not lost in the expression but recognize it as being the natural expression of rigpa, there's no source from which confusion can unfold.

Now that you understand, what's the next step? Practice! That's the factor that's still missing. Everything else is complete.

Among the three points—view, meditation, and conduct—conduct means the way of freeing, how to be free. The best situation is for a thought to be either freed upon arising, naturally freed, or freed beyond benefit and harm, so that the continuity of the view is not interrupted by the occurrence of thought. This is essential! But if it doesn't happen, if we really get distracted—and let's just say that we occasionally do get distracted from rigpa's continuity—then we need to conceptually re-mind ourselves, "Hey, recognize mind essence!" This is like the meta-phor of striking the gong one more time. And then let go. And when again we forget—hit the gong again. That's our life's task.

At some point, the continuity naturally lasts longer, eventually be-coming quite long. Honestly, it's not that the continuity gets longer but that the duration of the confusion gets shorter. Rigpa itself is not something that can grow or diminish; it's beyond all arising and ceasing. But that which obscures—the coemergent and conceptualizing igno-rance—can decrease; the duration of being confused can diminish. As we continue training, one day we find that we are fully enlightened. At that time, if you're in doubt about whether you're enlightened, then call me on the phone. I have that specific test for you, and no matter where I am in the world, I can remind you. But if you yourself know that you're fully enlightened, that's good, it's all right. Go to the buddhafields first, shake hands with the Buddha, say hello, look around, look back down at this world, and then notice, "Oh, no! Tsoknyi Rinpoche is still in sam-sara. How sad! He is still at Gomde in California, teaching. He's still confused. I'd better go back and help."

At that time, please come back immediately. Don't remain in the buddhafields enjoying yourself with all the dakas and dakinis. Don't just hang out there. Send down one emanation, a second, a third——what-ever is required to help, please do it. Help Tsoknyi Rinpoche if he needs help; help whoever else needs help. Let your activity for the welfare of beings be unceasing. As a matter of fact, complete enlightenment is not about loitering in a buddhafield—not at all. The fully awakened state is one in which activity for the benefit of beings is unceasing and never-ending. Take the example of Padmasambhava, who manifests in ten billion simultaneous incarnations in all kinds of forms. Not just as human beings—as insects, as different animals and other beings, as in-animate objects, in myriad ways. And not just in this world either. Bud-dha Shakyamuni mentioned that the difference between our world and the number of other places that have sentient beings is like a speck of dust on one fingernail compared to the whole body. There are beings everywhere, and in the same way, emanations are sent out to all these places.

When you train in the way explained here, you may at some point have the idea "I won't attain enlightenment, I refuse to attain buddhahood," but the process is already set in motion so that you still awaken. In fact, you are powerless to stop this process after a certain point; it's inevitable. Once you have fully developed and perfected the strength of rigpa, there is a stage at which all objects of distraction dissolve into dharmata, into the unconditioned nature. Anything that could catch your attention to move you away from rigpa is now automatically recognized as being an expression of rigpa itself. There is no longer anything whatsoever that can cause distraction. This is buddhahood, the state of complete enlightenment, the point at which the ground is realized to be the fruition. What the ground was has now become the actuality, no longer hidden, and that itself is the fruition. The three kayas are fully realized, in the sense that empty essence is realized as dharmakaya *in actuality*; cognizant nature is realized as sambhogakaya *in actuality*; and unconfined capacity is realized to be nirmanakaya *in actuality*. These are the three bodies at the state of the fully enlightened buddhahood.

STUDENT: Is the ultimate innate guru the expression of emptiness?

RINPOCHE: The statement "Whatever is seen is the form of the guru or the form of the deity" really means that mind is not clinging to things as being concrete and real. Rather, objects and events are just allowed to unfold as a magical illusion, as the scenery in a dream. This comes about as an expression of recognizing the ultimate innate guru. When realizing this in actuality, the fact that there are pillars, walls, ceilings, and so forth offers no obstacles; this apparent solidity doesn't harm anything. With no fixation on these as being concrete or real, there is no bind or fetter being created. That's the meaning of Tilopa's famous saying: "Son, perceptions don't bind, clinging does; so cut your clinging, Naropa."

When clinging is interrupted, then whatever occurs—sights, sounds, smells, tastes, or textures—can all be said to be the expression of emptiness. The statement "Whatever is heard is the voice of enlightenment" doesn't mean that we become deaf. There is still hearing, but you don't cling to this hearing; you don't fixate on the sound as being *something other*. You experience it in a freer, more spacious way. At this point, we can rightfully say that all sound is the voice of the guru. The movement of mind is the display of original wakefulness, enlightened mind. In the moment of recognizing rigpa, thoughts arise out of our nature and dissolve back into our nature. This happens naturally because of not clinging.

The pith instructions explain the way to get to this level. But they must be correctly applied, and this is possible only after we've come in contact with a qualified master. Trust and devotion are essential components in this mix. Devotion is the highest-quality love. When people fall in love with each other, they are so open, so happy to be together that their normal emotions are totally loosened up. When a man and woman are really in love, the usual feeling of separateness melts away, so they no longer feel as if they were two people, but more like they're just one. In the moment of being completely in love, ordinary concepts are dissolved or melted so they have no strong hold in one's mind whatsoever. One is sort of lost in that, totally opened up. Unfortunately, because the object of love between a man and woman is just an ordinary person, sooner or later it ends up in a samsaric direction. It doesn't lead further than that.

It is an entirely different situation when this love is directed toward the guru—the source of the instructions on recognizing the nature of mind—and toward these teachings. The moment of complete devotion allows thoughts to fall away, so that your mind is no longer enveloped in the peels of ordinary concepts. In this moment, there is a strong possibility of recognizing rigpa. If you have received instructions on how to recognize your nature, that possibility exists: it has been laid bare, laid open, so that the self-knowing state of wakefulness can be fully acknowledged. That is the reason for devotion.

Most of you have some kind of experience with love. When you were a teenager falling in love, wasn't love very strong? Teenage love is the strongest love. The boy and girl are *really* in love. They're so in love that they just gaze into each other's eyes, without many concepts of the world. The world simply disappears. There's not even a concept of me and you; they fuse into a single experience and are lost in that way, just gazing into each other's eyes. Every other thought has vanished. It's like mingling, melting together into one taste. This really does feel good.

Because of the love, you become so open that there's no hope and fear. The experience opens because of feeling love, and then you genuinely feel each other, you really can talk honestly. There's no game involved. You can speak honestly, openly, sincerely with each other, without playing games. That's just an example, okay?

Devotion in the spiritual sense is something like that, but it's not exactly the same. The object of the love is different. What is the object here? The sense of love springs from confidence in the fact that confusion can be liberated, so it is basically a love of the Dharma. The sense of devotion is very similar to that in true love. The gurus of the past have written many love songs about this. One is *Calling the Guru from Afar*. This is a different kind of love song from the mundane type, where you sing, "I love to look into your eyes; I cannot bear to be apart from you, not for a single moment; I must be with you always." It's not that sort of love song. It's more a love song of appreciating the value of how to dissolve confusion and realizing, "without this understanding, I'm lost." It's a love for what is true, what is real.

Take any love song that you hear and look into what it's actually about. Basically it has to do with honestly telling your feelings to another person—how much something means to you, what your state of mind is, what you really want, what you're longing for. In the same way, *Calling the Guru from Afar* is like a love song. It's like somebody who's in Europe writing to their lover in America, saying, "How I miss you, how it hurts to be here all by myself." In *Calling the Guru from Afar*, you just sing verse by verse, "How it hurts to be in samsaric existence, being so confused about what I really need, I'm thinking of you, please grant your blessings, why are you not helping me immediately, this is so difficult without being enlightened, being deluded like this." While chanting *Calling the Guru from Afar*, you must open fully; you don't hold anything back. You sing from a state of fully disclosing how you feel, 100 percent. There's no delusion held back in that song. Everything is laid open; you're baring yourself down to the very bone. In this openness you can receive the blessings.

When you get up in the morning, chant the love song, calling upon the guru with complete sincerity. If you cry, you cry, that's okay, but chant it anyway. And then as your heart, instead of being so constricted, begins to loosen up further and further, allow the peels, the conceptual wrappings, to simply fall away. Within this open state of mind, receive the blessings and let the realization of original wakefulness unfold.

That is the whole purpose of devotion: to undo the mind's rigidity. The attitude of the ego is so uptight, so tied up in itself. Devotion can loosen this up completely. This is a necessary process. Most religions, not only Buddhism, teach devotion as a way to open up one's heart.

Devotion comes very naturally for Asians who are brought up with Buddhism. I'm not saying that this is good or bad; this is just how it is. But for people who come from another part of the world, this sense of devotion may not come easily. On top of that, one might think, "This is actually not important. I'm smart, I'm well educated, I'm very intelligent—I can realize the basic nature of mind by my own power of intelligence." It's not going to be so easy to attain realization with that kind of attitude. Whether we like it or not, devotion is necessary. It is necessary because it helps us open up from deep within. Opening up is also done by means of accumulating merit. So we combine the feeling of devotion with merit and the intelligence of understanding the key instructions. It is not enough only to be intelligent: we need intelligence together with devotion and merit. There's a certain connection between the three.

Trust is the method of revealing that which is not evident. There are two kinds of trust. In one, we train our minds in a certain way and we come to trust. The other is just a spontaneous trust we have in something, without having to go through any kind of training. Both kinds of trust are taught in Buddhism, and both are very important. Let's take it as a given that we've trained in the first one: in this context, I'm referring to the second, the sense of spontaneous trust. When spontaneous trust deepens and grows much stronger, we can call it devotion. Therefore, devotion is based on trust, and trust is based on personal experience. This trust comes about through reflecting upon the self-existing wakefulness that my guru has pointed out to me. This is what liberates the very root cause of samsara—ego-clinging. Ego-clinging is based on fixating on duality, and this fixating can be totally dissolved. In other words, I can be completely free of the three realms of samsara by experiencing this self-existing wakefulness. How wonderful, how amazing!

Understanding this brings certainty. And this certainty is an expression of rigpa; it's how rigpa reveals itself. The very identity of this confidence, this certainty, is not separate from rigpa; they're a single identity.

After the meditation state and during breaks, we can look back on that experience and feel an even stronger sense of conviction. Reflecting like this, we realize that these minutes of composure in the state of rigpa really do cut through samsaric delusion; it really works. We can feel totally assured of this. This strong confidence is what makes us have trust, and it is out of this trust that we can have devotion.

Let's chant *Calling the Guru from Afar*. *[chanting]*

Stay in composure for a while. *[Rinpoche rings bell]*

After imagining that the guru's state of mind and our own are indivisible, mingle your mind with the guru in the state of rigpa. Generally speaking, there are two kinds of guru: the conventional symbolic guru and the ultimate innate guru. The relative guru is the physical one, the one from whom we take the refuge precepts or the bodhisattva vow, the one who explains the Dharma to us and initiates us into Vajrayana practice, the one from whom we receive the pointing-out instruction. This is the guru whom we see with our own eyes, who is composed of the five aggregates, the physical being to whom we direct our prayers, the guru with whom we can communicate directly.

The ultimate innate guru is the very nature of the guru's mind, which is fully endowed with all the qualities of original wakefulness. Our own nature is not different from his in any way whatsoever, neither in size nor in quality. To see this in our own experience, to lay bare the nature of our mind, the state of rigpa, the innate dharmata, whatever word we use—to realize that fully, in actuality, is called *realizing the ultimate innate master.*

PART THREE

DESSERT

RETREAT

Buddhism, when applied in practice, can be summarized into the *three superior trainings*—the trainings in superior discipline, concentration, and insight. I would like to explain how we can use these three trainings as the basis for retreat. The Tibetan word for retreat, *tsam*, means a boundary line. To begin a retreat means literally to draw the boundary. The experience of closing up this boundary line can be defined on three levels: outer, inner, and innermost. We often find these distinctions in the general Buddhist teachings. Especially in Vajrayana, there are frequently three levels or even more—the outer, inner, innermost, innermost unexcelled, and ultimate. Please don't have the attitude that the outer is something inferior, the inner is slightly better, and the innermost is really special. These distinctions don't indicate differences in quality but rather differences in subtlety. The outer level refers to that which is immediately obvious to anyone. Behind that, there's something that is sort of hidden. It wasn't deliberately hidden by anyone; it's just naturally out of sight. As we grow more familiar with the visible level, it dawns on us that there is another level, and behind that we eventually find yet another level. That is just how things naturally are; please don't think that any one level is somehow better than another.

The outer level of retreat is connected with the *training in superior discipline*. The Buddha spoke of the first training in these words: "A sense of discipline is like the earth itself. It is the ground from which all good qualities can grow forth." Discipline has to do with what is traditionally called the four main precepts[3] and the subsidiary ones. It's good if we can keep these.

Our behavior and how we speak should also be embraced by discipline of both body and speech. The first basic advice to a meditator in the Tibetan system is to make sure your body stays on the meditation

---

[3] Refraining from murder, theft, sexual abuse, and deception.

seat. Second, your body should be relaxed, and third, your mind should be in your body. Be relaxed but not overrelaxed, as when we're really tired and stretch out to relax. Here there is a sense of being self-contained and upright, just as a cup placed on a table stands upright—it's steady and simply *there*, relaxed and not uptight. You are not intoxicated with being relaxed, but you are very present at the same time. Often people don't understand this important balance between relaxation and presence. Some people get more stressed the more they meditate, while others emphasize being too relaxed, and they become more stupid. Physically our body should be very relaxed and at ease, while at the same time our consciousness should be clear and awake. It's said, "When the right circumstance is arranged in the body, realization occurs in the mind."

Discipline means keeping certain codes of conduct, both physical and verbal. By being in retreat and by training in being careful and conscientiousness, we are not killing anyone, or we are trying not to. We're not stealing anyone's belongings nor engaging in sexual misconduct. With our voice, we avoid lying, slandering, harsh words, and idle gossip. Keeping to these is what I mean by the outer retreat.

A retreat location should be fairly removed from other human dwellings, at least one and a half miles away. In retreat, it is good to remain silent. Not speaking the whole day suddenly frees up much more time. That means that we have more leisure to practice and we'll be more relaxed. There's no talking at my retreats. There's a special quality in silence. Quite a bit of talk is concerned with stirring up feelings of either desire or aggression; a lot of time is wasted on that. During silence, instead spend time in practicing. Another point is that gossiping dissipates the energy and power of speech, of mantra. Talking pointlessly disturbs other people's minds, and third, it creates thoughts in one's own mind.

The inner level of retreat relates to the *training in superior concentration*, being collected and not caught up in what happens outside. It also has to do with our own thoughts: having a certain presence of mind due to keeping mindful. The body is relaxed and on the meditation seat, and our mind is composed, meaning not involved constantly in something other, but is simply present. The mind is in charge now, not some other entity commanding our attention. This is what shamatha training is all about: being present.

The inner retreat is to give up superfluous activity, and you accomplish that by refraining from talking or carrying out other worldly activities. When you pay attention to something, then keep to that, instead of letting your attention drift off to all kinds of other matters. Firmly focus on whatever you are occupied with at that time. Keep your attention like a peg that's been driven into the ground in a meadow—it just stays there. Be undistracted. The training in concentration is to be independent rather than being steered by circumstances. Instead of allowing your attention to wander aimlessly, have it be in charge of itself. The unwavering quality we cultivate through the training in superior concentration is very precious and important.

Now we come to the innermost retreat, the *training in superior insight*, sometimes described as "beyond keeping and giving up." You acknowledge a sense of pervasiveness through every experience. This innermost retreat in fact means there are no boundary lines at all, since it pervades every single situation. You recognize the nature that transcends sometimes keeping and at another times letting go. Let's get this point straight, because the innermost retreat is the most crucial; it is the point on which everything stands or falls. We must bring this forth in a fruitful way. The outer and inner retreats are meant to create the conducive circumstances for that to happen.

The innermost retreat is about drawing the boundary so that dualistic thoughts, the thoughts that conceptualize a perceiver and the perceived, dissolve into our innate nature. When our dualistic thinking dissolves into dharmata, there is no longer any boundary to keep or to transgress. That is the meaning of the innermost retreat. We become capable of letting everything that takes place in our experience be liberated within a sense of spaciousness and expansiveness. We need this in order to progress.

To reiterate, the innermost retreat is the training in superior insight. This means to go totally beyond every conceptual boundary of what to keep or discard. You transcend the walls of conceptual attitude, to simply be basic space. That itself is Dzogchen retreat. The innermost retreat is to realize the Great Perfection.

The training in superior insight automatically includes the training in being collected and the training in being disciplined. In our external behavior we maintain discipline, but inside we should be very carefree, open-minded, and totally relaxed, at ease and not worrying so much about this and that.

My personal style of retreat is to be disciplined outwardly but relaxed inwardly, carefree on the inside. This is an essential point of living simply in a complex world. It is not the opposite—maintaining discipline inside while nonchalant on the outside. If we do that, we become uptight inside and frivolous on the outside. Do the opposite: be happy and carefree internally, and don't feel guilty about being carefree. People often think, "There is so much suffering in this world—how can I be carefree and happy?" From a certain perspective this is true, but it's a limited perspective. If your unhappiness and inner tension could somehow help suffering people, that would be fine. But if it doesn't help them, it's not necessary. It's better to be totally open, to have this openness of mind that is like an open circuit, like a connection to all buddhas and all beings, and to receive the blessings and then pass them on, making wishes and aspirations that this may benefit them all. That is the best situation. And it happens slowly, slowly, as we train in liberating all thoughts and emotions into the expanse of awareness.

Spiritual practice is not about just doing whatever we feel like, according to our habit or our mood at a particular moment. Dharma practice means dissolving those habits and moods. Otherwise, the habits never give us a second's rest. If they would just give us a break once in a while, we would be free to practice when the habitual inclinations took a holiday. But they don't; habits and moods are on twenty-four hours a day. It is up to us to interrupt them. In fact, spiritual practice is to cut through habits.

New habits are continuously being formed—habit, habit, habit, habit. To carry on with the Dzogchen teachings, our perseverance should be one of fortitude, which in Tibetan literally means "firm in one's heart," as firm as bone. With firmness of resolve we can achieve complete enlightenment in one lifetime, in this very body. We must find out when and in what situation to be diligent, to apply ourselves. In other words, we should understand the key points of spiritual practice: trust, compassion, intelligence, and diligence. Possessing these key points, we're suitable recipients for the Dzogchen teachings and we find ourselves moving forward on the path. That's how it is.

As I've often stated, Dzogchen has to do with how we experience phenomena and their unconditioned nature. Conditioned phenomena are the perceptible contents in our experience. It is a fact that all phenomena, whatever is perceived, never part from their unconditioned nature, dharmata itself. Everything is complete or perfectly contained within that. That is one meaning of *dzog*, the first word in Dzogchen. Another connotation is that all conditioned phenomena—including ignorance, emotions, duality, obscurations, and so forth—are completed, in the sense of being finished, vanished, dissolved, or purified within the immensity of the innate nature.

The word *chen* in Dzogchen, meaning "great," means that from the very beginning everything, whatever appears and exists, has never been anything other than pure perfection. There has never been a single day, a single moment when everything was not complete purity, pure perfection. It's not that everything has to be brought to a state of purity at some point, but rather that it always was and is. To acknowledge that this is how it really is, we need the third of the three trainings: the training in superior insight. The main job in my retreats is this third training, which is to discover the state of the Great Perfection.

Any questions?

STUDENT: Could you explain more about retreat in terms of the three vehicles?

RINPOCHE: Actually, my style of retreat could be defined as practicing all three yanas at the same time. First, we lay the basis with the Vinaya, meaning with a sense of discipline. Then we adorn that with the Mahayana attitude of compassion, and finally we bring forth the fruition of the Vajrayana.

Vinaya refers to the very basis of Buddhist practice. You could draw a parallel to the Theravadin teachings, but discipline really has to do with how you conduct yourself. You move about in a gentle and respectful way, so that when you relate to people you don't use harsh words, facial expressions, or body language. When sitting down, you sit with a straight back, in a nice posture, not a lazy slouch. When meditating, you don't submit to one thought after another, which would be daydreaming. Nor do you let yourself be absentminded. When teachings are being given, you listen carefully. When practicing, you pay attention.

On a deeper level, discipline involves releasing the attitude of separateness, the conceptual world of "he" and "me," "I" and "that," in which things are always kept apart in our experience. You let go of this attitude in order to realize one taste, the single nature of all things. After experiencing the equality of all phenomena, you can appreciate their multiplicity. First let go of the separateness to allow the realization of equality.

This principle is important whether we are practicing Theravada or training in the Mahayana attitude and trying to behave like a bodhi- sattva. Understand here that the multiplicity, the manifoldness, must first be realized as one taste. After that, within the one taste of all things, their distinctive features can now arise in multiplicity again, but in a different way because you no longer hold the rigid notion of a personal entity and the identity of phenomena. The superficial reality we produce and carry in our minds right now is like garbage that needs to be recycled within the big recycling machine of one taste. Once it's been straightened out, cleaned up, and is able to be reused, it's a different matter. It's like clean recycled paper that can be used again. Right now we have empty bottles lying in one area, chocolate wrappers somewhere else, plastic bags strewn all over the place. Just having these around is not good enough. They need to be recycled.

It's the same with our concepts. We form so many notions in our minds of "me" and "you," "that" and "this," east and west, south and north, yesterday, today, tomorrow, above, below. These concepts within which we envelop ourselves, these concepts that we regard as having so much reality, are actually one big illusion. As long as we maintain that constricted way of experiencing reality, we postpone the chance of being enlightened. There is no truth to what we see or hear really. The Buddha said the objects of sight and sound are not to be regarded as ultimate truth, as a verifiable reality. No enlightenment is possible while we are clinging to these as solid. Some people may wonder, what does this word "enlightenment" actually refer to? Really, it is nothing that special. It's simply when the factors that tighten us up, that constrict us, that confine us, are released. Then we can say we are free. Enlightenment is just another word for being free.

STUDENT: What is the purpose of an offering feast?

RINPOCHE: We make a feast offering, a *tsok*, in order to be in harmony with all the masters of the lineage, the dakinis, and the guardians of the teachings. The Vajrayana feast mends any rift, reconciles any dishar- mony that may have taken place. When people don't get along for small reasons, they get together and throw a party so that everything is cleared up, forgiven and forgotten. In the same way, we may have fallen into disharmony with the teachings, or there may be disharmony among Dharma friends. All this can be cleared up by throwing a *ganachakra* feast. We make a party where we drink a little wine, eat good food, and have a good time together. This is the outer meaning.

The inner meaning of feast has to do with the fact that the food and drink, which have the nature of means and knowledge, enter your mouth and the mandala of your physical body in the form of unconditioned nectar. The nature of great bliss permeates the 72,000 channels in your subtle body, and this feeling of ease and bliss suffuses your physical being so that all the channels that were bent, withered, or tangled are straightened out and fully opened up. The deities that dwell in this mandala of your body, all the dakas and dakinis, are given this offering of unconditioned great bliss that is indivisible from emptiness. Imagine that they all get intoxicated with the taste of great bliss and are fully satisfied. This complete internal harmony is the inner meaning.

For the innermost level of feast, you acknowledge the basic space of your being, called dharmadhatu, the immensity of your empty nature, as the offering tray for the feast offerings. The feast articles themselves are the cognizant, awake quality that is present within this emptiness. Your unconditioned nature, manifest in actuality, its increase in experience and vision, your awareness reaching culmination, and the exhaustion of concepts and conditioned phenomena, as well as the six lamps and the display of awareness—all these are the innermost feast articles. In short, when these articles don't leave their tray, everything that appears and exists is part of the innermost feast. In this way, when everything is spontaneously experienced as being pure—a purity that is free of dualistic clinging to subject and object—everything on the innermost level is in harmony as well.

ADVICE TO THE DRIED-UP YOGI

According to the extraordinary teachings of Dzogchen, all phenomena are naturally contained within rigpa. The panacea is therefore to know rigpa, and this knowing is called "the single sufficient king." Recognize the empty essence, and from within the continuity of emptiness, phenomena unfold as its expression. This key point, that all phenomena are part of rigpa's spontaneous presence, is extremely precious. But "Dzogchen training" without genuinely acknowledging rigpa's empty and spacious quality makes its expression juiceless—rigpa's compassionate brilliance and intelligence fails to manifest. There is the danger of one's incorrect "rigpa" becoming dry.

Tulku Urgyen Rinpoche's teachings were expressed primarily through his realization. He was probably of the instantaneous type, meaning that from the very first, when he was young, he recognized the empty essence, the cognizant nature, and their indivisibility. The actual substance of his initial understanding became what he taught throughout his whole life. He spoke about this directly and emphatically to his disciples, teaching the essence of naked awareness. We in comparison may have recognized that essence, but we get caught up in its expression repeatedly. At our level, as ordinary people, we need to know the vital difference between essence and expression; we must recognize the essence of rigpa and grow accustomed to it. Whenever we are just about to follow the expression, the movement, we should recognize rigpa's wakefulness. That is what we ought to do continuously. If we are able to train like this repeatedly, we will progress.

A crucial point I've maintained throughout these teachings is that mental movement can arise even though you are familiar with rigpa. Without moving away from the continuity of rigpa, this *seeming motion* should be allowed to arise. It is not a real motion in the sense of being solid; rather, it is permeated by the scent of rigpa. There *is* cognizance during a mental movement, of course—if there were not, then rigpa would be blocked, obstructed. But, as the Dzogchen scriptures often say, "If you do not know the essence in the expression, then the expression turns into thought and deludes you." It is the expression, *not* the empty essence, that you can be either deluded or freed.

I would like to mention a particular problem that so-called advanced Dzogchen practitioners could face at some point in the training. This is how the Dzogchen yogi's trouble could begin: the cognizant nature seems to freeze, to turn into ice, while the empty quality is like a vacant blank, and you feel obstructed, blocked. Even though you recognized that your mind is empty in essence and you *know* it, somehow you have missed the vital point that the cognizant quality's expression is a self-arising self-liberation, so the cognizance seems to freeze in its emptiness. In this frozen state, there may be no overt thought activity going on— no gross attachment, aversion, or stupidity nor any strong clinging. There is not anything in particular. Still, this is an obstructed state because rigpa's unimpededness is lacking. In the genuine openness of rigpa, everything arises and is liberated. Whatever arises in your mind—be it a sense of ease, well-being, discomfort, joy, sadness, painful emotion, irritation, or anything else—is allowed to arise. The essence is not lost and it is not closed off. Being frozen in the empty state, however, you may still be lucid, but what you are experiencing is *not* rigpa. It does not help to maintain this blocked state; it will only hamper the expression of enlightened qualities.

If you were not cognizant at all, this state would turn into just plain old stupidity. You would be lost in the all-ground for a while, from where you return into the patterns of negative emotions. The cognizance in this case is quite lucid. However, if it freezes into *feeling* empty, it is a mental act and is not total nondoing. This is the mental action that maintains the blank, vacant state. If your training is to rest like that, you do not give birth to any compassion whatsoever. You feel neither respect nor devotion. You are temporarily stuck in a frozen state of nothing whatsoever. Now, compare this to the juicy qualities of compassion and devotion that flow forth from an authentic practitioner! In Tulku Urgyen Rinpoche, you sensed that nothing was obstructed. No matter when you saw him, morning, night, or whenever, he was fresh and juicy—not like a dried-up yogi who is blocked up and closed off in his private space.

Normally, our cognizance—let's call it Mr. Cognizant Nature—keeps hold of the past, the future, anger, pride, or jealousy. In this particular brand of "petrified shamatha," the cognizant nature manages a state of nothing whatsoever, and he holds in mind a blank nothingness as his object. The empty quality remains stuck in vacancy. Usually, Mr. Cognizant Nature is in anger, pride, jealousy, past thoughts, and future thoughts. Now he thinks, "This is no longer good. I should stop, I should meditate." But along the way he gets stuck in being empty, leans too much to the empty side, so that there is no longer a unity of being empty and cognizant. The cognizance turns into the subject, the emptiness its object. Fixated like that, there is not a single good quality, except for one: blatant negative emotions do not arise. Unlike true rigpa, this state is not free of the cognitive obscuration. Although new emotional obscurations are not formed, the previous ones are not purified either. In fact, nothing is being purified.

This frozen, juiceless state is a state of enforced abiding. You dwell in the present moment. It is better than shamatha, a little higher even, but it can be more dangerous than clinging to a regular sense of calm, because this state involves a very subtle, problematic type of clinging. You are not being mindful of a *thing*; the knowing quality is fixed on *being empty*. It is not exactly an emotional fixation; it is a sort of locking-in on being empty. So what is the method to unlock your awareness? What is the way to prevent falling into this uninspired vacantness? There are two methods: the general methods of cultivating compassion and *lojong*, mind training, and the Vajrayana method of guru yoga—"traveling on the highway of devotion." Use them to quickly progress in view, meditation, and conduct.

Guru yoga involves supplicating with devotion, and in the beginning this sense of devotion is mind-made. Nevertheless, as you notice that your mind is locked in, think, "This is not good. It is time to sing *Calling the Guru from Afar*." Supplicate your teacher and practice guru yoga. With the attitude "please grant your blessings," the ice slowly melts, and juice flows through your mind. Supplicate in a deep-felt, wholehearted fashion, so that your previous mental states all melt, dissolve. Then recognize the essence of rigpa, and the mind-made devotion also falls apart. The blessings slowly transform your state from the locked-in feeling to being wide open. Among the many enhancement practices the most essential is guru yoga.

Your Dzogchen training must bring forth these three qualities: devotion, compassion, and intelligence. And with their support you will experience impartial, pure perception. Bodhichitta, the deep-felt wish to liberate all sentient beings, arises through training in compassion. "All these sentient beings without exception have been my own mother and father." With this attitude, abandon the ego-oriented thoughts of "me" and try to equalize yourself and others. Third, since the essence of Dzogchen is by nature intelligence itself, you should not be ignorant about anything whatsoever—not dull, obscured, unknowing, absent-minded, oblivious, or even lost in thought. Rigpa is an aware state, a wide-awake state.

The three qualities—devotion, compassion, and intelligence—should come about naturally. Although you may not have much attachment, anger, or stupidity, the absence of the three qualities is a sign that you might be doing "freeze training." If the three qualities do not come easily, from time to time you have to manufacture them. Sometimes remain in composure, then destroy the meditation state and instead do the compassionate practice of tonglen, exchanging yourself for others, as in the traditional Kadampa style from Atisha. Occasionally alternate between training in pure perception and resting in the view by training in the threefold sky practice. At that time, whatever happens, do not fixate, do not meditate: practice nonmeditation. Interchange and alternate among these three.

In truth, devotion, compassion, and intelligence should come about naturally, but their natural arising is a bit difficult at the beginning. The Dzogchen texts mention that on the "exterior" we should maintain a training in rigpa that is uncontrived, while on the "interior" we sometimes start a session with a fabricated meditation. Whatever the case may be, you must definitely train in loving-kindness and compassion during the postmeditation. Since they are rooted in intelligence, love and compassion naturally and gradually blossom the more you genuinely train in rigpa. How does compassion expand? As you train further in the state of rigpa, a tender feeling can emerge that is not based on a sense of "I." You feel a bit sad, like Milarepa, who sang of unceasing sadness. This is not the grief of losing one's father or mother, or the unhappiness of having no food, or the despair of ending up in hell. Nor is it the sadness of feeling sorry for someone who has died. The feeling I describe is more open than that; there is no particular object for your compassion. An atmosphere of tenderness just naturally permeates you, like juice. But you are not sinking into this tenderness and losing the sense of intelligence. Your lucid intelligence is crystal clear and at the same time very tender. You also experience a deeper devotion, a commitment that springs from appreciation. As with compassion, let it be lucid and clear. Do not become rapt in its excitement like Hare Krishna devotees.

Another problem meditators encounter is known as *straying into the all-ground*. According to the extraordinary teachings of the Great Perfection, your training should be alive and vivid, not obscured and dull. While you are clear, awake, and totally unobscured, the three qualities I mentioned above should be present—and if they are, then everything is fine. The problem comes up when one doesn't practice according to the Dzogchen teachings and instead follows the old habit of letting the essence stray into the all-ground. You may be sincere and devoted and compassionate, but if your training is anchored in the all-ground, you are merely extending the basis for further samsara. From the all-ground, the ego again rears up. Such training does not free you from samsaric existence.

Now you might think, "It shouldn't be like this; I should destroy artificial emotions and emphasize a supercorrectness!" That attitude leaves no room for compassion and devotion, and those qualities remain incomplete, leaving your training in danger of being very dry. The key point is that all three qualities must be present in the vividly awake essence. If all of these qualities are there, it is a truly good practice.

This is a very difficult point to understand immediately. Sometimes there is devotion or compassion, but there is a danger of trying to control it, claiming ownership. "The teachings say to be compassionate. Before I didn't have any compassion, and now I do. I must be an advanced practitioner now." When Mr. Cognizant Nature then assumes ownership of compassion or devotion, the practitioner has gone astray. Don't do that.

The Dzogchen teachings often speak of empty essence. Why? It's in order to reduce grasping immediately. It's so easy to suddenly leap into grasping; we get involved repeatedly. In the empty essence, we grasp. In the cognizant nature, we grasp. In bliss, we grasp. In compassion, we grasp. In devotion, we grasp. In every situation, we grasp. Now we must break apart this grasping tendency. Destroy, destroy, destroy. But there is a danger of straying into vacant blankness if we get too preoccupied with avoiding the grasping. In order for that not to happen, bring forth devotion and compassion. When your devotion and compassion become too obsessive, destroy them as well.

STUDENT: How does compassion in this practical context include an acceptance of or love for oneself?

RINPOCHE: How does compassion first appear? In the beginning, the first compassion is for oneself. It appears with a sense of joy, of delight, and when this delight expands it encompasses others as well. Where does this delight come from? It comes from appreciating how it is to be free. True freedom comes about through confidence in liberating any and all thought states.

Most people are actually afraid of themselves. Not in the sense of being afraid of their own hand or head or such, but in a different way. Of course, there are exceptions, like being afraid of looking at this old head in the mirror getting older every day. When I look in the mirror I see there is less and less hair there—it's truly scary. Really, joking aside, being afraid of oneself, as I said earlier, is a matter of "I can't get along with what happens in my mind. Something is wrong in the relationship between me and my experience."

We all have a subtle fear to begin with: existence itself is tinged with fear. But that fear can get mixed up with unnecessary factors, with some other aspects in your being. There is some confusion about how one experiences. "I"—what does it refer to? It is not necessarily this body, but somehow we experience "I feel," "I sense," "I feel bad," "I feel good"—about "my relationship," "my possessions," "my house," "my world." And this relationship to the whole affair can feel quite awkward, insofar as you are not really clear about what is what. Within that confusion, you are uncertain as to what will happen next—"Why am I here? How do I operate? What is the solution? I don't really know what is going to happen or how to deal with it"—and somehow you are scared of it.

When you are scared of it, that fear is *you*. You don't find any other experience than that to define yourself. Somehow you are scared of yourself. The situation is uncertain, unclear. And within this feeling various thoughts arise, of being annoyed or proud, jealous or closed-minded, clinging to this and that. It is very unpleasant. You feel, "I would rather not be this way." But since you don't know how to avoid being this way, these feelings keep coming at you—"This is not right, it shouldn't be this way, but it keeps being so"—over and over again. And then you start to lose self-confidence.

From my point of view, this is actually the main dilemma for human beings. Animals do not suffer in this way. We think, "I shouldn't feel this way," but because we do not know how *not* to feel this way, we are not free. We should be free, but we're not. This shouldn't happen, but it does. It shouldn't be so painful, but it is. And it just goes on and on. The worst part is that you realize that those awkward feelings are no good and shouldn't be there, but they are, and it is painful. If you just didn't notice the pain, it would be somewhat okay; you could just carry on. The worst part is that you do notice how painful it is, and not knowing how to be free makes it more painful. It is like being in a real hell.

Because of this acute discomfort, you pursue something you heard of called meditation practice. You meditate and meditate and try to learn about and train this mind. Your old habit of giving total credence to perceptions loosens to some extent. You start to blame your thoughts less; there is a sense of befriending your thoughts, because honestly, these thoughts are also you. You need to love, to give space to these thoughts, and in doing so you are helping yourself. Now when a thought arises it is sometimes liberated. This happens a few times, and you notice, "Hey, a thought can arise, but it's not so harmful, it doesn't matter so much." One thought arises and it is liberated; another one comes, and it too is liberated. You begin to be in harmony, to develop a friendship with the occurrence of thoughts.

You now begin to notice a harmony among the thoughts as well, so that even angry and proud thoughts can become friends. A desirous thought and a loving thought can also be reconciled—you have plenty of space for them. Through the recognition of empty essence, there seems to be more space for everyone. Giving space automatically transforms into a sense of love for the thoughts. Previously, it didn't feel like there was any room for a single thought or emotion: the whole situation was claustrophobic. This is far more comfortable. Recognizing empty essence gives more room for the whole picture that is the sense of love for thought. You feel at ease from within because there is more harmony. You become intrinsically harmonious. You yourself have become harmony, and you feel deeply at ease with yourself.

The difference between fear and harmony is in how you handle your thoughts. When in harmony with them and at ease, you actually *can* be very peaceful. As you experience a greater and greater sense of peace, you become lighthearted: "My whole experience used to be so frozen and rigid, but now it is completely at ease within me. This is great! Ah, I love myself!" In the right atmosphere, this feeling can deepen gently and naturally—not aggressively, which would distort the whole situation. You feel delighted, at ease but not clinging to this sense of ease either, and all because of the Dzogchen instructions that allow thoughts and emotions to be naturally liberated. Because of these instructions, you experience a growing sense of spacious mind and a profound delight in being at ease. Sometimes the teachings describe this as giving rise to a feeling of overwhelming, almost unbearable devotion, compassion, and joy.

There is a certain spiritual attitude that makes it obligatory to please others selflessly, to try to obliterate yourself, to want only to please others. This forced unselfishness is like squeezing toothpaste out of the tube. There is something missing—half the compassion is missing. There is something absent—the quality of natural liberation. You are trying to be unselfish and care for others, by squeezing and squeezing and squeezing. There is no new juice left. At some point you may regret this altogether, saying, "What am I doing here? What's the use?" This spirit of self-sacrifice looks very good, and it *is* of course a good attitude; I am not saying it is bad. I suggest that instead you allow compassion to flow from a sense of being free, from within your own spacious state of being. The root of compassion is this quality of freedom. In knowing how to naturally liberate any and every thought state, there is a sense of delight, and that is the root of unconditioned compassion.

In this state of freedom, your former confusion is settled harmoniously. It's completely cleared up, and in addition, there is an increasingly strong sense of confidence. As this confidence grows stronger, you find yourself turning into a *real* warrior—a compassionate bodhisattva warrior. Compassion that lacks this fearless confidence is a chicken-hearted loving-kindness.

The true bodhisattva spirit grows out of this personal sense of freedom. You discover that you don't feel so needy anymore. You don't crave another refueling—with shamatha or with other people's love and attention—because you know within yourself how to be free, how to be confident. With this sense of security and freedom, you begin to direct your attention to the needs of others. The compassion expands. This is my point about inner simplicity as the basis for living fearlessly in a complex world.

This principle of fearless simplicity involves training in the two accumulations *as a unity* and experiencing the fruition of such training. We have found a true, effective remedy for ego-clinging, negative emotions, the twofold ignorance, and adversity. We have persevered in the two accumulations, and we have grown confident in liberation. We are now open and spacious, and from within that sense of fearless simplicity, we can accommodate all phenomena. We can naturally care for others unpretentiously; no one is a threat any longer.

This spirit is definitely permeated by a sense of joy, because you know from your own experience how painful it all was previously, and now it isn't. Taking hold of the real solution is very delightful. This is the genuine experience of knowing how to be free—the ego gives up, saying, "Okay, now I am finally satisfied." All the hardness has melted, like butter on a hot plate. This doesn't mean that you sit and savor its taste. Rather, you open up even further. You understand very clearly, *experientially*, how the mechanism of dissolving confusion and being free works. It's very workable. With this insight you no longer feel like just leaning back into a personal state of passive peace. "So many other beings are still not aware of how to be this way. How wonderful it would be if they just could!" You grow increasingly keen on sharing with others this reality of how to be free. There is a willingness to reach out to other beings. You have arrived at active compassion.

This fearless and simple frame of mind is very carefree, very open, very moisturized, not dry at all. Compassion is Dzogchen moisturizing cream. It's full of juice. It might differ entirely from the time you first trained in emptiness, a mind-made emptiness, a juiceless style of being vacant and open, a training that in itself was never going to turn into the real Dzogchen state. But now it's almost unexplainable, yet after a while, you begin to feel confident from your deepest being as to how it is. Because of this openness, this complete loosening up, it is like you are thoroughly saturated. Tibet is a very dry place, so people rub butter on leather, for example, to moisturize it. It's as if compassionate butter has reached into every single nook and cranny, in the sense that your entire being—every thought and emotion, every part of yourself, your innermost being, your heart, your spirit, everything—is saturated by this compassionate openness. Every thought and every emotion is saturated with a sense of caring, not superficially but deeply and naturally. Through recognizing, training, and attaining stability in rigpa, every single area is liberated. This liberation extends through your whole brain and your entire nervous system. There is no corner left dry in your stream of being.

At this time, there is a certain free quality to the empty essence that permeates your entire being, so that you feel extremely carefree. Out of this, real compassion grows. It is also from this shedding the burden that devotion comes, through this delight and sense of rejoicing in how you are. You feel that this Dharma is so great. You really appreciate these teachings deeply—"Wow!" Delight and appreciation mingle. This is based on confidence too, in that you are not scared of yourself; you are willing to face anything and everything your mind may stage. You have a technique to liberate it. You don't have to be annoyed with your phenomena. Rather, you are able to be in harmony with whatever arises. That is the basic sense of love for yourself.

At the same time, you have confidence: you are not scared of anything anymore. Somehow phenomena seem to work well for you. And the sense of appreciation grows: "How wonderful! How great! Marvelous! Awesome!" It's almost as if you are taking refuge in that confidence. It is a very relaxed, delightful feeling combined with certainty. These feelings all combine to create a stronger and stronger appreciation. You feel, "How wonderful these Dzogchen teachings are! They are so beneficial! I have practiced for five or six years and I have already gained so much benefit. So the buddhas and bodhisattvas and all the masters, the yogis and yoginis who have trained for so long—how wonderful their state of realization must be!" You rejoice in their awakening. This feeling of strong rejoicing and appreciation is called devotion. It is a sincere interest, a deep admiration, which is like your first love. This deep admiration opens your heart even more; it completely intoxicates you.

Throughout this whole affair, rigpa is never abandoned. It is there all the time. In fact, at this point you can say the qualities of rigpa have begun to play. This is the point where the display begins to manifest, and it feels pretty good. You are very open, you don't hate samsaric phenomena, and the will to practice grows even stronger. In fact, you enjoy samsaric phenomena, but you're free of attachment to that enjoyment, no longer chasing after it, hankering after it, wanting to hold it captive. It is more like when you watch a movie: you are entertained by the movie, but you don't attach a solid reality to it. The daily display of samsaric phenomena is like a motion picture; you relate to it as if it were a movie. It is *seemingly* real, but when you pursue it is not really so.

Once you understand rigpa experientially, you know what is meant by the ability to enjoy the phenomena of samsara. Before you recognized rigpa, there seemed to be only two ways of relating to samsaric phenomena: one is dualistic grasping, the other is the feeling of futility and wanting to keep it away from yourself.

Please understand that the compassion and devotion that arise from experiencing the awakened state are not what we conventionally know as compassion and devotion. It is together with true intelligence, the real knowledge of how to be free—that is why they can become true compassion and true devotion. Otherwise, of course we feel compassion, of course we have some degree of devotion, but it is more like we either are forced into or manipulate ourselves into these feelings for a specific reason; they don't happen spontaneously and sincerely. The devotion and compassion that arise out of true intelligence are unshakable. They arise out of true confidence.

Intelligence here means a sense of being capable, of knowing how and what is happening when a thought or emotion begins to take shape. You are no longer blind to what is taking place. Nor is it like in the past, when you got annoyed or irritated, when you got wrapped up in certain feelings for hours at a time before you could finally let go. It's not like that any more. There is a sense of being awake to the situation that you can call intelligence. You are seeing clearly how it works—not only how it unfolds but also what the solution is, and how it is possible to simply let the clinging dissolve. You are not ignorant about that at all. This intelligence comes from within. You can almost say it is in the air, *together with* the arising of, for example, desire, which otherwise could cause so much trouble. The negative emotions create so many complications and pain when one gets caught up in them, chases after something, and loses track of oneself. Intelligence here means to see very clearly what leads to negative states, what has bad consequences, and what the right way is. All this is laid out quite clearly in your field of vision, so that of course you choose—not conceptually, but with a certain immediacy—the right way rather than the blind alley. This intelligence is not like being able to memorize ten thousand phone numbers or figure out intricate systems. It is natural, from deep within. It's a feeling of not being blind, a fundamental absence of blindness. That intelligence is a natural attribute, a natural atmosphere that arises from recognizing rigpa.

Compassion, devotion, strong appreciation and admiration, unfold in this way; and so does intelligence, a real brightness that grows further and further. This is not the same as developing the intellect through formal education, which is a part of the sixth consciousness; that is entirely different and has more to do with being less and less unaware. The "intrinsic unawareness" is dissolved through intrinsic awareness, the coemergent ignorance through coemergent knowledge. As the habit of *simply not knowing* diminishes, the *simply knowing* gets stronger and stronger, more and more evident. Intelligence here is not an external component we try to bring into our state. It is more a natural quality of rigpa itself that manifests increasingly.

In the beginning it is possible to be wrong, to get into a frozen, stiff, dried-out, mistaken rigpa. After a while, though, when these three qualities are present, it is no longer possible to make that mistake. The best is if all three—compassion, devotion, and intelligence—are naturally part of rigpa. Sometimes one of them might predominate so that there is more compassion, devotion, or intelligence. But all three of these are called intrinsic qualities of rigpa.

When training in ultimate truth, one could go to the far end of the scale where nothing matters. When training in relative truth, one could cling to everything as having a concrete, solid meaning. Both of these are too extreme. While we need to know the difference between them, we must balance and harmonize ultimate truth and relative truth. Everything the Buddha taught can be personally verified. We can have certainty by understanding the two truths because they include everything, including the Four Noble Truths. At a certain point we have to practice in a way in which the two truths are indivisible. According to Dzogchen teachings, to recognize the empty quality and thereby not cling at all is to respect ultimate truth. At the same time, experience unfolds unobstructedly in very amazing ways. To recognize that as well is to respect relative truth. These two should be experienced as an indivisible unity.

Mingling Practice
with Daily Life

Here are a few bits of advice on mingling practice with daily life. There are many manuals as well as your personal teacher's instructions on how to mingle recognizing rigpa with daily life. In spite of these numerous methods, it is not that easy to combine this practice with everyday life. The extraordinary teachings of the Great Perfection state that in all situations one should recognize the dharmakaya awareness and that there is no need to depend on any other method. Whether there is anger, desire, stupidity, pride, or any other negative emotion, recognize dharmakaya awareness and your negative emotions are self-liberated, liberated upon arising, or directly liberated. This is indeed how it is for the skilled yogi, but for a beginner on the path, practicing like this is exceedingly difficult. Liberation of thoughts is more likely to occur during sessions than in the postmeditation or daily activities.

The hardest time to remember to practice, as well as the most beneficial time, is when we are unhappy or mentally uncomfortable. We experience depression, exhilaration, strong pride, or rivalry, or we simply feel stressed and overwhelmed by a lot of work. Our mind excessively churns out thoughts: "I must do this, I must do that." It is hard to recognize rigpa in the midst of this unceasing obsession with what needs to be done. On these occasions you need some additional mind training, lojong. When you have piles of work to do and a stream of thoughts about it, remind yourself of impermanence. Immediately ask yourself, "Who knows when I am going to die? If I died today, would anyone finish my work?" Understand that mundane work is endless and futile. Think that all is like a dream and a magical illusion. Convince yourself through mind training that things are not really so overwhelming, and then recognize rigpa. That is my first piece of advice.

At other times, when you are feeling depressed, sick, or unhappy or have a wind disorder, simply invite in your suffering and say, "Oh, how wonderful! Thank you so much, suffering! I really enjoy this. Whatever happens, whether you eat my flesh or drink my blood, suck the marrow out of my bones, just go ahead and do it. No matter what suffering befalls me, come on! Come right in and carry away my ego-clinging. If you want to flatten this body of aggregates, go ahead. Even if you want to drive this mind crazy, okay, go ahead, it makes no difference to me." If you can respond like this, completely carefree, the difficulties diminish. At that point, recognize self-existing rigpa. This is my second piece of advice.

Sometimes it happens that the older practitioner experiences good fortune and success. Your lama says, "Very good, you really understand meditation." Others respect you and sing your praises. Suddenly—*pop!*—pride wells up and you become overly confident. Believing yourself better than you actually are is like being a lamb dressed up like a lion. Another practitioner realizes this and shouts at you, "You are no lion! You are only wearing a lion's costume!" Immediately you feel embarrassed, deflated. This is really an opportunity to be a first-class practitioner by appreciating that other person who exposed you. Think, "Fantastic! You really know! You are really good." Apply the mind training of pure perception and then rest in the wakefulness of rigpa. I feel that this is also good advice.

Always be watchful and conscientious. According to the Kagyu forefathers, watchfulness and conscientiousness are effective at different times. There is the king of mindfulness, which is wide-awake rigpa in which everything is self-liberated in the recognition. This is first-class mindfulness. If you are not yet able to train in this, then there is the state of knowing the mind as being happy, unhappy, at ease, or uneasy. This is mind knowing itself, like a mirror. You are simply watching yourself. You may not know the nature of mind, but you can still determine how your mind behaves by being watchful. For example, if you are angry, immediately you know the anger. This knowing is not necessarily liberated, although it may be. Even if the anger is not freed, you admit being angry, and in that process the anger can be lessened. The main problem is when you do not even notice that anger has arrived. Being unaware in this way, you completely fall under the influence of the emotion.

Presence of mind also makes it possible for the king of mindfulness to naturally liberate thoughts. The foremost practice is to be able to remain in the inseparability of rigpa and mindfulness. If not, then through applying deliberate mindfulness, you are made aware of your mind and how it behaves. Tulku Urgyen Rinpoche often quoted a famous saying of the Kagyu masters: "Being mindful is like herding sheep and goats." You notice where the sheep and goats are. This is truly beneficial, because it keeps you from being totally carried away by distraction. While training in rigpa, when in a single instant you get distracted from the continuity, you may occasionally find it quite helpful to apply a sort of watcher instead of being completely unaware of the distraction.

Now if you always keep a watcher, this maintenance act makes you unable to dissolve all thoughts. Nonetheless, the watcher does help with bringing practice into daily life situations. Therefore, alternate between deliberate mindfulness and the effortlessness of rigpa. Naked awareness either is or is not present. It is never both at the same time. If there is not rigpa, there is a thought—we have only these two options. While undistracted in awareness, it is impossible to have thoughts. Until you are stable in rigpa, apply deliberate mindfulness when distracted, as suggested by the Kagyu masters. Obviously thoughts can arise, but when thinking you can now be aware of these thoughts. By being watchful, you can immediately know coarse thoughts. Your mind will become calm. When your mind becomes dull, you will know this. Then again, remain calm. This enhancement practice is very beneficial. Adeu Rinpoche gave me this advice.

Broadly speaking, there are six types of mindfulness, but they can be condensed into two: deliberate and effortless mindfulness. The latter is Dzogchen's extraordinary king of mindfulness—being inseparable from rigpa—which can be applied wherever you are, in all situations. It is truly the best. However, it is quite important to train in deliberate mindfulness whenever you are unable to sustain rigpa. Isn't it true that you make fewer mistakes when mindful? Without mindfulness, you are swept away by appearances. When someone says an unkind word, be mindful and know whether or not you are angry. If you are not even aware that you have become angry, you have already been carried away. With mindfulness you at least know that you are angry, that anger is not okay, and that you can do something about it. Be deliberately mindful, and you'll find that it is easier to mingle practice with daily life. This is another key piece of advice.

Then, in the postmeditation or break time, supplicate your guru one-pointedly; experience deep-felt devotion, mingling your mind with your teacher's mind and having the confidence that he is close to you. With deep devotion sing *Calling the Guru from Afar*, mingling your mind insepa-rably with that of your teacher. In this way, every negative emotion, even intense anger or desire, will crumble and vanish. Tell anger, desire, and stupidity to go away. Invoke your teacher; supplicate and receive the blessings. Then rest in equanimity.

At other times, do the tonglen practice of sending and receiving, ex-changing your happiness and insight with the suffering and ignorance of sentient beings: "How sad; these poor beings, so confused and unaware; they are fooling themselves." Feel sincere compassion for them. Even if you do not have compassion for them, produce it. The Dzogchen meditator finds fabricating a bit awkward, because the teachings tell us to practice the true and avoid the fake. But honestly, faking it can be quite helpful if you play it right. Remain in the genuine, and then do this "good imitation" a bit. Especially when it comes to engendering the correct motivation, contriving can be helpful. Definitely manufacture the proper motivation. Often Westerners feel guilty pretending. They do not like being false. They say they want to be honest and that it doesn't help feigning compassion, which should come naturally. This is not the correct attitude. You need to *train* your mind in being compassionate. Aspire, yearn; make the prayer "Even if I don't feel compassion, please make it arise in my being." Cultivate compassion, create it, and pray that it may fill your heart! Pray to your teacher for compassion to develop in you. Do this and slowly, slowly, true compassion will spring forth.

We do all have the potential for genuine compassion within us; we just need to make it grow. Right now it is rather undeveloped. It's like when you beckon a small child to come; you offer candy and say, "Come here, take this sweet!" Any child will respond to that. It is a skillful method. Compassion, love, self-existing awareness are all intrin-sic to our basic nature, and we need to nurture these qualities. The empty essence, cognizant nature, and unconfined capacity must be brought to maturity. Use both methods—sometimes rest in the empty awareness and sometimes say, "Come here," almost pulling these quali-ties out. The pulling belongs to the postmeditation, while resting in the essence belongs to the meditation session. We cannot always be in ses-sion, so this is a convenient way to practice in the postmeditation. It is necessary to force the qualities forth in the breaks. Then allow the qualities to be naturally present in the meditation session.

The same principle applies to the development stage practice. Let the visualization arise, and sometimes rest in the essence. Actually, the manifest aspect does unfold unobstructedly from this essence. This is a very important point: don't overemphasize the manifestations but allow them to arise within the empty awareness. Or, when the essence seems to dissolve into the all-ground consciousness, immediately recall the deity. If you have seriously strayed into the all-ground consciousness, it is better to get up and do virtuous activities such as accumulating merit: sing *Calling the Guru from Afar* and generate compassion. It is better to perform general spiritual actions than to remain in the all-ground, bland and half mindless.

It is simply the nature of things that at the present stage, where you are now, you cannot stay a long time in rigpa. Why? The inability to sustain rigpa reflects not having enough merit. If you find that you immediately get distracted every time you let go, you should increase merit by generating it whenever possible. When you are distracted, you may get lost in a semblance of rigpa, a facsimile of it. You may think that it is rigpa, but actually you are lost in the all-ground consciousness. When you notice this, immediately break it up. Recite OM MANI PADME HUNG; do prostrations; do *rushen*; shout PHAT; generate devotion, compassion, and renunciation; gather the accumulations—then once more compose yourself in uncontrived awareness. Alternate like this throughout the whole day. At night before sleeping, make a wonderful dedication, devoid of politics, without the notion of gaining something in return. Pray sincerely to reach the state of buddhahood in order to benefit all beings. This is some more important advice.

We speak of mingling the practice with daily life because we usually get carried away during postmeditation. If there is no division between sessions and breaks, there is no mingling to do in daily life. Actually, the problem is the seeming duality of meditation and postmeditation, sessions and breaks. Once you have amassed sufficient merit and are inseparable from rigpa, there are no longer *either* sessions *or* breaks, and there is nothing to mingle or not mingle with in daily life—not at all! Dilgo Khyentse Rinpoche no longer had to mingle his practice with daily life, because whatever he did was within the domain of self-existing wakefulness. Adeu Rinpoche can sit in a *puja* for four or five hours and not lose the state of equanimity. Since he does not stray from composure, he has no need to mingle it with daily life. He merely sits in the puja, drinks tea, and remains in rigpa, having already mingled the practice and his life.

ASPIRATIONS

The thought that nonclinging is the main focus of Buddhist practice can turn into a misunderstanding of rigpa. With the idea of "clinging to nothing," the misguided practitioner could become hard, cold, and dry, as I explained earlier. Such a person confuses this juiceless, vacant state of nonclinging, of blocking out feelings, for the realization of Dzogchen and could become quite irresponsible and heartless. This dysfunctional meditator feels isolated, cut off from everything. One doesn't know how to relax and still be responsible. There *is* a way to be responsible while not clinging, but if the point of nonclinging is misunderstood, then the unattached way of experiencing turns into frozen ice and the whole affair gets very stiff. That is a danger. You can be respectful toward how things function and unfold while at the same time recognizing the emptiness of it all. Without clinging, you still allow everything to unfold.

This relationship between you and outside phenomena is fundamentally based on compassion. True compassion is not selfish, because there is no clinging to the self. Whether compassion is selfish or not depends on clinging. Some compassion appears to be unselfish, but it isn't, because the "compassionate me" is always ego. When ego dissolves, true compassion enters. This is a very important point that I want you to understand. While we train in the awakened state of rigpa, our essence is crystal clear; at the same time it is saturated with the juice of true compassion. It is through this compassionate attitude that we relate to the world.

Sometimes we engage in mind training in a determined sort of way as indicated in Shantideva's *Way of the Bodhisattva*. I think this is very helpful for Dzogchen practitioners. While you are training your attitude, don't get caught up in anything. Develop compassion, develop the four boundless states, but always in the same state of rigpa. This energy of compassion and loving-kindness sometimes becomes so strong that you might feel as if you are going to faint–but don't. That genuine feeling of compassion enhances your realization of emptiness. Sometimes you feel such strong compassion that it almost intoxicates you, but don't let it. Let the warm moisture of loving-kindness and compassion thaw the frozen meditation state.

The scripture entitled *Entering the Middle Way* says, "In the beginning, compassion is like a seed; in the middle, compassion is like water and fertilizer; in the end, compassion is like the fruit." In the end, compassion is the buddha activity. Without compassion, one is cut off. For compassion to be real we must be free of clinging, that is for sure, but the one-sided focus on nonclinging prevents compassion, renders it inadequate. When compassion arises you might think, "Oh, no! This is an ordinary emotion, I should not have it!" That becomes the nihilistic path. Conversely, you could also regard whatever you feel as being *so* precious that it smothers the genuine empathy you feel. Then it does not radiate freely, because the natural clarity drowns in this "divine" state of compassion or ecstatic devotion. Avoid that sidetrack as well.

In short, we must generate compassion. Even though the Dzogchen teachings don't generally encourage the artificial creation of anything, in this case it is necessary. Once you have recognized rigpa, deliberately generate compassion whenever possible, because it is an enhancement practice that strengthens the recognition of rigpa. I keep emphasizing this point because I think it is extremely important.

Another important point is to make prayers of aspiration. Without aspiration one's meditation lacks something important, a certain vital richness. Your aspirations must be inspired by the altruistic spirit of bodhichitta. Express them in the presence of a holy object or in a sacred place. For example, when you go to Bodhgaya, first offer one thousand flowers, one thousand butter lamps, and one thousand alms to beggars. Sit next to the Vajra Throne and, with the sacred place as your witness, offer a mandala with a completely open heart to all the buddhas and bodhisattvas. Then simply sit, let go of your ego completely, and let go of the idea of offering. Now make the sincere aspiration "For the sake of all sentient beings, may I realize rigpa." Don't pray selfishly; do not use such a precious circumstance to be egotistical. Instead, make this wish: "Even if I don't become realized in this life, may I realize rigpa in the next life to benefit countless sentient beings." The combination of that circumstance and your pure aspirations will be very, very powerful and even can influence world peace.

Unfortunately these points are missed in the West. The sincere force of our aspirations, the influence of all the buddhas and bodhisattvas as the support, the sacred place itself—all these together create a kind of powerful energy that also enhances our potential for being stable in rigpa. Westerners, though, often don't give much thought to such matters as aspirations and accumulation of merit; they think these things are mostly for beginners. In fact, making aspirations is an advanced practice for advanced practitioners.

Aspirations and creating merit are not only for enhancing rigpa; they also work for people with low self-esteem. In a developed society, there is really no mention of making aspirations and creating merit, is there? The basic attitude in the air in the West is: "go and get it." Whoever wants to go and get it, can. This premise is taken as a given: everyone has the same opportunities, everyone has the same potential, the same smarts, the same possibilities; the chances are equal and open to everyone. "You can do it just like everybody else; you have the intelligence, you are a human being, you can shape your own success; take it into your own hands." We hear this said, but what is the reality? Those who are capable go happily along and of course are perfectly fine. For them, there is probably no better system than this materialistic society. But it can be very painful for those who cannot face up to life so aggressively. They feel incapacitated somewhere deep inside, as if they are not complete human beings. Instead they need to hear, "You can still do something. You can create more merit, you can make pure aspirations." They should be told to do these activities as an antidote to low self-esteem.

Now merit-creating endeavors combined with aspirations are more than merely tools to improve one's self-image; they are major factors in attaining buddhahood. Prayers, compassion, and meritorious actions are extremely important because they propel us forward: "The more I practice, the more I learn, and the more I see. Wow! This makes a lot of sense!" Merit also creates perfect situations, spiritual as well as worldly. Otherwise we are bound by our karma and conditioning. We are under the power of causes and conditions. No matter how much we want to deny this, we cannot escape our habitual tendencies. With lack of merit, we walk the conditioned path, clutching a dry, intellectual, juiceless Dzogchen. My teacher, Nyoshul Khen Rinpoche, did the ganachakra puja offering every day. Even Dudjom Rinpoche, a fully realized master, engaged in regular practices to create merit.

There are natural forces at work here in the conditioned reality. Take the example of how you create your living situation in the West. You are experts at making yourselves very cozy and secure for your present life. Merit created through skillful means and wisdom, on the other hand, is for more than physical comfort; it is to improve the conditions for your mind. You *can* actually improve your state of mind through creating positive causes and conditions, through the force of merit. As merit ripens in your mental state due to your having gathered the accumulations and purified the obscurations, realization comes automatically. I suggest that you practice the relative while embracing it with the ultimate, the recognition of rigpa. In this way, relative and absolute enhance each other. In the case of rigpa practice, relative merit helps you to sustain the ultimate essence longer until you finally attain stability.

I feel very sad sometimes that this aspect is missing in the West. The creation of merit is an essential point. My spiritual tradition attaches profound meaning to the principle of merit. I think we should all move forward to the level where accumulating merit is combined with meditation practice. The Westerner's intelligence is very sharp, better than the Tibetan intellect. But honestly, your merit is inadequate. Don't you notice how you are always handicapped, feeling a little frozen? Even though you try your best, circumstances pull you down. It is taught that emptiness expresses itself as cause and effect. If one does not have much understanding of emptiness, then one does not really believe or have much confidence in cause and effect. Conversely, the more one realizes emptiness, the more conviction arises about cause and effect. *There is a need to work equally with merit and wisdom.* If you expand the merit aspect of your practice and join it with the wisdom meditation, I trust that soon there will be many realized masters in this country!

Any questions?

STUDENT: When a being wakes up to his essential nature and becomes a buddha, how come all beings are not awakened at that point? Or are they in some way?

RINPOCHE: Why do other sentient beings not awaken? It is because they have bad karma. You may have just parted from that group, but the others are still there doing their own business. They all have the ability to wake up, but they are not using it. As you awaken, you have the ability to bestow blessings on all sentient beings, to wake them up. Somehow, though, these blessings do not get through to them due to their karmic experience. The sun has the ability to illuminate all of California, so why is there no sunlight inside my cup here? The sun has the power to shine, right? Why is there no light inside my cup? Because the lid is on. It is completely covered. Can this wooden mallet illuminate all of California? No, of course not—but seen from the cup's point of view, "The mallet is equal to the sun, in that neither of them does anything for me; neither of them illuminates me." But isn't it true that there is a huge difference between the mallet and the sun?

Right now, at the time of the path, while we are not enlightened, we need to connect through blessings and positive aspirations. We connect through making wishes; we make bad connections, good connections, we say "Hello, how are you"—all kinds of different connections. By making pure wishes, we connect karmically with others. Now, let's say you get enlightened, then through your positive connections, you are able to benefit whomever you are linked to. Otherwise, you can try to benefit someone, but they are like the cup with the lid on—you cannot shine inside them.

A past incarnation of the Karmapa would travel to different places in Tibet, and some people would throw stones at him. A few even hit him and drew blood, which is not a very good type of connection to make, but on the other hand it is at least some sort of link. The Karmapa, being a great bodhisattva, wouldn't curse the guy and say, "May he drop dead and go straight to hell!" Instead he would say, "Poor foolish guy! Out of his ignorance he doesn't know what to do. May he be benefited somehow!" In this way, a link was created. He would include the guy in his prayers and develop more compassion for him, which would strengthen the link.

Tibetans try to create spiritual links in so many ways. They give a white scarf, offer something, bow down, light butter lamps, and so on. They really try their best. A lot of them don't really know why they're doing this, but they just do it like everyone else. At the beginning there probably was someone who understood why. In countries where the Dharma has matured, it often happens that the wisdom quality within the culture diminishes and the methods become overemphasized. Therefore it may seem as if the method aspect is purely ethnic, when in fact it isn't and it never was. There is a reason for these methods, but because one is simply told, "do this," the reason recedes into the background, and the methods may end up looking like merely cultural practices.

During a tantric ceremony practiced in a Tibetan monastery, a certain small percentage of the monks may not know its purpose. Their teacher told them to do it, so they do it. Seen from the outside, we as onlookers may think they are "doing their cultural thing," but if you look at it from the inside the ritual is completely in tune with the natural state of rigpa. Starting with refuge and bodhichitta, every aspect of tantric ceremony is interwoven with the wisdom of the nature of things, from the beginning to the very end. For anybody who is aware of why and how, it is a perfect way to grow accustomed to being in harmony with reality. For someone who doesn't know, it could merely appear to be an ethnic ritual. Like all cultures, Tibetan culture has certain traits that are unique. Some are influenced by Dharma, while some actually are Dharma practices that were absorbed into the culture. We cannot categorically say, "That is just cultural. It isn't Buddhism." We may believe we can cut so-called cultural trappings away, but there are so many different aspects in which the two are interwoven. That is one of the issues in the countries where the Dharma has become old.

Anyway, we speak of "planting the seed of liberation," in the sense of opening up to the possibility that the lid of our cup can be removed, that it *will* be removed. Planting the seed of liberation is the attitude of opening up toward a sublime object. This is not necessarily a human being; it can also be the atmosphere of compassion, the thought of the Three Jewels, and so on. As soon as a sentient being's mind links with one of these, then the possibility for liberation has been opened. The seed is planted. This does not mean that the potential wasn't there—of course it was there the entire time. We all have buddha nature; all sentient beings have always had this potential, but there must be an opening up. This opening occurs in connection with a sublime object, because the sublime object or spiritual person has that ability. Not all objects have it, just as, for example, this stick cannot shine. We therefore try our best to connect with sublime objects that have the ability to illuminate us and the inspiration we gain therefrom helps us remove our negative karmic patterns. Linking ourselves to further ordinary objects doesn't plant the seed of liberation no matter how many times our mind fixes on them. Exactly when that seed of liberation will grow and fully bloom is not known for sure. It could take a billion lifetimes, or it could happen in this same life—it's not certain. The fact that we are all here attending these teachings means that quite probably we have, in innumerable past lives, already planted seeds of liberation. For some of us it is quite likely that the crop is about to ripen. I feel it is a definite possibility.

The Dzogchen teachings mention that unless one has already accumulated an abundance of merit in past lives, one will not even hear the term "Great Perfection," let alone meet the teachings. All of us must be extremely fortunate.

STUDENT: Is the state of enlightenment beyond karma?

RINPOCHE: First of all, let's distinguish between two situations. One is rigpa as a brief glimpse and the other is the unending rigpa of true and complete enlightenment, buddhahood. These two are different. A single instant of rigpa helps to perfect the accumulation of wisdom. Please understand that "accumulation" here means beyond the duality of accumulator and something being accumulated. Even though wisdom here, yeshe, is the natural state itself, there is an accumulation in the sense of perfecting our stability in this natural state of original wakefulness. It is *accumulated* by recognizing rigpa instant by instant. This "wisdom accumulation" is beyond karmic action. So what accumulates it? Not the law of karma that works as relative truth, but the law of the innate nature. This law is a natural property of the basic nature. To give an example, the law of fire is that it burns. Whatever comes close to a flame isn't cooled down, it heats up—that's its nature. This is not anyone's making, it's a natural law. One could call it the flame's natural properties. What is the natural law of the awakened state? Let's say that at some point you are fully enlightened and rigpa is uninterrupted; at that point there is no karma. After enlightenment, in this endlessness of rigpa, is everything now chaotic? If karma has been transcended, do bananas turn into oranges? Does everything turn upside down? No, it doesn't. There is a different type of law from karma, the rules of which are still being naturally followed by all buddhas. Thus the law of dharmata is to be in tune with the intrinsic nature of everything, unerringly and unmistakenly.

STUDENT: How does activity for the benefit of beings manifest after enlightenment?

RINPOCHE: Compassionate activity to influence other sentient beings and to ripen them is part of that natural law. It is a natural property of the awakened state. There is also something called the ripening of former aspirations, which is sometimes misunderstood. It is not that compassion is the product of former aspirations—that would mean that one would have no compassion unless one had made prayers in the past. A buddha's compassion is not created by former practice. It is a natural property of the awakened state; yet the activity to benefit others coincides with former aspirations.

Let's say you have five hundred enlightened buddhas. In the identity of their enlightenment, there is absolutely no difference between them. Their degree of compassion, their realization, their wisdom, their capability and so forth are exactly the same. Yet their activity and how they connect with sentient beings can be immensely different. What does that depend upon? It depends upon former aspirations and how many beings they are linked to, and upon how much they directed their good energy toward benefiting other beings while they were bodhisattvas on the path. As a matter of fact, you can notice this if you look around in the world right now. Some people have a high level of realization, but they are not really connecting with other people; they just remain self-contained. So perhaps when they are enlightened, the reach of their activity will be less. I am not sure about that, but it is at least possible. A bodhisattva who tries his or her best to benefit and to connect with as many beings as possible will at the time of enlightenment have a wider reach of activity.

STUDENT: Considering that we are all obscured, how does wishing other people well and dedicating merit really work?

RINPOCHE: It helps a little bit directly, and it helps immensely in an indirect way. The moment you empathize with someone's suffering there is immediately compassion in your stream of being—that is already one benefit. Among 100,000 sentient beings, you *are* one sentient being, and in addition your compassion will enable you to benefit other sentient beings. At least it helps one sentient being. But you are also aiming your mind at complete enlightenment, in addition to feeling sorry about the suffering of others. That means that you are moving in the direction of buddhahood with the intention of benefiting other beings. If you keep moving in that direction, the state of enlightenment will be fully perfected at some point. Then, because of the connection with the other beings you held in mind, the link is there, and when the time is right you will be able to benefit them. Exactly when that happens is not necessarily known today. It is not necessarily like immediately being able to extinguish a fire on their mountain by flying over it once so that everyone is happy—a huge miracle. But, on the other hand, if you really mean it when you make good wishes and send all your good vibes and prayers and whatever you can imagine, showering down goodness, then, if they are open, it is possible that they may feel something. This is not impossible. First you have to have an emptiness wire; second, make sure that the other line is not engaged, their telephone is not busy. Assembling all the right circumstances takes time. It is a bit difficult to have that opportunity. Maybe you have the merit, but you don't know where to send it because you don't have a telephone wire or a satellite.

When dedicating the goodness, the virtue that we have created, there has to be something created, and we must know how to dedicate it as well. If the others are not ready to receive it, they may not receive it immediately. But there is one guarantee: the moment you develop compassion, at least you are benefited immediately. Your mind is changed in a positive way: that is an instantaneous, guaranteed benefit of compassion. Whether the other beings are benefited immediately is not guaranteed, although they will be at some point. You will certainly benefit them in the future, but it may take some time.

STUDENT: Could you explain a little more about the power of blessings and guru devotion as a way to enhance the state of rigpa? How does guru yoga enhance rigpa?

RINPOCHE: There's a definite need for blessings if one wants to realize the nature of mind. Phenomena may sometimes "stain" emptiness. In order to free yourself from this stain, blessings from a teacher are very important. Your mind needs a certain force in order for it to open up and be influenced, a teacher who communicates with your mind. This is possible because both minds are of the same material. To be truly effective, you need someone's realized mind to influence your mind, to invoke the blessings that influence your mind to release clinging. You need a blessing to let go.

First, you must understand the word "blessings." You may not like the word, so we could use another term, like special atmosphere, or a special energy that can inspire or influence you. A physical place can be blessed when great masters have practiced, meditated, and attained realization there. We can, however, receive various kinds of influence. As you well know, one can be influenced positively or negatively: there can be a good influence or a bad influence.

Blessing is somewhat miraculous. Prior to the recognition of rigpa, the preliminary practices—in this case, the guru yoga practice—clear the hindrances and form the conducive circumstance for recognizing the view. Through the blessings, the cognitive nature gets even sharper. Through the blessings, the continuity of rigpa gets even longer. The whole point is in blessings. Whether you get blessings or not is an open question. Receiving blessings is like being revived, being brought back to life. This is not a technical explanation, like if you flick a switch in guru yoga then the cognitive nature brightens up even more; flick another switch and it is extended by so much. There is undoubtedly a connection here, but the very essence of this connection consists of blessings. It is the blessings that make the miracle possible. To prepare for this small miracle of blessings, you need to make sincere supplications. The devotion that is generated by this opens you up. By being opened up through devotion, you are able to receive the blessings, and the blessings take care of all the rest.

The key point is the attitude of surrender, which is not easily understood here in the West. For some reason there seems to be a big block about that. Anyway, surrender simply is: "You know best! Throw me whatever you want. It doesn't matter to me anymore, I submit completely." That attitude is what opens one to the blessings. It is important to understand that surrendering is not merely to your physical teacher. Surrendering only to the one physical person whom you happen to connect with could be a bit too limited, or it could even be somewhat risky if he happens to be an outright bad person. To surrender to someone like that could have severe repercussions; that's *not* what I mean here. You open up to the entire Buddha, Dharma, and Sangha, all four kayas, the entire lineage of enlightenment.

Rather, you are surrendering to the *guru principle*, so to speak. You say, "Okay, I give up now! I surrender completely." The real purpose here is to lead everyone to enlightenment. But from the point of view of the disciple, you no longer care what is going to happen: "Just take over and you can do with me what you will. Give me bad luck. I don't care." Of course, an enlightened master is not going to give one bad luck, but from one's own point of view one relinquishes all conceptual hopes and aims, letting go of the whole affair. It is that sense of release or commitment that actually opens one up to be suffused with blessings.

Otherwise, the normal materialistic attitude is: "If I press this button, then I get that. If I press the other button, I get such-and-such." It gets very technical if you are always trying to do the right thing, to press the right buttons in your practice. With that kind of control attitude, it is very questionable how much blessing you actually receive. Unless you can trust the other person 100 percent, you don't have 100 percent pure feeling, nor 100 percent love. Without compete trust and love, it is hard to be 100 percent open. To receive blessings, you need to be *totally* open, intoxicated with devotion, almost like your first true love.

PERSEVERANCE

The general vehicles of Buddhism emphasize perseverance, which as a matter of fact is one of the six *paramita*s, the transcendent virtues. As you well know, the six paramitas are generosity, discipline, patience, perseverance, concentration, and insight. We have covered the fifth and sixth paramitas in great detail—concentration in the form of shamatha training and the true insight of rigpa, which, in the sense of prajna-paramita, is to discover that mind is totally devoid of any constructs, having no root and no basis.

I would like to bring up a point about perseverance and effort: there is the possibility of mistaking the two. Dzogchen practice is the path of effortlessness, but that does not mean that we lean back and do nothing. Actually, there is a way of persevering without effort, a way of *effortless perseverance*. In order to understand this correctly, I would like to define the difference between effort and noneffort. I also want to address the principles of perseverance and transcendent perseverance.

Generally speaking, perseverance is the remedy against laziness. When do we feel lazy? One situation is when we are supposed to be composed in meditation. There is an invitation to be lazy that we give in to, and then the state of composure, the meditation state, is lost or dissipated. As a matter of fact, laziness arises because of a habitual pattern. It arises as a pattern, gets accepted in the moment, and one then gets carried away by it. But resting very nicely in the state of unfabricated rigpa is itself the perfection of diligence, transcendent perseverance. Why? Because when the tendency to be lazy recurs it is naturally freed. As laziness is self-freed, there is no need to apply the normal remedy against being lazy, which is conceptual diligence. If we deliberately try to be diligent, then rigpa becomes conceptual. Therefore, there is no need to be specifically diligent at that time. Remaining in the state of rigpa is itself the perfection of diligence.

Another example is when we get distracted from rigpa during post-meditation. We don't really feel like meditating. The alarm clock is set for six in the morning, but when it goes off we feel, "I can just lie here another five minutes—it's okay." I am an expert at that! That is the moment when we need normal perseverance: transcendent perseverance does not even come into question. We must tell ourselves, "Get up!" We need to be tough with ourselves. Try setting two or three alarm clocks for the same time, scattered about the room where you can't reach them. That is a good trick, because then you actually do get up. Once you stand up, you may feel sluggish. Once again, there is an invitation for the mind to get caught up in that laziness. Instead, invigorate your state of mind, thinking, "Hey! I am not going to give in to this emotional pattern. I am not going to accept this call to laziness." Get up immediately, and if you have a hand drum and bell, ring them. Imagine that all the buddhas, bodhisattvas, dakas, and dakinis at that very moment appear in the sky before you, in such a huge number that they fill up the infinite sky. Now they tell you, "Why are you still asleep?! Wake up! You have already spent half of your life sleeping, and now you want to sleep more? Get up, get out of that stupidity!! You are thirty years old, and you've slept for fifteen years. You have no idea when you might die—you might die in two minutes. Who knows? Get up! Do some spiritual practice or do some work; there's is no point in being lazy." All the dakas and dakinis harass you until you get up.

In actual fact, this is a traditional practice to create the circumstance to be more persevering. It is called the wake-up practice, and there is a chant that goes with it: "Don't sleep! Don't sleep! Wake up from ignorance!" It is a short chant, with a few lines about the precious human body, impermanence, your good fortune, and how your life is wasted unless you practice. While chanting you sound the bell and drum, imagining that the dakas and dakinis are there in your room with you. This is the practice to do immediately upon waking up. Just get up and immediately do the chant.

Did you see the movie *Groundhog Day*? It is possible to have a tune playing instead of an alarm when you wake up. You could put on a tape with the chant, "Don't sleep! Don't sleep! Wake up from ignorance!" Why not? Immediately after this chant, you should recognize mind nature. Next give your mind a little love, develop some loving-kindness and compassion, some shamatha, and then gently allow the very identity of this calm state to turn into intelligence. In other words, let be in rigpa. Once the state of rigpa is an actuality, you do not need the extra thoughts: "How can I improve this? How can I prolong it? I must really be diligent in rigpa." That would only worsen it. In other words, during the state of composure, which is rigpa itself, we do not need deliberate diligence, because transcendent perseverance is already present. It is only once we get distracted from the state of rigpa that we need to remind ourselves. If we use deliberate diligence during the state of rigpa, we actually worsen the state by making it conceptual. During composure there is transcendent diligence, and during postmeditation we need normal diligence.

You know the phrases "Try hard" and "Don't do anything." We need to know when each of these is applicable. "Try hard" when you are lazy—cut it . . . chop-chop. We have this tendency to be lazy, to whine and complain. It needs a chop, which is not such a big deal. We don't have to be too considerate toward the lazy tendency. The best remedy against laziness is the preliminary practices of the four times 100,000. Once you finish these in a reasonable amount of time, your laziness is all chopped up, so that you can persevere and completely let go. The ngöndro chops into pieces this pattern of giving in to laziness.

We should reach a certain readiness so that we are willing to practice immediately, no matter where we are, without having to prepare a whole setting and *then* practice. It was pointed out to me that in the United States, unless something is planned it will not happen. It appears that everyone is always occupied with other affairs that were planned previously. Therefore, the state of rigpa needs to be planned and put into the daily schedule so that there is a morning and an evening period devoted to rigpa. Ask your secretary to remind you: "Sir, it is rigpa time: your meeting with rigpa is at 10:45 A.M." What's wrong with that? It is part of an important itinerary, isn't it? Otherwise, practice twenty-five minutes or one hour every day. Do it in the context of a guided meditation and apply the visualizations for refuge and bodhichitta. During the daily session, you can make these a bit shorter, so that out of half an hour you spend three or four minutes on refuge and bodhichitta. Then simply let be in the meditation state. If it is rigpa, fine, otherwise practice shamatha. Try your best to allow the continuity of rigpa to get longer and longer. You can call this the "official practice" and fit it in your daily routine. But apart from this "planned daily awakening," we need to be ready to recognize rigpa anywhere, anytime. Your physical posture doesn't matter: you do not have to position yourself first in order to recognize.

Sometimes people say, "I am going through a hard time right now, but after two more years, I will retire and become a dedicated meditator." This way of thinking is actually a deceptive form of laziness. If you obey this thought, you will wait two years before practicing in earnest. Then, after two years have passed: "Look at my body. I am sixty, but unlike the old days, people now live to ninety, so I still have thirty years to go. Thanks to modern technology, diet, dietary supplements, exercise, and so on, making it to eighty is no problem. I have at least twenty years to practice. Twenty years is a lot of time! I have an easy five years before I must bother to practice seriously." Carrying on like this, one day you discover that your life is over.

I am not particularly trying to give you bad news—people do think like this. Therefore, the advice is to practice immediately, no matter what situation you happen to be in. Wherever you are, if you have five minutes, practice, without a lot of preparation. The moment you have the thought to practice, do it. If you only practice after staging it, you might never get around to it. Preparation is just another way of taking counsel from your ego. People like to ask Mr. Selfishness for guidance on how to lead their lives, and then he gives nice advice that's surprisingly close to your wish. Mr. Selfishness is very clever; he knows psychology very well. In fact, he is the best psychology teacher ever. He knows, "If I say it like that, my host will like it." Ego tries to please your inclination, and then of course you follow it. Try to find another way rather than asking selfishness for advice.

I am not talking about the rest of your life now, just a single day. But if you ask Mr. Selfishness how to practice for even one day, he won't even let you do that much. Ego knows you like to practice, so he plays along and says, "Practice is good; I like it, but you must be comfortable and do it right. Your environment should be clean and peaceful. If not, your mind will wander. Make sure everything is right first and then practice—then I am happy too." Mr. Selfishness has a very shrewd way of arguing, so you think, "Wow! That's a good idea." You make a shrine room in your house, but it takes two years to complete. You worked hard and it was very expensive, so your money is all gone. You practice a bit. Then you decide, "I'm still young, so I should work and make more money before practicing seriously." You keep postponing your practice. You make some money, but then think you should buy a tangka for your shrine. You delay another year, and on and on it goes. Then one day you finally sit down to practice, but you notice the incense bothers you and you worry you might be allergic to it, so you get up. There is no end to the excuses people come up with. This is the mentality of placing comfort before practice. If you keep yielding to that, you will never find the perfect opportunity to practice.

In Tibet there is a small mammal, a predator that eats mice and other small rodents. When it wants to catch a mouse, it sits at the entrance to the mouse hole as if it is meditating and waits. Then, when a mouse sticks its head out, the bigger creature grabs it. "There must be more in there," he thinks. "Rather than eat this one now, I'll save it and catch some more." So he sticks the victim under his butt and sits on it and goes on waiting. When the remaining mice don't come quickly, he leans forward to look in the hole, and the one wedged under his butt sneaks off and escapes. Another mouse comes, and he grabs it and sits on it. He manages to catch ten mice, one after the other, but they all escape, and he ends up having nothing to eat. Why? Because he keeps preparing for what he will eat later and ignores the present. He ends up going to bed hungry.

With that attitude toward practice you will never practice. Wherever you are, whatever you are going through, whatever the setting, practice right there. When you go see the doctor and sit in the waiting room, practice right there. If you have an interview with Tsoknyi Rinpoche and are waiting in line, practice there. When you are on the telephone and get put on hold, practice then. If you are in rigpa when they finally say hello, you can immediately reply—but if you are in stupidity meditation they will think no one is there and hang up on you. Wherever you are, practice. When you go back home, do not lie in wait for the right time to practice, because that right time never comes. Please remember that. That is the perseverance we need: to practice on the spot.

I feel that we have a particular obstacle in our modern age—a laziness called instant gratification, the need to feel gratified on the spot. There are so many gadgets and so many situations we can put ourselves into that give us instant satisfaction. That itself is not the problem; the problem is actually that our minds get accustomed to immediate feedback, and we become bound by expecting it. This is one of the major obstacles to practicing on the spot. In the old days there were other obstacles for spiritual practitioners, like being forced into service by the king of the country, being a serf for the local chieftain, being enslaved by the head of the family and having no resources to walk off and practice. These days we have personal freedom; we can make good money and take care of ourselves. Instead we have other problems that hinder Dharma practice, and one of them is the tendency to seek instant gratification. When you use a gadget, you expect it to work immediately. If it is a bit cold, you immediately put on more clothing. If there is a bad smell, you immediately get the air freshener to get rid of it. Really, though, a slight odor won't kill you. Or your seat is a bit hard, and that bothers you. It is not going to kill you or flay the skin off your buttocks, but you feel you must get up right away and get a thick cushion. If you feel a bit sleepy, you must immediately get a cup of coffee. Responding to that urge or tendency to seek instant gratification gives only temporary relief. Doing so, you get occupied with all these petty little affairs, and it seems difficult to get beyond them. Of course we can use things for our own comfort—that is not what I am talking about. It is the obsession that is the problem.

A certain degree of perseverance is necessary to reach perfection in meditation training. There is a famous story of Milarepa giving a teaching to Gampopa, one of his chief disciples. Milarepa had six major caves that he frequented. He would never settle in one place for long but would move every six months or so. While he was staying in an area called Nyalam in south central Tibet, Gampopa asked Milarepa questions about spiritual practice, and they had many discussions. Finally Milarepa said, "The time has come when you don't need to stay with me any longer. You can now go wherever you want. You don't have to go anywhere in particular, just go and practice. You and I will probably not meet again in this life, but now you must leave." It seemed that Gampopa had to disconnect from his attachment to his teacher, and that is why Milarepa told him to leave. Milarepa said, "You are leaving in the morning, but I will escort you part of the way. I usually don't do that, but since this is our last meeting, I will."

The next morning they walked up the ridge. When they reached the top, Milarepa said, "I have one extremely profound instruction that I have not yet given you." Gampopa said, "Shouldn't I first make a mandala offering? Is there a special torma I should use to make a shrine?"

Milarepa replied, "No, you don't need to prepare anything." They walked a bit further. Gampopa thought, "This is strange. I have been with Milarepa for many years now and I never got the feeling that there was anything I haven't yet received." Gampopa himself was extremely learned in all the scriptures. He had already become a *pandita*, a great scholar, but it was only after meeting Milarepa that he attained realization. Because of his vast spiritual education, he had concluded that there were no important teachings left to receive. He wondered, "What could this last teaching be?"

At a certain point on the trail Milarepa stopped and said, "I won't go any farther, as I do not stay in the villages of worldly people." Then, he abruptly pulled up his simple cotton robe so that his backside was exposed to Gampopa. "Touch it!" he said. Gampopa reached out and felt Milarepa's callused buttock. It was as hard as a yak's horn from his years of meditation practice. Milarepa said to him, "You have all the teachings, but if you want to be equal to me, your father, your butt needs to be like mine! Persevere as I did!" That was his last teaching: no realization without perseverance.

CONTACT ADDRESSES FOR TEACHINGS AND RETREATS

For information regarding programs,
recorded and published teachings in the lineage
of Tulku Urgyen Rinpoche and his sons,
please access one of the following websites:

Tsoknyi Rinpoche
WWW. TSOKNYIRINOPOCHE.ORG

Lotus Treasure
WWW.LOTUSTREASURE.COM

Rangjung Yeshe Gomdé,
WWW.GOMDEUSA.ORG

Rangjung Yeshe Gomdé, Denmark
WWW.GOMDE.DK

Rangjung Yeshe Publications
WWW.RANGJUNG.COM

Tsoknyi Rinpoche's recent activities to support Dharma include: helping re-build Tsechu Gonpa in the Nangchen region of Eastern Tibet after it was destroyed by an earthquake in 2010; compiling, editing, and publishing a complete set of over 100 important texts for the Drukpa Kagyu lineage in 2016; publishing a new book, *Open Heart, Open Mind* in 2012 and creating an online course, *Fully Being*, in 2016; participating in Mind-Life seminars; completing the construction of a large monastic campus in 2017 for over 135 young Nepali girls to learn Dharma and Western education; and continuing to teach Dzogchen to students around the world. For more information on his activities and teachings, please visit tsoknyirinopoche.org and tsoknyinepalnuns.org.

TSOKNYI RINPOCHE AND HIS TEACHERS

Kyabje Dilgo Khyentse & Tulku Urgyen Rinpoches

Tulku Urgyen with Tsoknyi and Mingyur Rinpoches and their mother

Tsoknyi Rinpoche with Adeu Rinpoche of Nangchen

Tsoknyi Rinpoche with Nyoshul Khen Rinpoche Yangsi

Nyoshul Khen

This reprint has been made possible by a
generous donation by Owsley Brown